AF342678

Glamorous Sorcery

MEDIEVAL CULTURES

Series Editors

Sponsored by the Center for Medieval Studies at the University of Minnesota

Volumes in this series study the diversity of medieval cultural histories and practices, including such interrelated issues as gender, class, and social hierarchies; race and ethnicity; geographical relations; definitions of political space; discourses of authority and dissent; educational institutions; canonical and noncanonical literatures; and technologies of textual and visual literacies.

Volume 25
David Rollo
Glamorous Sorcery: Magic and Literacy in the High Middle Ages

Volume 24
Steve Ellis
Chaucer at Large: The Poet in the Modern Imagination

Volume 23
Edited by Barbara A. Hanawalt and Michal Kobialka
Medieval Practices of Space

For more books in the series, see pages 233–34.

Glamorous Sorcery

Magic and Literacy in the High Middle Ages

David Rollo

Medieval Cultures, Volume 25
University of Minnesota Press
Minneapolis
London

Part of chapter 1 appeared in "William of Malmesbury's Fables of Literacy: Gerbert of Aurillac and the Excavation of the Campus Martius," in *Translationes Studii: Essays in Honor of Karl D. Uitti on the Occasion of His Sixty-fifth Birthday,* ed. Renate Blumenfeld-Kosinski, Kevin Brownlee, Mary Speer, and Lori Walters (Amsterdam: Rodopi, 1999); reprinted with permission from Editions Rodopi. Part of chapter 3 appeared in "Benoît de Sainte-Maure's *Roman de Troie:* Historiography, Forgery, and Fiction," *Comparative Literature Studies* 32, no. 2 (fall 1995): 191–225; copyright 1995 by The Pennsylvania State University; reproduced by permission of The Pennsylvania State University Press. Part of the conclusion appeared in "Three Mediators and Three Venerable Books: Geoffrey of Monmouth, Mohammed, Chrétien de Troyes," *Arthuriana* 8, no. 4 (winter 1999): 100–114; reprinted with permission from *Arthuriana.*

Published by the University of Minnesota Press
111 Third Avenue South, Suite 290
Minneapolis, MN 55401-2520
http://www.upress.umn.edu

Library of Congress Cataloging-in-Publication Data

Rollo, David.
Glamorous sorcery : magic and literacy in the High Middle Ages / David Rollo.
p. cm. — (Medieval cultures ; v. 25)
Includes bibliographical references and index.
ISBN 0-8166-3546-3 (alk. paper) — ISBN 0-8166-3547-1 (pbk. : alk. paper)
1. Latin prose literature, Medieval and modern — England — History and criticism. 2. Literature and history — Great Britain — History — To 1500. 3. Benoît, de Sainte-Maure, 12th cent. — Criticism and interpretation. 4. Great Britain — History — To 1485 — Historiography. 5. Anglo-Norman literature — History and criticism. 6. England — Intellectual life — 1066–1485. 7. Literacy — England — History — To 1500. 8. Magic in literature. I. Title. II. Series.
PA8045.E5 R65 2000
478'.0308—dc21 00-009010

Printed in the United States of America on acid-free paper

11 10 09 08 07 06 05 04 03 02 01 00 10 9 8 7 6 5 4 3 2 1

To

Julia and Rosemary

Contents

Introduction

According to Georges Duby, the sophisticated lay culture that developed in twelfth-century England and France was a direct consequence of improved fiscal control.[1] As systems for calculating and coordinating levies gained greater efficiency, the francophone baronies of the era augmented their disposable wealth and began to appropriate some of the literate prerogatives previously restricted to the clergy.[2] Learning became an object of acquisition, as younger sons were sent in increasing numbers to receive a formal education at cathedral schools;[3] and, toward the end of the century, the education they thereby acquired itself became a commodity liable to trade.[4] Not only did the royal courts enlist the services of the literate in the spheres of dynastic historiography and political administration; even minor landholders took clerics into their employ, primarily as tutors for their children, but also on occasion as private scribes of regional histories.[5] One of the results was a considerable corpus of Latin writing, produced in a secular environment for the edification of a lay public.

But, as Duby also demonstrates, this historical fact of patronage creates something of a cultural paradox. Although representatives of the landed barony acquired these insignia of learning, few of them displayed an advanced literacy and the competent understanding of the Latin language it would presuppose: inheritance by primogeniture required first sons to submit themselves to a seigneurial training in arms that would prepare for the eventual succession to title and territory, and under these circumstances relatively little time was devoted to their formal education.[6] As a consequence, it remains unclear by what means these titular magnates understood the often extremely sophisticated Latin texts that were written for their benefit:

> What could have been the practical function of a work such as the *Historia Gaufredi ducis,* in Latin? Was it read? Where, in what circumstances? How—in translation, with annotations? This

> work shows Geoffrey Plantagenet besieging the castle of Montreuil-Bellay: the "educated count" *(litteratus consul)* requested that a copy of Vegetius be brought from the abbey of Marmoutier. To be sure, it was not claimed that he read this book himself: he had it read to him by a monk. In Latin? Translating, commenting on the text? (259–60)

Thus, Duby implies, at least some of the Latin writing dedicated to seigneurial magnates may have gained general intelligibility only through oral paraphrase and glossing in the vernacular. In such cases, the Latinity of the text would certainly provide evidence of the cultural aspirations nurtured by the patron. But it would not prove his or her linguistic competence. Alternatively, Duby ventures, the increase in supply could perhaps be taken to suggest an increasingly informed and increasingly discerning demand, with the implication that the landed barony of the era in fact commanded a more advanced literacy than has previously been recognized:

> Among the lords and ladies to whom Hildebert and Baudri of Bourgueil dedicated their sophisticated poems, were there really so few who could enjoy these works without an interpreter? The canon who composed the history of the lords of Amboise about 1160, specifically citing Boethius, Horace, Lucan, Sidonius Apollinaris, and Seneca, and who strove to make the affective bond forged by vassalage resemble Ciceronian *amicitia*—did he not expect that the grace and vigor of his Latin composition would be appreciated by persons other than his clerical colleagues? Must we not assume a significant enlargement of the lay audience, people sufficiently cultured to be able to communicate with and appreciate the language and knowledge of the schools without an intermediary? (259)

Duby abstains from committing himself to either of the positions he hypothesizes. Yet the issue he raises is of great sociological and literary importance, even though it remains difficult to scrutinize with historical accuracy. As M. T. Clanchy and Franz H. Bäuml have demonstrated in studies that implicitly engage Duby's questions,[7] many early analyses of medieval lay literacy were compromised by reductive anachronism. Today one is either literate, meaning able to read and write, or illiterate, meaning incapable of either. However, this clarity of distinction is ill-suited to the medieval context.[8] The ability to read did not always take as its corollary the ability to write.[9] Conversely, writing was widely regarded as a demeaning activity best fulfilled by functionaries, and if, therefore, a given magnate never signed his or her name, it does not inevitably follow that he or she was incapable of doing so.[10] Other difficulties have arisen through failure to distinguish between complete and partial literacies. To define, in classic fashion, the medieval *litteratus* or *litterata* as a man or woman who could read and write Latin is methodologically expedient.[11] Yet it fails to account for the fact that a basic grasp of Latin lexicon and syntax was at times a sufficient qualification for these epithets, even if this partial control of the language was accompanied by the inability to read, to write, or both.[12] Further compounding these problems, even those who were fully literate in the modern sense could have been inadequate to the task of understanding the full complexities of given works produced for their benefit, since grammatical competence does not presuppose a skill in applied hermeneutics, a discipline that required years of study to master and remained the esoteric domain of the clerical minority. Therefore, as Bäuml refreshingly emphasizes, the formulaic hyperbole with which authors celebrate the literate accomplishments of prospective benefactors cannot necessarily be taken at face value.[13] Because flattery tends to be self-interested, often entails exaggeration, and at times accommodates calculated falsehood, prefatory eulogies of lay literacy do not prove that the literacy eulogized was anything more than a polite fiction designed to transform a hope for patronage into a remunerative reality. Further, because potentially venal, the act of dedication cannot be taken to imply that the work dedicated necessarily glorifies the behavior, character, or aspirations of the semiliterate potential benefactor. On the contrary, it may bespeak an extreme irony. While it is no doubt justified to state that on many occasions medieval authors did indeed enlist their scribal talents to the edification of secular powers, it is also at least hypothetically legitimate to posit particular cases in which they did not. By its very nature, superior learning could lead to the production of texts that aggressively challenged the interpretative capacities of their inscribed patron, ultimately to yield a message that is the very opposite of flattering.

In the present study, I propose to reengage some of these problems, but with a complementary emphasis on an epistemological tension that is central to the culture of the High Middle Ages. As even my minimal paraphrase of Bäuml's arguments has shown, much of the information pertinent to the lay literacy of this era is derived from texts written by representatives of the clerical minority. I would like to add that many of the clerics responsible for such works project themselves as manipulators of hieratic and contextually invisible powers. To intimate what these may be, it is apposite to call briefly on the testimony of the twelfth-century English historian, William of Malmesbury. In the short section of the *Gesta regum Anglorum* devoted to tenth-century Italian politics, William observes that Pope Silvester II was considered by many to have owed his prodigious scientific achievements and economic success to necromantic talents. Yet he counters this view with a simple rebuttal: "But any of us could believe this to be popular fantasy, since the common people tend to slight the fame of the lettered, saying that anyone they see to excel in a given field must converse with a demon."[14] Subliminal to the popular opinion William paraphrases is a distrust of literate accomplishments that are perforce arcane and exclusive, and these are rationalized by the disadvantaged as magical, malign, and deceptive gifts of the devil.

It is precisely this ambient charge of sorcery that I wish to integrate into the study of medieval literary reception, concentrating on twelfth-century Latin and Old French works produced in the British Isles and the Continental domains owing fealty to the English Crown. Some writers, I demonstrate, strove to dissolve the hieratic aura that had come to be associated with their clerical status, ultimately to demystify and to educate. Others, I show, exploited magic as a metaphor of their own to configure the epistemological and financial prerogatives they believed themselves and their literate peers to enjoy. My primary topics of analysis are the particular degrees of literacy the authors in question explicitly or otherwise adduce as prerequisites to the understanding of their texts; the means whereby such thresholds of understanding are expressed through self-reflexive themes of performance and reception; and the consistent presence of sorcery in these thematic rehearsals, with surrogate author projected as magician and the written medium he controls designated through a lexicon that collapses the verbal arts with glamorous sorcery *(gramaire/grimoire)*, performative conjuring *(praestigia)*, intoned spells *(incantationes)*, and drugs capable of seducing, bewitching, transforming, or curing those to whom they are administered *(medicamenta/medicamina)*. As this last point makes clear, I am not preoccupied with the perceived reality of magic itself, either to the twelfth-century community or to individual authors. I am exclusively concerned with its literary function and the sociological implications of its metaphorical use.[15]

My interest in the literate and their relationship with the public has in large measure been inspired by Brian Stock's seminal *The Implications of Literacy.*[16] Stock's purpose, however, is to demonstrate the interdependence of oral and written traditions in the development of a hermeneutic textuality. Thus, he does not directly broach contemporary appraisals of reception, concentrating rather on metamorphoses in patterns of thought and, through them, social negotiations.[17] Nonetheless, he appeals for a renewed sensitivity to issues of dissemination and understanding, and he lays a particular emphasis on the contemporary public for whom medieval texts were produced: "To investigate medieval literacy is . . . to inquire into the uses of texts, not only into the allegedly oral and written elements in the works themselves, but, more importantly, to inquire into the audience for which they were intended and the mentality in which they were received" (7). Consistent with the frames of inquiry Stock proposes, I shall investigate literacy in its sociological implications. But I shall do so exclusively through the prism of highly literate texts. I make this caveat because my analyses are not intended to retrieve precise data that can be objectively adduced to define how various sectors of the twelfth-century public responded to writing that was prepared for their benefit. Rather, they demonstrate how and by whom particular authors imagined and suggested their writing should or should not be understood, and they are therefore glosses of literary strategies and not disclosures of historical fact. As a result, my principal focus is on literate *self*-perceptions that are textually constructed through the hypotheses of encoded readers and listeners, and the social conclusions I draw concern the duties, privileges, and powers of lettered clerics as they were explored and obliquely defined from the evidently partial perspectives of the clerical community itself.

Analysis of reader/listener response in the context of medieval writing inevitably bears the influence of Hans Robert Jauss, who, some thirty years ago, as both theorist and medievalist, first argued that each literary work must be appraised in its relationship with prior normative structures.[18] Reading thus becomes an engagement with a horizon of expectations that must be attributed to the original recipients of a given text and analyzed as a paradigmatic criterion that is variously reproduced, realigned, or flouted in the generation of new meaning (and, ultimately, in the creation of new horizons and new conventions to be manipulated).[19] Although Jauss devotes part of his analysis to the vernacular genres of the Middle Ages,[20] the test cases he uses in his detailed studies of the evolution of expectations and aesthetic responses are selected from post-Enlightenment literature.[21] Within the context of the vernacular High Middle Ages, however, this evolutionary process was often realized in a manner that finds no equivalent in the later writings Jauss considers, since in many cases it had to be negotiated across the barrier of linguistic difference. Vernacular writers of the twelfth century regularly challenged expectations (and, prospectively, obliged them to alter) by making implicit or explicit reference to works that were either ill understood or totally arcane to unlettered recipients because couched in Latin. Under these circumstances, the study of response resolves into the study of not only literate competence, particularly in the domain of intertextuality, but also linguistic accomplishment.[22] If a given author structures his or her work through allusions to antecedent paradigms that would by necessity remain inaccessible to his or her chosen public, then familiarity and recognition break down, and expectations are replaced by the unexpected and unrecognizable. Certainly, as Jauss points out, the initially outlandish comes to be neutralized by later generations of recipients. But this prospective evolution by no means compromises Jauss's own stress on the original moment of challenge, on the point at which an implied public could be confronted with a level of expectation it could not match.

Such confrontations are found to particularly striking effect in romances, which, by the contemporary evidence provided by medieval authors, were prepared for noble men and women who had at best a rudimentary literacy. Yet, as many modern critics have demonstrated, these works are densely allusive literary artifacts, and much of their significance is comprehensible only through the Latin antecedents they intertextually invoke. Under these conditions, the lucid understanding of the romance would presuppose an understanding of an extraordinarily wide corpus of often extremely recondite Latin texts, ranging from those of the classical *auctores*[23] to the works of Saint Augustine[24] and allegories of creativity by such Neoplatonic writers as Macrobius and Martianus Capella.[25] But, if this is so, then romances would necessarily militate against the *full* comprehension of the illiterate or semiliterate. By this I do not mean they would be utterly devoid of sense to the disadvantaged listener, but that they would always carry a residue of significance that would be immediately intelligible only to those displaying a high degree of competence in Latin. To be sure, through the very act of transposing the obscure, a given author could be moved by a desire to elucidate the previously unknown for the benefit of those who lacked the proficiency to do so for themselves. But he or she could also be employing the barrier of linguistic impenetrability to promulgate meanings that were *by design* inaccessible, thereby challenging not so much expectations, but the interpretative capabilities of his or her public.

DEGREES OF LATIN COMPETENCE

The problems of understanding I delineate above are also found in the Insular Latinate writings of the period, although here the internal hierarchy of understanding is constructed between, on the one hand, readers who were hermeneutically proficient and, on the other, readers who were grammatically competent yet could not grasp the full complexity of the work. I devote my first two chapters to these divisions, addressing the following categories of recipient: the accomplished *(litteraturae peritus)*, controlling intertextual mechanisms and endowed with a complete mastery over the polyvalences of tropes;[26] and the unaccomplished *(parum litteratus)*, capable of reading but incapable of the interpretative acts solicited from within the text.[27] There is also the category of the implied listener of Latin, though it is rare.[28] When evoked, the listener serves as a counterpoise to the reader and is less proficient. In this case, differences in hermeneutic engagement arise not from implied ability but from the mode of reception, since, certain authors imply, listening granted a more restricted access to significance than reading. The listener of the Latin text could of course be divided into subcategories corresponding to the accomplished and unaccomplished readers, since under any circumstances listeners obviously bring to bear varying levels of competence. Yet this is never an encoded concern in the Latin texts I treat. The third category I consider is the surrogate for the author, a thematic figure who is the peer of the accomplished reader and is always endowed with the figuratively magical powers I have briefly rehearsed. The reason for this consistent choice of metaphor is clarified by the interpretative positions outlined above: by its very nature, magic implies recondite, even superior knowledge; it is the possession of a minority; it is powerful, however illusory its consequences; and it instills respect, if not fear.

My first chapter is devoted to certain anecdotes that William of Malmesbury inserted into the *Gesta regum Anglorum,* written at the juncture of the first and second quarters of the century. I begin by analyzing William's apocryphal biography of Silvester II with three primary motives. First, to demonstrate that William employs the seemingly frivolous context of the anecdote as a medium for sophisticated thought, in this particular case to create a performative parable of literate control. Second, to show how the theme of magic functions as the diegetic term in a complex allegory of reading, in this case contrived to reflect the literate proficiency that must be brought to bear to uncover successfully the subterranean didacticism William has placed beneath the verbal surface of his tale. Third, to reveal that William turns this conflation of literacy and sorcery against the accomplished and successful reader, finally to warn against what he considers the demonic hubris of literate arrogance, the idolatry of those who would use their education only to the furtherance of worldly ambition and who adopt a supercilious view toward their true, divinely sanctioned vocation—to educate those lacking the skill to educate themselves.

I further pursue this concern with learned hubris by investigating William's use of rhetoric as a metaphorically necromantic device that is capable of effecting unlimited metamorphoses. The logic of the rhetorical maneuver I consider is of course already inherent in the function of the trope, which, assessed in the most straightforward of terms, realizes a superimposition of senses and evokes two signifieds from within one verbal structure. Throughout the anecdote from the *Gesta regum* that I consider in this light, the operative trope is the word *asinus,* meaning both "donkey" and "idiot," which bridges diegesis and reception to create superficially unflattering effects on the unaccomplished reader. Those who fail to engage the anecdote with a sensitivity to the trope themselves emerge as figurative dumb asses who maintain a steadfast belief in the reality of magic; those who read with the clear vision William invites see that the only transformative power operative is that of rhetoric itself. Yet again, however, William maneuvers the accomplished to recognize in themselves an unduly supercilious view of those who are less proficient, on this occasion by elaborating a parallel set of intertextual signals to reveal that the truly asinine disposition is displayed by the educated who refuse to allow others to benefit from the clarity of insight that advanced literate competence bestows.

In chapter 2, I demonstrate that William's anecdotal exploration of the rhetorical *medicamentum*—both stupefying drug and medicinal cure—finds its functional analogue in the most celebrated scene in the slightly later *Historia regum Britanniae* of Geoffrey of Monmouth. This concerns the conception of Arthur, orchestrated by Geoffrey under the guise of Merlin and textually described as a drama of reception that mobilizes the *medicamina* of rhetoric either to seduce the reader into credulity or to grant him or her the clear vision necessary to see that this apparent history is in fact a meticulously constructed fabrication. In the second half of the chapter, I consider the implications of Geoffrey's initiatives in the light of John of Salisbury's *Policraticus* (ca. 1159), the most extended discussion of magic, semiotics, and government to have been produced during the era. Assessed according to John's categories, Geoffrey emerges as an exemplary representative of a new secular counterculture, and his "magical" power to create ex nihilo is to be understood as a sign of the new—and for John dangerous—authorial prerogatives of fictional writing that gained their clearest expression in the vernacular romances composed in the latter half of the century.

William and Geoffrey explore differences in receptive proficiency within the ranks of those at least capable of reading the language in which they write. Such divergences could be even more pronounced in the audience of an Old French text, since the use of the vernacular presupposes an effort to accommodate those who have an incomplete mastery of Latin—presupposes, therefore, a considerable hermeneutic gulf separating, on the one hand, the author and his bilingual peers and, on the other, those who were at best partially literate and who explicitly or otherwise form his inscribed audience. In chapter 3, I consider these potential problems of romance understanding.

Literate Readings of the Romance

It is a perfectly legitimate undertaking to approach twelfth-century Latin writings as scribal artifacts bearing complex rhetorical and intertextual structures. However, according to Paul Zumthor in *La lettre et la voix,*[29] no such liberty is by any means guaranteed in a vernacular context. This study stands as something of a summation of Zumthor's earlier work, but with primacy placed no longer on "le texte," but on "l'oeuvre," conceived as a plenary "socialisation" that embraced performer, audience, and community through the unifying agency of the voice.[30] In Zumthor's view, the methodological shift from the analysis of discursive modes to meditation on a totality of poetic experience is an imperative, necessitated by what he considers an ongoing process of critical distortion. With some exceptions, he argues, modern medievalists tend to ignore the fundamental orality of the medieval text.[31] Internalizing a printed culture that invests the written word with a hegemonic primacy and locates its most cherished values in the literary artifact, they perform across time the gesture of transforming the medieval other into a surrogate of the modern self, with the effect of reenacting the imperialist reflexes that inspired their discipline at its origins.[32] For these reasons, Zumthor states, their readings of medieval texts are irretrievably compromised: the immediacy granted by the shared experience of the voice is displaced by a visual scanning that is both linear and solitary,[33] and ever mobile meanings are ossified by a false engagement founded on the comforts of a totalizing and ultimately totalitarian hermeneutics.[34]

Whether Zumthor is justified in his comments remains open to debate simply because he abstains from naming those he rebukes. Furthermore, the path to rehabilitating performative modes in the way he suggests opens onto a secondary set of difficulties: since the performative circumstances of medieval delivery and reception are situated in the medieval past, then we today can appreciate medieval "vocalité" only through leaps of the modern imagination (which could be vitiated by any number of nonmedieval criteria), efforts at physical reconstruction (which could tend toward a cultural patronage bordering on Halloween caricature), or an acknowledgment of absolute alterity (which would deny appreciation for anything but alterity itself). Zumthor is certainly not ingenuous to these problems, and he avows that his injunctions lead to something of a critical aporia[35] and back to the problems of cultural perspective he himself investigated in earlier studies:[36] any silent and solitary act of reading a work that at its origins constituted a performance that was both vocal and communal is perforce an act of distortion; yet it is the only mode of reception to which the modern critic—by necessity the modern *reader*—is truly competent. The first step to negotiating this problem, Zumthor argues, is to recognize its existence; then, he concludes, at least the possibility of reconstitution could be envisaged, not with an end to seizing the medieval work in its inevitably lost historical specificity, but to witness, in however vicarious and incomplete a manner, the form of vocal and gestural "socialisation" that has been obscured by the modern proclivity to approach the grapheme as the sole vehicle of meaning.[37]

Zumthor considers this performative reconstitution a matter of particular urgency in modern approaches to the *chanson de geste* and the lyric, for him the exemplary genres of oral "socialisation." With regard to the romance, however, he is more circumspect. As the privileged arena for modern analysis,[38] this would seem the most likely candidate for anachronistic abuse. But, as Zumthor himself acknowledges, it bears an ambiguous and marginal relationship to the communal ethos and vocal immediacy he addresses.[39] Certainly, it depended on performative vocalization for its initial dissemination and was therefore "socialized" through the same physical mechanisms as epic and lyric forms.[40] Yet, in its twelfth-century manifestations at least, it was the product of a profoundly Latinate, bilingual culture that was both peripheral to the majority and, appraised in the most negative light, potentially elitist.[41]

The clerical ethos Zumthor associates with the romance does not necessarily bespeak an antagonism between author and audience. On the contrary: as a point of mediation through which representatives of a literate culture addressed the anxieties and aspirations of the illiterate and semiliterate, the romance constitutes a generic interaction between the two social spheres. This mediating principle is one of its primary internal themes, creating a formal self-reflexivity through which communication becomes an obtrusive textual concern. To engage the romance under these conditions is to engage a commentary on intelligibility, understanding, and, ultimately, cultural cooperation. Witness in this regard the prologue to the *Roman de Thèbes:*

> Qui sages est nel deit celer,
> Ainz por ço deit son sen monstrer,
> Que, quant serra del siécle alez,
> En seit pués toz jorz remembrez.[42]

[Those who are wise should not hide it. Rather, precisely because of it, they should show their wisdom in order always to be remembered once they have left this world.]

Por ço ne vueil mon sen taisir,
Ma sapience retenir;
Ainz me delét a aconter
Chose digne de remembrer.
Or s'en voisent de tot mestier,
Se ne sont clerc o chevalier,
Car aussi pueent escouter
Come li asnes al harper.
(9–16)

[For this reason, I have no wish either to hide my knowledge or to hold back my wisdom. On the contrary, it shall be my pleasure to recount something that is worthy of memory. So now let all those leave who in their station are not clerics or knights, for in listening to me they could only be like the ass that listens to the harpist.]

The author's division of society according to cultural prerogative illuminates what has rightly come to be viewed as the distinguishing function of the earliest romances—the mediation between an increasingly leisured feudal aristocracy and a written corpus of learning previously confined to a restricted Latinate culture.[43] The fact that *Thèbes* is a translation first and foremost implies that the public for which it was prepared was incapable of negotiating the Latin of Statius. But this does not, of course, mean that the accomplished *litterati* of the era were excluded from the circle of the text's reception. As he himself suggests by citing both *clerc* and *chevalier,* the author wrote to accommodate an audience demonstrating a range of literate abilities, and this desire to address a number of receptive positions is corroborated by the text itself. By dramatizing the themes of genealogical dispossession, military conflict, and the relationship of the individual to the body politic, it explores the values endorsed by the feudal magnates of the era in terms that are accessible to all. Less transparently, it also displays a web of learned references that could only have been in the first degree recognizable to the lettered.

Yet, confirming Zumthor's warnings of elitism, responsible mediation is not the only role ascribed to the educated in the vernacular writing of the High Middle Ages. A more ambiguous presentation of literate power is found in the work of an anonymous redactor of *Floire et*

Blancheflor, probably active in the late twelfth century or the early thirteenth. This is Barbarin, a performing magician in the employ of a royal court. As a calque on *barbarus,* his very name suggests the linguistically outlandish, esoteric, and incomprehensible; and these subtle resonances of opacity are in turn amplified by the specific conditions in which he chooses to perform:

> Quant il ert en grant assanlee,
> de son nés issoit la fumee
> tele c'on nel peüst veoir
> ne ja son estre apercevoir.[44]

> [When he was in a large assembly, smoke would come out of his nose so that people could not see him and lost sight of what he was doing.]

These fumes amount to something of a smoke screen in their own right, and they should not blind us to the set of tropes the author is using. For Barbarin can also conjure forth magical images, one of which has unambiguous literary implications:

> Une harpe tint en ses mains
> et harpe le lai d'Orphey;
> onques nus hom plus n'en oï
> et le montee et l'avalee;
> cil qui l'oent molt lor agree.
> (862–66)

> [He held a harp in his hands and strummed the lay of Orpheus. Never did anyone hear more of it in its rising and falling modulations. Those who heard it loved what they heard.]

All this would indeed be delightful, if not innocuously enchanting, were it not for a far less benign permutation on the theme of Orpheus that has already been provided. Barbarin may perform. But he expects to be paid in return, and the commodity he offers as his part of the transaction may not be what his client initially presumes:

> Qui li donast .XII. deniers,
> sa teste trencast volentiers;

tantost com il l'avoit trencie
et a home l'avoit baillie,
demandoit lui: "Ai toi gabé?
As tu ma teste?" "Oïl, par Dé!"
çou li respondoit li vilains;
quant il regardoit en ses mains,
trovoit u laisarde u culuevre:
par ingremance faisoit l'oevre.
(813–22)

[For anyone who gave him twelve deniers, he would willingly cut off his own head. As soon as he had cut if off and given it to the other, he would say "Have I fooled you? Have you got my head?" "Yes, by God," the bumpkin would say. But, when he looked in his hands, he would find either a lizard or a snake. Barbarin did all this by magic.]

Beneath his necromantic garb, this "encanteres molt sages" (line 810) is a figure for all those who sell their literate talents for money. He is the modern Orpheus, enchanting the ears, subordinating things to the command of his words. Yet the severed head of song that he purveys to the illiterate, to the *vilains* here so inappropriately placed in the royal court, is never to be trusted and may turn out to be the serpentine voice of deception. The performer only appears to sell himself, operating from a position of invisibility and rendering his moves and motives obscure to others. Under these circumstances, it is he and he alone who benefits from the transaction, since the dupe of the jape is the oaf who believes money can buy a trustworthy voice.

Assessed together, the author of *Thèbes* and the redactor of *Floire et Blancheflor* dramatize the alternative faces of the *litteratus* in his relationship with the monolingual. The purveyor of the vernacular may be the self-effacing medium through which the values of the community are expressed. Or he may be a sorcerer of words who employs his craft as a crucible for financial advancement by selling a debased product to those who cannot scrutinize its integrity.

A pioneering study that engages romance as a figurative magic has been provided by Michelle A. Freeman in a monograph on Chrétien de Troyes's *Cligés*.[45] Freeman anticipates my interests by demonstrating that

Chrétien diegetically reflects his own authorial procedures through the Byzantine sorceress Tessala and configures his text as a magical draught.[46] Although I shall return to Freeman's work in the conclusion to gauge Chrétien's Continental response to certain Insular predecessors, it is apposite at this early stage to state how my own focus on the "magical" vernacular differs. While Freeman studies the draught as a sign of authorial self-consciousness and thereby lends weight to her contention that *Cligés* is primarily to be read as a performance of scribal prowess, I shall approach the vernacular as a potential vehicle for exclusion and literate control. The text I shall consider is one of the most successful romances of the entire Middle Ages, Benoît de Sainte-Maure's mid-twelfth-century Anglo-Angevin *Roman de Troie*.[47] Benoît's work is particularly relevant to my field of inquiry, since it circulated in the Middle Ages with alternative prologues, each of a very different epistemological implication. In some of the earlier manuscripts (including one from the late twelfth century), the author expresses his intent to translate the history of Troy for the benefit of "cil qui n'entendent la letre" (35), for those who, while not necessarily analphabetic, cannot understand the full complexity of written artifacts, by inference including the Latin works of Dares and Dictys. In some slightly later redactions, however, the negative verb is changed to a positive and the romance offered to "cil qui entendent la letre," to those who can indeed comprehend such texts in all their subtlety.

These alternative prologues place *Troie* in two apparently divergent traditions, and they suggest methodological approaches that can be used by the twentieth-century critic. An effort could be made to hypothesize horizons of reception obtaining among the illiterate or semiliterate, preparatory to engaging the text as a depiction of the values endorsed by highly self-conscious and increasingly leisured feudal magnates negotiating the transition between barony and aristocracy. Such a reading would tend to concentrate on thematic issues such as social mobility, genealogical dispossession, kingship, and varied inflections of individual autonomy. Alternatively, study of the work could consider first and foremost the scribal context of its production. In this case, the author and the authority he arrogates would become the focal points of interest, and criticism would tend toward the analysis of literary self-consciousness, intertextual allusion, and inherited systems of meaning. I consider, however, that a synthesis of both approaches is necessary. *Troie* is structured of all the "magical" prerogatives I have already outlined in a Latin context, and it explores in its themes precisely the gulf of understanding that its vernacularity is prospectively designed to bridge. And it is to be read as both a performance of, and a meditation on, the relationship between the clergy and the barony, between two communities that at this period in history were becoming not only increasingly interdependent, but also, at times, openly antagonistic. The relationship at issue is already reflected in the two groups of recipients that emerge from the alternative prologues: "cil qui entendent la letre," who find their peer in the inscribed author and his "magical" diegetic surrogates; and "cil qui n'entendent la letre," comprising the greater part of the audience. This distinction is far greater than that obtaining between the divergent readers of the Latin text, since it involves not only a difference in hermeneutic competence but also the relative limitations implied by auditory reception. With this distinction in mind, I seek to establish whether *Troie* is indeed the work of enlightenment that its earlier prologue implies or whether it is in fact a work of occlusion.

LATIN AND VERNACULAR FANTASIES OF LITERATE CONTROL

In the remaining two chapters, I shall use some of Duby's conclusions to open an avenue of sociological inquiry that Duby himself does not pursue, demonstrating that certain of the young men who answered a clerical rather than chivalric vocation employed the learning they thereby gained to flaunt particular talents and powers beyond the grasp of the less educated.[48] Amplifying the initiatives of Ralph V. Turner[49] and applying them to a literary context, I argue that feudal dispossession led to a collateral empowerment, as land and title were replaced by the new prerogatives of literacy—not only, as Turner has demonstrated, social and financial advancement, but also, in particular cases, a conspicuously displayed control over what is to be known by others and what is not.[50] And these prerogatives were themselves frequently explored in writing through metaphors of not only magic but also mercantile opportunism.

In chapter 4, I consider three clerics whose literate prerogatives led, directly or prospectively, to social and financial advancement. The first is Thomas Becket as he is presented in William FitzStephen's *Vita Sancti*

Thomae, Cantuariensis archiepiscopi et martyris. While other biographers attest Becket's spectacular rise from a mercantile background to the position of archbishop of Canterbury and primate of all England, FitzStephen is unique in projecting his career through a set of topoi adapted from the dynastic, baronial tradition initiated by Geoffrey of Monmouth in the *Historia regum Britanniae.* Following Geoffrey's precedent, FitzStephen presents London as the New Troy. Yet he makes Becket one of the world-renowned rulers that Geoffrey's Diana predicts to govern the new *imperium,* and this despite the obvious oxymoron of the bourgeois monarch he thereby creates. This emphasis on social mobility prepares for FitzStephen's subtle portrayal of Becket as the effective ruler of England during his chancellorship.

Similar concerns underlie my reading of Richard FitzNigel's handbook on fiscal administration, the *Dialogus de Scaccario.* Here too, the author celebrates the social mobility granted by education and suggests that the members of the Exchequer are the effective lords of the land. But he does so with a marked emphasis on the cabalistic prerogatives of these secular clerics: raised from even the most plebeian origins, they are guardians of mystic secrets *(sacramenta)* binding together writing and political control, and they oversee the quasi-religious consubstantation of king and finance literally to forge the monarchy to the contours they design. These points lead me to return to the *Roman de Troie,* in which Benoît too explores the financial prerogatives of his own clerical status by developing a figurative alchemy of writing and, ultimately, by elaborating his own vernacular analogue to the Royal Treasury itself. He is not concerned, however, with a numismatics of kingship: rather, he imprints his own authorial likeness onto the written coinage he circulates in the textuality of his romance.

Finally, I devote chapter 5 to Gerald of Wales, the most prolific Latin author associated with the Anglo-Angevin court. Gerald, I demonstrate, fashions himself as the *daemon* of contemporary letters (and, through them, politics), and under this guise emerges as the most manipulative figure of magical literacy of the period, deliberately performing precisely the necromantic *praestigia* investigated and censured by William of Malmesbury. But he takes this written sorcery beyond anything anticipated in the *Gesta regum* and exploits his erudition to create texts that are calculatedly designed to subvert the temporal pretensions of the semiliterate to whom they are dedicated.

1

William of Malmesburyx

Magic and Prestige

William of Malmesbury's eminent position among twelfth-century Insular historians has long been established and critically endorsed, and his writings still partly constitute the foundation for modern studies of Anglo-Norman England.[1] Yet his major work of secular history, the *Gesta regum Anglorum,* at intervals displays curious detours into anecdote, picturesque tales that evoke such curiosities as necromantic hags, animate statues, talismanic rings, eternal flames, and sempiternal corpses.[2] These have elicited a far more nuanced response from critics. In some cases, they have met with puzzled agnosticism, bracketed as superficially frivolous yet with a potential for ulterior meaning;[3] in others, they have been dismissed as inconsequential entertainments, mere interludes contrived to break the implied monotony of documented fact;[4] and in one instance they have been treated as no more than the figments of an impressionable mind reflecting the superstitious tendencies of a credulous era.[5]

However eccentric and regrettable they may seem to modern historiographic sensibilities, these tales are urgently in need of reevaluation. It can be stated with no discomfort that William was clearly an intelligent and erudite writer, and it is defensible to venture hypothetically that his intercalated anecdotes are as much the products of this intelligence and erudition as the historical narrative that surrounds them. To substantiate this hypothesis, it is necessary to engage these tales on their own terms, without anachronistic judgments of value and without the—possibly—anachronistic modern credence in medieval credulity. Of course, no one can prove that William did not harbor unqualified belief in the outlandish phenomena he describes. But critical analysis of his anecdotes could potentially disclose structures of meaning that would suggest that they are neither simple entertainments nor the products of a naive imagination. It could, in fact, identify these tales as calculated literary artifacts, *fabulae* orchestrated to yield a subjacent sense that could perhaps illuminate the historiographic context in which they appear. Such a possibility is corroborated elsewhere in twelfth-century letters: by the account of one of William's contemporaries, the Continental philosopher and poet Alain de Lille, four types of Latin *fabulae* were indeed being produced by the mid–twelfth century, one of them directly related to the historical narrative. This being so, it is legitimate to employ Alain's categories as paradigms against which to appraise the tales of the *Gesta regum* as a first step to explicating their function.

Alain broaches fable in the *De planctu Naturae* as part of a lengthy commentary on poetic reference, proffered by Natura for the benefit of the narrator/protagonist. Two categories of fiction are unconditionally rejected: naked *falsitas* sold in a brothel of literary production by a pimping poet and *falsitas* clad in a garb of probability that is designed to induce dull acquiescence in the consumer.[6] Set against these perceived depravities are two types of acceptable fiction. One is theocentric in design, a fabulous narrative intended to disclose a higher truth:

> Don't you know how the poetic lyre strikes a false note on the superficial rind of the letter, but on a more profound level communicates to listeners a secret of higher understanding, with the result that, once this shell of falsehood has been discarded, the reader may find secreted inside the sweeter kernel of truth?[7] (837)

Natura's *cortex* is pragmatically false, a narrative of things that never happened or could never happen. But this untruth is a purposeful construct of the Christian poet, designed to conceal a *nucleus* of truth to the glory of God. Compared with this "truthful falsehood" (which can be plausibly read as Alain's gloss on his own practice), the other acceptable fiction Natura mentions is relatively insignificant:

> Occasionally, poets bind together historical events with an elegant suture formed of entertaining fictions. Through the artful

> conjunction of differing elements that this creates, the narrative assumes a more pleasing design.[8] (837)

In this case, untruth is tolerable primarily because it is of little consequence: it is playful, if not frivolous *(ioculatio fabulosa)*, and it serves only as an interlude in the documentation of facts *(historiales euentus)*.

Of course, these remarks are not made with pointed reference to the work of William of Malmesbury. Indeed, they apply to the practice of narrative poets rather than prose historians. Yet, formal issues aside, they do furnish contemporaneous and therefore viable models of signification. Alain's two categories of depraved *falsitas* must for the time being be set aside: because they are predicated on the absence of ulterior meaning, their pertinence to the present context can be argued only if analysis fails to demonstrate that William's tales are more than inconsequential frivolities. The same stricture applies to Alain's *ioculatio fabulosa*. Although this category perfectly corresponds with the type of light entertainment some critics have argued William's anecdotes to be, and although it is particularly relevant to the *Gesta regum* because they are presented as an interlude to the historical narrative, it is by inference as vain and empty as the carnal text (even if far less devious). For this reason it too must be bracketed until other avenues of inquiry have been thoroughly explored. Remaining, therefore, is the pragmatically false yet ultimately significant narrative that Natura delineates through the metaphor of the *cortex* and *nucleus*, the rind and the kernel, verbal surface and secreted truth.

With this paradigm in mind, I shall now analyze one of William's anecdotes in detail. It concerns Gerbert of Aurillac, the French monk who rose from obscurity to become Pope Silvester II and who, as I mentioned in the introduction, was popularly viewed to have owed his worldly and economic success to necromantic powers.[9]

The Treasure Trove

After sketching the pontiff's career and his prior achievements in France (2.167–68), William devotes extended attention to his interest in the seemingly frivolous pastime of the treasure hunt: once pope, William states, Gerbert employed his mystifying powers to disinter the buried riches of pagan Rome, and his most spectacular find was inspired by an ancient statue:

> On the outskirts of Rome, on the Campus Martius, there was a statue, either of bronze or iron (I am not sure which). It was pointing with a finger of its right hand and also had written on its head "Strike Here."[10] (2.169)

As William proceeds to explain, this written command had led earlier generations to conclude that they were obviously being instructed to strike the head, with the inference that this would somehow or other grant them access to treasure. Yet the multiple dents caused by their misguided ax blows clearly demonstrated the extent of their misprision.[11] It was left to Gerbert to understand what had escaped everyone else: "hic" did not designate the head or, for that matter, any other body part; rather, it was the spot on the ground indicated by the shadow of the outstretched finger at midday. Accordingly, Gerbert marked the place to dig with a stake and returned at night with one of his servants. They began excavations and eventually came upon the entrance to an underground vault containing the fabulous treasure of Octavian.[12]

Far more may be at issue here than a tale of lucrative archaeology. William employs the pointing statue to differentiate between two degrees of literate competence, between those who halt at the letter of the text and those who perceive that the signified may lie beyond. This diegetic emphasis on the interpretation of signs could itself be a signal to indicate that the tale is invested with a specular function, becoming both admonition and commentary on the means of its own decoding and emerging as a purposeful challenge to a new group of readers. Consider in this regard the terms in which William describes the pope gaining access to the subterranean vault:

> Soon, with night falling, he hurried back, accompanied only by his personal attendant carrying a lantern. There, the earth opened up to his usual skills and exposed a wide door for them to enter.[13] (2.169)

At hand is a miraculous variation on digging holes in the ground, realized without any dependence on a spade. In an effort to understand this apparent prodigy, the reader could adopt one of two positions. He or she could passively concur with the popular view and conclude that Gerbert is using some ungodly power. Alternatively, he or she could actively imitate Gerbert himself, abandon the letter of the text and follow the clue of the pointing finger, which finds its analogue not in the tangible realm of classical antiquities, but in the proem to that celebrated treatise on the relationship between Christianity and the pagan art of the trope, Augustine's *De doctrina Christiana.* Here, the church patriarch uses a metaphor of his own to counter two groups of potential detractors:

> To those who do not understand what I am writing, I say this: it is hardly my fault if they do not understand. It is as if they wish to see the old or new moon or some faintly shining star that I am pointing at with my outstretched finger, but find their sharpness of vision insufficient even to see the finger itself. They should not fly into a rage with me for that. And as for those who, even knowing and understanding these precepts of mine, fail carefully to look at the obscure parts of the Holy Scriptures, they can be likened to people who are able to see my finger but cannot see the stars it is pointing at.[14]

From this, it is legitimate to posit that William has transposed the figure of Augustine himself to the Campus Martius and that he employs the statue as an iconological index for the theoretical directions prescribed in the *De doctrina.* It is also provisionally warranted to suggest that the diegetic actions of Gerbert at least partially reflect sequential stages in the decoding of the tale. After all, in recognizing that the statue points only to indicate something else, Gerbert has shown precisely the sensitivity to displaced significance that is central to the advice Augustine offers Christian exegetes in their efforts to interpret signs.[15] With these avenues for inquiry in mind, let us therefore briefly consider Augustine's central preoccupations.

Throughout the *De doctrina,* Augustine approaches hermeneutics with two primary concerns—the astute interpretation of scriptural language and the subsequent exposition of its Truth through preaching. In the process, he rehabilitates for the Christian cause modes of discursive exposition already productively analyzed and codified in the classical tradition under the rubrics of *grammatica* and *rhetorica.* Augustine conceives of rhetoric as the forensic discipline of oratorical delivery, and, like Donatus before him, diverges from Quintilian by absorbing tropic ornamentation into the field of grammar.[16] It is to this extended domain of "grammatical" expression that he devotes the greater part of the first three books, remotivating the pagan discipline as a theoretical paradigm for scriptural exegesis.[17] The reasons for this are simple: like the profane fictions of the classical poets, biblical discourse often shrouds its message in veils of obscurity. The distinction between the two is of course absolute: pagan texts are woven of superstitious fallacies, while the Truth of God is One and Transcendent. Yet, for reasons of intellectual satisfaction and monitory force, truth is often most efficiently expressed through the tangential agency of verbal figuration. Augustine does not explicate the tropes and the figures of thought through which this is achieved, but he does briefly mention as examples *allegoria, aenigma, parabola, metaphora, catachresis, ironia,* and *antiphrasis* (3.29).[18] All of these, including those functionally dependent on tonal inflection, Augustine refers to as "tropi" (3.29). His *tropus* therefore embraces far more than the restricted domains of metaphor, metonymy, and other discrete figurations of deflected sense. An entire discursive sequence can be tropic: many of the biblical passages Augustine discusses are minimal narratives to be interpreted as *allegoriae* signifying the workings of the Word. Therefore, in emphasizing the importance of *tropi,* Augustine is addressing not simply individual units of lexicon, but also deflections from the literal extending over entire narrative sequences. If this tangential force of biblical discourse is not recognized, the result may be nonsense:

> To know tropes is necessary to anyone wishing to unravel the ambiguities of the Scriptures because, faced with a meaning that appears absurd if read literally, we have to search in an effort to determine if the sense that escapes us is perhaps expressed by some trope or other. It is in this way that much underlying significance has been found.[19] (3.29)

To move beyond the literal is a theological imperative, since figurative language itself was imposed by the Holy Spirit to nurture a clear-sighted awareness of the distinction between truth and falsehood. To read the figurative is to work toward communion with God; to halt at the literal is to capitulate to the misery of the contingent. Verbal surface, therefore, is often a barrier to intellection, and to fall passively into its snare may be an act of hubris denying the need to transcend the flesh of the letter to attain the Truth of the Word:

> When words with a figurative meaning are accepted only with their literal sense, they are understood according to the flesh. Nothing is more aptly called the death of the soul than the very thing that raises it above the beasts, the intelligence itself, submitting to the flesh by following the letter. He who follows the letter takes literally words invested with a transferred sense, and fails to make what is meant by the proper refer to another meaning. It is surely indicative of the wretched servitude of the soul to take the sign for the thing and to be unable to lift the eyes of the mind from the world of flesh in order to drink in the light of eternity.[20] (3.5)

This last remark reintroduces Augustine's own particularly favored trope—sight as a figure for understanding. As the prefatory motif of the pointing finger has already implied, lucid intellection depends on an ability to see beyond the primary signified of any sign, and, as this later passage suggests, the understanding of God can only be achieved through a *caritas* that allows the Light to bathe the eyes in an epiphany of communion.

Augustine's warning to look beyond the literal of course anticipates Alain de Lille's injunction to discard the false shell and to search for an underlying truth. Moreover, both suggest a possible interpretation for William's emphasis on excavation: even from the minimal paraphrase I have so far offered, it will have become clear that the anecdote of Gerbert and the Campus Martius dramatizes a quest that moves from the surface to a level that is literally subjacent. But for this—possibly—allegorical model to have any significance, it is necessary to attach a contextually valid meaning to the object of the quest, to that *thesaurus* left as a subterranean legacy by pagan Rome. Evidently, because William inaugurates this excavation with an icon that forcefully recalls Augustine's image of his own hermeneutic directives, it is reasonable to search the *De doctrina* itself for a metaphor that will lend the interred riches of the Campus Martius an ulterior significance.

This secondary quest of intertextual hermeneutics does indeed prove rewarding. The following are the terms in which Augustine characterizes the pagan disciplines he proposes to enlist to the Christian cause:

> To be found among the writings of the gentiles are more than simply the contrivances of superstitious imaginations and the burdensome figments of empty artifice, which every one of us should abhor and repudiate when we leave the society of the gentiles to submit ourselves to the leadership of Christ. There are also the liberal arts, which fully lend themselves to the expression of Truth, setting down social precepts of great utility and even disclosing a considerable number of truths regarding the worship of the one and unique God. These, the gold and silver the gentiles have to offer, were not created by them, but were excavated, as it were, from the mines of all-pervasive Divine Providence and then abused in the perverse and aberrant worship of demons. It is precisely these arts that the Christian, when he divorces his mind from the wretched society of the gentiles, must take from them and devote to the just cause of spreading the evangelical Word.[21] (2.40)

This use of gold and silver as metaphors for the learning inherited from the pagans explicates the remaining enigma of the Campus Martius, and it is now fully defensible to state that William purposefully employs Augustinian motifs to create a coherent allegory. Indeed, advice that he gives at the end of the tale fully substantiates the hypothesis that the allegory at issue bridges diegesis and reception, with Gerbert's thematic actions reflecting the very process of reading:

> The masses are of the consistent view that Gerbert negotiated feats such as this through black magic *[adversis praestigiis]*. But if anyone does diligent research into the truth, he will see that Solomon, who had received his wisdom *[sapientiam]* from God himself, was not unaware of such powers.[22] (2.169)

By citing the precedent of Solomon, William aligns Gerbert with a tradition not of sorcery, but of preeminent wisdom. As a result, he comes grammatically close to exonerating the French pope of demonic dealings, and by contrastive juxtaposition he suggests that the *adversa praestigia* of popular belief are in fact an illicit synonym for *sapientia*. This movement from the magical to the scholarly is then accelerated by performative means. Having advised the reader actively to search out the truth concerning Solomon in order to reassess Gerbert's talents, William identifies a precise bibliographic source for the appropriate facts, citing the work of the Jewish historian Josephus ("ut enim Josephus auctor est"). Of importance here is not so much the identity of this account of Solomon's wisdom, but the terms in which it is offered as an object of reading. William's use of the verb *videre* ("si quis verum diligenter exsculpat, *videbit*") places an Augustinian emphasis on seeing and is a functional catachresis for understanding, and this understanding will come from a diligent research that is itself expressed through metaphor—*exculpare* literally means "to hollow out" or simply "to dig." This trope creates a suture between the anecdote and its reading, and Gerbert's excavations thereby achieve their full figuration. The tale of the Campus Martius is no less than a parable of scholarly inquiry: the wealth that is excavated is identified through Augustinian displacement to be learning itself, intellectual treasure first elaborated by the pagans but ultimately to be enlisted to the service of God; the subterranean vaults, those repositories that are to be dug open and their riches reappropriated, function as a trope for texts, and the ability to gain access to these recondite vaults of knowledge does not devolve from black magic, but from the application of *sapientia*. These metaphors in turn configure the successful interpretation of the very text through which they are established. In order clearly to see and clearly to understand, the reader must undertake figurative excavations of his or her own, must first follow the clue of the pointing finger and actively engage the *De doctrina* in a quest for truths that will grant the parable its meaning. Thus enriched, he or she must then return to the tale and unearth the displaced senses that William himself has buried therein.[23]

Once again, therefore, William addresses disparate degrees of hermeneutic ability, although on this occasion with pointed reference to his own text. On the level of theme, early readers of "hic percute" were never able to locate subterranean riches and simply hammered on obdurate metal. Similarly, certain readers of the anecdote may fail to follow the pointing finger, may fail to perceive the presiding presence of Augustine, and may simply conclude that they are perusing a tale with no ulterior significance, a fiction as unrewarding as the impenetrable surface of the statue itself.[24]

If suspended in these terms, however, the tale of the Campus Martius would be no more than an ingenious and somewhat elitist riddle, satisfying to those who are hermeneutically accomplished, but obscure to those who are not. Furthermore, it would yield little that could be viewed as in any way edifying, still less theocentric. There is certainly a message to be gleaned, but, again to use Alain's vocabulary, the message is hardly "altior"—subterranean yet ultimately of a higher, divine significance. But everything I have so far explicated is in fact part of a wider stratagem through which William progressively forces the clear-sighted reader to identify with Gerbert himself, eventually to reveal his tale to be a didactically efficient and thoroughly Augustinian commentary on clerical hubris.

This collusion between *litteratus* and protagonist has by this stage already been implicitly prepared. When first mentioning the popular view that Gerbert owed his success to black magic, William makes a predictable caveat: "But any of us could believe this to be popular fantasy, since the common people tend to slight the fame of the lettered, saying that anyone they see to excel in a given field must converse with a demon" (2.167).[25] By balancing the distrust of the *populus* against the accomplishments of the *litterati,* William recognizes the arcane prerogatives enjoyed by the literate in a semiliterate society, and he dismisses the popular view as an unreasoning suspicion ultimately arising from fear. It is because perforce hieratic and exclusive that literacy mystifies the disadvantaged. And it is in his own capacity of rational *litteratus* that William speaks in defense of talents that he too shares: employing the literate medium of Latin to paraphrase the views of the uneducated, he inevitably identifies himself with the accomplishments that others view with such distrust and aligns his own writing with the learned tradition that Gerbert exemplified. Indeed, he goes so far as to cite the *Consolatio philosophiae* and indicate that no less a figure than Boethius himself was suspected of demonic collusion.[26] The *litteratus* therefore mentions a prestigious antecedent in order to exonerate another, and he implicitly expresses his own fellowship with both.

It is therefore at first glance disconcerting to discover William immediately proceed to cite yet another artifact of literate culture in order to contradict Boethius and reaffirm popular suspicion:

> This is the view of Boethius. But the unprecedented circumstances of Gerbert's death lead me to believe that he was indeed guilty of some sacrilege. Why, with the end approaching — as I explain later — should Gerbert have had himself torn to pieces, have been the gruesome butcher of his own body, unless he did so with an awareness of some rare sin? Thus, in an old volume that came into my hands and that contains the names of all the pontiffs and their years, I read the following set down in writing: "John, who is also Gerbert: four years, one month, and ten days. He ended his life shamefully."[27] (2.167)

By implication, it would seem that this extreme act of penance arose from an equally extreme sense of guilt and a pitiful desire for absolution, most plausibly the result of the demonic familiarity that popular tradition attests. Gerbert's black magic would indeed seem a historical fact, precluding any literate effort to rise to his defense, and this because the *vetustum volumen* of pontifical tenure attributes to Gerbert a degree of contrition that can be interpreted only in negative terms. It appears, then, that the distrustful view of the *populus* is in this instance justified, and it appears that the twelfth-century *litteratus* writes the biography of an eminent antecedent only to acknowledge that his own literate peers do on occasion owe their talents to the devil.

There is a problem here, however. As William Stubbs argued over a century ago, William seems to have confused Gerbert with one of his immediate predecessors, John XVI, antipope to the imperially sanctioned Gregory V.[28] This confusion specifically concerns Gerbert's plea for dismemberment, which owes its circumstantial details to the very real and contemporaneously documented mutilation of the antipope, who was seized by his rival's supporters, blinded, and deprived of ears and nose. William, therefore, appears guilty of indifferent research: he first confuses Gerbert with a mutilated predecessor and then compounds his error by interpreting this falsely attributed mutilation as a divine punishment for diabolic hubris. Yet, it is one thing to be in error, but it is quite another to flaunt emphatically a text that will make this error plain to any responsible reader. The reference to the *vetustum volumen* comes from a conscientious historian who at a slightly later stage invites his readers to corroborate for themselves the information about Solomon that he has derived from Josephus ("if anyone diligently digs for the truth, he will see"). Mention of the unnamed but unambiguous "ancient volume" begs the same type of responsible corroboration, and anyone who consults the papal lists will know that John XVI and Silvester II were quite emphatically not the same person.

Such transparent bibliographic incompetence attracts suspicion for two reasons: first, William was clearly well versed in papal history, himself having supervised a written record of pontifical tenure;[29] second, by his own account, he visited the libraries of most of the major English cathedrals and abbeys when compiling his history of Insular ecclesiastics, the *Gesta pontificum*,[30] and therefore had every opportunity of perusing any number of documents relevant to the papacy. Even if we accept it as plausible that William could somehow or other misread all available records, it is difficult to imagine that no one attempted to correct his error between the appearances of the first redaction of the *Gesta regum* in 1125 and the second and third some ten to fifteen years later.[31] Certainly, it can be objected that the *Liber pontificalis* produced under William's direction also includes this problem of mistaken identity (and does so in identical words). However, all of the points made above apply even more forcefully to this text: it strains the imagination to picture William carefully collating facts with an end to producing his own historical account of the papacy, yet still failing to notice that he has confused Gerbert with a signally obscure antipope. In short, because we are dealing with a historian who otherwise approaches his material with a meticulous attention to corroborative detail and who otherwise shows himself to be something of a contemporary authority in specifically the field of research that is here at issue, we cannot conclude that this error results from incompetence. On the contrary, we must consider it a calculated stratagem on William's part.[32] If the historian has (apparently) confused Silvester II with John XVI, then the entire account of Gerbert's plea for dismemberment is at once open to question, not only as an accurate portrayal of the past, but also, and more importantly, as evidence of Gerbert's sinful compact. If Gerbert did not in reality command that his body be mutilated, then we have no reason to presume he lived in fear of eternal damnation, in which case there is also no reason to presume he ever traded his soul to the devil. All these factors combined point to Gerbert as a genuine scholar and not as some kind of slave to Satan.

I submit, then, that the ostensibly grievous error that has so troubled critics is in fact no error at all. I also suggest that this purposeful confusion is to be assessed as yet another challenge, through which William invites his readers to corroborate his bibliographic evidence and to perceive that the charge of sorcery is false. The result is again to impose a distinction between passive acceptance and clear-sighted reading. Those who lend credit to William's citation of proof are left to accept the reality of sorcery. Those who actively search for truth not only see that at no point does sorcery obtain; they also once again demonstrate the learning that is popularly viewed as magic and open themselves to precisely the charge of demonic collusion they know to be contextually unjustifiable. They have, in short, become avatars of Gerbert himself, not only in their successful excavations, but also in the suspicion their success may bring.

Provisional Conclusions

William, therefore, selectively rewrites Gerbert's biography in order to address two interrelated issues. The first and more obvious is thematic. Despite popular belief, Gerbert did not sell his soul to Satan, and, despite superficial implications to the effect, he did not use necromantic powers to appropriate the material wealth of antiquity. Rather, he was an accomplished *litteratus* who heeded particular cultural directives in order to gain intellectual treasures. Concurrently, William on the level of grammar expresses apparent facts that are contradicted by ulterior meanings. Throughout, he addresses only those capable of bringing to bear a degree of literate proficiency. To understand the anecdote, it is necessary to recognize the pointing finger, to show a familiarity with the work of Augustine, and to perceive the functional presence of certain tropes. To understand that Gerbert did not die shamefully, it is necessary to recognize bibliographic error, to show a familiarity with the lists of papal tenure, and to perceive the absurdity of the resultant confusion.

From this a certain ethical problem arises. Since William writes only for a proficient minority, then he writes in a manner that is perforce exclusive, leading his peers to acknowledge the extent of their competence and to perceive the idiocy of identifying literate skill as a dark and satanic art. He seems in fact to be inviting the accomplished to bask in the pride of superior interpretative acumen, to congratulate themselves for having negotiated a difficult reading and for having demonstrated the crude and foolish misprisions of the less sophisticated rabble. He seems, in short, to invite them to enjoy the prestige of their position.

All this is true. But here too the stratagem is attentively orchestrated. By manipulating the reader to a position of self-esteem, William prepares what is in effect a subterranean didacticism. As he progresses through the tale of the Campus Martius, he unveils two types of scholarly hubris, one concerning Gerbert, the other concerning the reader who clearly sees the extent of Gerbert's corruption. As the final result, he in both cases demonstrates that literacy may be pushed to the point of idolatry, and that to pass beyond the surface may bring sins of its own.

Although William implicitly reveals that Gerbert's powers were certainly not demonic in origin, he does nevertheless explicitly state that they were devoted to demonic ends:

> With the devil's aid, [Gerbert] promoted his own interests, so much so that he left no plan unfinished that he had devised. He found the treasures buried long ago by the gentiles and, employing magical power, he cleaned them of dross and exploited them to the satisfaction of his lusts. This is an example of the despicable arrogance the unprincipled show by testing the patience of God, who would rather see them repent than perish.[33] (2.168)

Here too the figurative context is unmistakably Augustinian, Gerbert's excavation of pagan riches recalling the patriarch's image of the gentiles extracting their knowledge from the mines of divine Providence.[34] The two metaphors do not precisely correspond, since the intellectual riches dug up by the pagans were buried by God, while those disinterred by Gerbert were buried by the pagans themselves. But this slight shift of emphasis is in itself significant, as it establishes a historical process of figurative excavation and burial inaugurated by God himself and carried through the ages by those, both pagan and Christian, who then commit the silver and gold he has allowed to be mined to new, now bibliographic repositories. It is precisely as an intellectual placed in this tradition that Gerbert perverts Augustinian precepts. The general sense of his actions is clear: by excavating the vaults left by the pagans and employing his necromancy to clean the gold they have left, he metaphorically engages the legacy of pagan knowledge and uses his learning to recuperate all that is worthwhile. But he does so only to the satisfaction of *cupiditas* and thereby reproduces the aberrant perversion of divine Truth that Augustine cites as the practice of the pagans. By this I of course do not mean that Gerbert was literally an idolater, but that he ranged himself on the side of the devil by channeling his learning exclusively to the furtherance of personal ambition and material opulence and by failing to heed Augustine's instructions to direct pagan knowledge to the service of the evangelical Word. The ultimate result is simple: by abusing learning to consolidate worldly power, Gerbert has contrived to literalize Augustine's trope, transforming epistemic riches back into the material gold and silver by which they were configured.[35]

As William proceeds to indicate, Gerbert pushed this crime of venal scholarship so far that God himself ultimately intervened to curtail such a flagrant abuse of his gifts: "But Gerbert found where his Master would humor him no further. God obstructed his endeavors with the same art he himself had employed and, to use a popular saying, was like the crow pecking out the eyes of another."[36] Given the context of divine intervention, the image is curious. But it is cogent, nevertheless, introducing as it does one of the master tropes of the *De doctrina,* sight for understanding. Augustine first uses this metaphor in his proem when taking leave of his detractors:

> Let both groups stop criticizing me and pray instead they be given, by divine intercession, sight to their eyes. After all, even if I can move my limb to point at something, I cannot sharpen the eyesight of others to let them see that I am pointing or to let them discern what I want to indicate.[37] (Proem)

Augustine employs vision to signify the cognitive process of apprehending the message he undertakes to impart in the *De doctrina* itself, and he hypothesizes two types of deficient reader. The first is simply too blind even to understand the straightforward sense of his text, metaphorically rendered by the finger itself. The second is evidently more accomplished and has already been addressed in greater detail in the immediately preceding period: "And as for those who, even knowing and understanding these precepts of mine, fail carefully to look at the obscure parts of the Holy Scriptures, they can be likened to people who are able to see my finger but cannot see the stars it is pointing at."[38] The reader of this category is obviously competent and understands the import of Augustine's precepts. Yet he or she fails to follow them through and ignores the divine Truth they are designed to serve. Gerbert shows precisely this enlightened blindness: he sees with the figurative lucidity Augustine suggests, but he omits to direct his knowledge to a truly Christian cause.

It is fitting, therefore, that God himself chooses to put an end to the pontiff's profitable excavations quite specifically by depriving him of the talent of clear vision he has abused. As already mentioned, Gerbert opens the—figurative—vaults of pagan Rome "with his usual skills" ("solitis artibus"). Yet on this occasion, the golden reward that is thereby disclosed is itself highly unusual:

> They saw an immense palace, with golden walls, golden windows, with everything made of gold. There were golden soldiers that gave the illusion of life as they played with golden dice. There was a metallic king reclining beside his queen, with a meal set down before them and their ministers standing by. There were vessels of great weight and value, displaying workmanship that surpassed nature. Further back in the palace, there was a carbuncle, an eminently precious and rarely found stone, which banished the darkness of night. In the opposite corner stood a boy, who held a bow with its string extended and an arrow ready-aimed. While this precious art enraptured the eyes of the beholder, there was nothing that could under any circumstances be touched, even though it could easily be seen.[39] (2.169)

Gerbert, the scholar of personal idolatry, is on this occasion confronted by golden idols and at once understands that his designs have been thwarted by a supernatural force: "For, as soon as anyone attempted to extend his hand to touch, all of these images would seem to leap into life and rush at the offender. Daunted by this prospect, Gerbert abandoned his plans" (2.169).[40] However,

> Gerbert's attendant, on the other hand, did not hold back, and grabbed a knife of exquisite craftsmanship that he saw lying on the table. He obviously thought that one petty theft would pass unnoticed amid such plunder. But shortly thereafter all the images thunderously leapt forward, and the boy shot his arrow at the carbuncle with the result that everything went dark. If

> the servant had not quickly followed his master's advice and dropped the knife, they both would have suffered severe injury. And so, with his unbounded avarice left unsatisfied, Gerbert left, his lantern leading the way.[41] (2.169)

By reaching out his hand, and therefore transgressing the interdiction Gerbert has understood, the servant sets in motion a shift from appearance to reality: the *imagines* conjured forth by metaphor take on substance, the figurative gold of knowledge becomes a treasury of material artifacts, and the textual repository becomes a literal underground vault. The servant in effect destroys the metaphorical fabric of the excavation: the knife and the table, for example, resist any ulterior sense, and the literal signified now gains absolute primacy. Since it is God himself who has overseen this supernatural metamorphosis, then all its affronts to plausibility can be rationalized: following Augustinian directives, Gerbert with the help of an acolyte reads a pagan text with an end to extracting its epistemic riches; but this text is abruptly transformed into the literal vault of Augustine's metaphor, and God chastises the pontiff with a punishment that fits the crime. Thus, while Gerbert appropriates the figurative gold of knowledge with an end to later transforming it into literal wealth, God intervenes to literalize the entire undertaking, transforming reading itself into a literal excavation. As a result, Gerbert discovers himself abandoned by the divinely bestowed lucidity of intellect that had previously guided him, and, blinded by the darkness of irrational fear, he is now as powerless as the *populus,* and magic for the first time asserts itself, here manifested as golden artifacts that spring to life. God therefore not only confines Gerbert with literal meanings: he in effect makes him fleetingly illiterate, preventing him from seeing anything but the work of sorcery. As a final sign of his displeasure, he plunges the chamber into darkness and obliges Gerbert to flee this nightmare of literalized figuration.

The resultant darkness also extends to the text. Not only does the French pope abruptly encounter the literal. So too does the reader, who initially attempts to apply Augustinian theory to glean ulterior significance from metaphors that have ceased to obtain. Accordingly he or she is once again maneuvered into a position comparable to Gerbert's, his or her metaphorical digging beneath now foreclosed by the obtrusive presence of artifacts that escape anything but a literal meaning. As a consequence, the reader too is fleetingly left groping in the darkness of incomprehension, confronted by metal that proves to yield nothing, acting out a series of frustrated gestures as unrewarding as the ax blows diegetically imparted to the pointing statue by those who fail to see clearly. It is only at the point at which the very significance of incomprehension is perceived that lucidity is restored and the final message of the tale is understood to be the chastening barrier of the literal itself. While God punishes Gerbert, William admonishes his accomplished peers, inviting them to reconsider the *De doctrina* and to apply Augustine's theoretical directives to the experience of frustrated interpretation they have just undergone. They have followed the hermeneutic index, identified a set of interactive tropes, and perceived a coherent subjacent meaning. But they abruptly find that these metaphors disintegrate and ideally perceive the limits of literate perception, the point at which *grammatica* becomes tantamount to darkness and ignorance if pushed beyond the confines of predicative theory. By these means, William manipulates his reader to the directives of *caritas,* inviting others to meditate on the ways of Providence and employing the barrier of the literal as a warning against its Augustinian analogue, the scholarly pride of rejecting the Word for the idolatry of the flesh. The reader therefore emerges from his or her textual excavations enriched with the wealth of the parable itself, with the enlightenment that can come from the darkness of fleeting ignorance. Thus, he or she does indeed extract metaphorical silver and gold, and this wealth is the knowledge that knowledge itself should only ever be silver and gold in the realm of metaphor. Hence the admonition of the vaults and of the text: "nihil erat quod posset tangi etsi posset videri"—what is unveiled is only to be understood by the eyes, and is never to be transformed into tangible riches.

Moreover, having arrived at the admonition never to literalize figurative gold, the advanced *litterati* find themselves in possession of a parabolic message that is in fact quite comprehensible on the verbal surface. After all, the thematic didacticism of the story is retrievable from the most literal plane of reading: Gerbert is obviously highly educated, as William has made clear by devoting the preceding section to his scholarly achievements; he is obviously driven by greed and ambition, as William makes clear by alluding to his cupidity ("cupiditas") and by depicting God himself finally punishing this tawdry self-interest ("sed reperit tandem ubi magister suus haereret, et, ut dici solet, quasi cornix cornici oculos effoderet"). The accomplished therefore perceive that they have been led through an extraordinary labyrinth of displaced meanings in order to extricate a moral that the modestly literate would also and far less tortuously understand. Or, to switch to the configurations of the parable, they discover that the silver and gold William has granted as the reward of the quest are already in the hands of those who were never required to dig in the first place. The consequence is twofold: the interpretative hierarchy that William has seemed so anxious to maintain disappears, and the clear-sighted have been led back into fellowship with the less accomplished. The circular trajectory that William thereby achieves gains its full significance in the coda to the tale:

> The masses are of the consistent view that Gerbert negotiated feats such as this through black magic. But, if anyone does diligent research into the truth, he will see that Solomon, who had received his wisdom from God himself, was not unaware of such powers. I believe that it was God who gave Solomon his control over demons, as Josephus testifies, stating that it was so strong that, even in his own time, there were men who expelled malign spirits from the bodies of the possessed by holding up to their noses a ring bearing a seal revealed by Solomon. I believe, then, that he could also have given this knowledge to Gerbert, although I do not affirm that he did.[42] (2.169)

Although William here refuses to commit himself, he has already used the tale of the Roman vaults to make it abundantly clear that Gerbert's powers were of divine origin, offering his readers a parable demonstrating God's punishment of those who would abuse the talents he has bestowed. At hand, therefore, is the final gloss to all that has preceded. Gerbert, who became slave to the devil in his surrender to *cupiditas,* was in fact originally selected by God to exorcise the devil in others, and his powers, considered by some to have been malign and necromantic, were in fact originally a divinely inspired gift of enlightenment. Since they are advanced as an epilogue to the tale of the Campus Martius, these additional comments must be assessed according to the metaphors William has already invited his clear-sighted reader to identify. As a result, the accomplished literacy that has been configured as magic here shifts into another metaphorical domain, now identified as a benign medicine, as a cure to the intellectual darkness that still obtains as a true legacy of the devil, and the Ring of Solomon is the talisman of the literate themselves, representing the ability to drive the demons of superstition and ignorance from the minds of the unenlightened.

Through this Judeo-Christian talisman, William's manipulations of the enlightened reader achieve their full significance. By guiding the clear-sighted through a riddle only then to lead them back to parity with the less accomplished, William erases intellectual elitism and reveals the ease with which advanced literacy itself may be tantamount to a sin of the flesh, a form of scholarly hubris that is different in nature but equal in degree to the crime of Gerbert. The literate must avoid such complacent sufficiency, must apply the precedent of Solomon to the Christian cause laid forth by Augustine, must devote their talents to the charity of predication. If not, they will have turned from God as absolutely as Gerbert himself, capitulating to the fleshy sin not of lucre, but of arrogance, self-esteem, and supercilious superiority.

Written Prestige

As a critic of material opulence, William is scarcely remarkable, emerging as but one of the many ecclesiastics of the era who wrote against the snares of the secular world. He is unusual, however, in his admonitions against the elitism of superior learning and the pride that may accompany the control of the literate talents he designates as *praestigia*.[43] In William's lexicon, this word chiefly carries its classical meaning of "conjuring tricks" or "magical spells." But, because in context signifying accomplishments that are not only hieratic and arcane but also economically rewarding and conducive to worldly advancement, it also accommodates a negative appraisal of everything we today would understand by prestige: an aura of rank and privilege that could perhaps be used to dazzle the disadvantaged and create respect or fear where none is warranted. William designates those who are particularly impressionable to these flaunted powers as the *populus* or *vulgus*, meaning the masses who lack formal education of any kind.[44] Yet, by establishing an internal receptive hierarchy, he also draws attention to the vulnerability of some of the literate themselves. These, the less accomplished who would halt at the surface of the pointing statue, are never categorized by social standing.

But they can be tentatively identified. The circle in which the *Gesta regum* was first disseminated was almost certainly monastic, initially comprising the brethren of Malmesbury Abbey itself and then extending to other institutions. At some point after its completion, William dedicated the work to Robert, earl of Gloucester, implying that he believed his writing would also be of interest to at least one member of the landed barony.[45] In all likelihood, then, William prospectively wrote for a wide public embracing the clergy and the laity, and this suggests that the disadvantaged *litterati* hypothesized in the tale of the Campus Martius found their actual equivalents in representatives of both.[46]

William never states the causes of their disadvantages, since throughout the anecdote he first and foremost addresses his peers. However, by persistently emphasizing clarity of vision, he gestures toward sight as the sensorial mode that must be brought to bear, implying that his anecdote should be subjected to the rigorous analysis of close *reading* to be understood in its full complexity: "si quis verum diligenter exsculpat, *videbit*" (2.169). If this is so, then the disadvantaged could plausibly fall into two categories: the deficient reader, who attempts a close analysis of this kind but lacks the requisite hermeneutic skill to identify the tropes and intertextual pointers that structure meaning; and the listener, who would be potentially capable of unearthing sense if given the opportunity, yet who is hindered by the less direct and personal mode of aural reception. But this is no more than an inference, and it perhaps borders on anachronism in its undefended assumption that the medieval listener was less proficient than the medieval reader. It is of course impossible to gauge precisely the mnemonic potentials and aural sensitivities of a medieval public. But, because the voice remained the primary mode of communication throughout the High Middle Ages and hearing the primary mode of reception, we can infer that those who formed William's public were more proficient in listening and memorization than we are today,[47] and we must cautiously brook the possibility that listeners indeed existed who were capable of grasping the subtleties of the tale without the relative luxury of reiterative comparison that reading would afford.[48]

However, and despite these speculations, further internal elements strongly suggest that William is indeed preoccupied by the reader. The metaphorical *praestigia* he himself performs, those bendings of hermeneutic perspective realized through intertextual pointers and tropic superimpositions, were themselves related to the semantic field of sight in twelfth-century etymology; and this too implies that visual, rather than auditory, apprehension is central to William's concerns.[49] The following, for example, is the classic definition of the *praestigium*, as given by John of Salisbury in the *Policraticus:*

> Mercury is said to have invented conjuring *[praestigium]*. The word comes from the fact that he could dull *[praestringere]* clarity of vision. He was the most skilled of magicians, making anything he wanted invisible or transforming things so they appeared in a different shape.[50]

As an avatar of Mercury, the "prestigious" scholar can disguise meanings by metaphorically dulling the eyesight in those who read the words he commits to parchment, and he can use the trope to disguise one thing in the verbal form of another. Under this new guise, he still shares the talents of William's Gerbert, potentially mobilizing an applied *scientia* to uncover figurative riches. But he can also avail himself of the mercurial ploys that are intimated by John to become the performative *praestigiator* in his own right. Throughout the story of the Campus Martius, William plays such a role, clouding the vision of certain readers and shifting the shapes of certain figures of reference. But he is a sorcerer only by association: Gerbert is the figurative magician, and other *litterati* are identified as such only if they display talents similar to his. William qualifies because he writes such an accomplished tale, and the proficient reader qualifies because he or she demonstrates literate accomplishments in arriving at an appropriately lucid interpretation.

However, William does construct a more openly necromantic persona for himself in a slightly later anecdote. The tale at issue is presented as a vast quotation, and it therefore marks something of a narratological departure from the material already considered. I have so far used the name "William" to refer to the narrative voice of Gerbert's excavations, and I have done so because a thorough narratological analysis has been unnecessary to my designs. But this "William" is, properly speaking, a strategic surrogate that is fabricated by the real author and on occasion made to relate first-person experiences and to express first-person views he himself does not share.[51] These interventions primarily come in the passage that introduces the *vetustum volumen*, which I shall now quote in the Latin with first-person markers underscored:

> Haec Boetius. *Mihi* vero fidem facit de istius sacrilegio inaudita mortis excogitatio. Cur enim se moriens, ut postea *dicemus,* excarnificaret ipse sui corporis horrendus lanista, nisi novi sceleris conscius esset? Unde in vetusto volumine quod in manus *meas* incidit, ubi omnium apostolicorum nomina continebantur et anni, ita scriptum *vidi*: "Johannes, qui et Gerbertus, annos quatuor, mensem unum, dies decem; hic turpiter vitam suam finivit."[52] (2.167)

With the exception of the "dicemus" (which refers to a future narrative intervention that is indeed made), these first-person pronouncements are fictions in their own right, disingenuously presented as authorial acts and opinions that William challenges the reader to deconstruct by elsewhere exonerating Gerbert: no ancient volume containing facts to this effect was ever found in historical time, and William was not led to share the view that Gerbert had himself dismembered to atone for a necromantic pact he allegedly made with the devil.

To have belabored these points in context would have unduly impeded my arguments. But they nonetheless illuminate a less-developed permutation on the narratological strategy I shall now consider in what I shall call "The Anecdote of the Ass." Here, William explicitly transfers responsibility for his tale to another voice, claiming he is offering a verbatim reproduction of a story he heard from an Aquitanian monk when he was a boy.[53] The delegated narrativity that results enables William simultaneously to perform an exercise in rhetorical enchantment, to distance himself from its negative implications, and to comment on the ethical problems it poses. Here, too, degrees of literate competence are addressed, and once again an interpretative hierarchy is created within the tale. But on this occasion William exposes more than the pride of lucid interpretation.

The Anecdote of the Ass

In *Gesta regum Anglorum* 2.171, the monk relates how a couple of women innkeepers in Italy made a young man into an ass, and a golden one at that, at least in the money he earned his owners by performing amazing antics for the benefit of passers-by. So entertaining was this asinine performer that its fame quickly spread and the old women sold it at a profit. One evening, while its new master was getting drunk, the ass broke its bridle, ran off, threw itself into a pond, and realized it was human. With his humanity thus restored to his own eyes, the young man related his experiences to one of his owner's servants, who passed the story on to his master, who confided it to Pope Leo, who, having it confirmed by the old women themselves, in turn told the acclaimed scholar, Peter Damian.

The tale is doubly specious. First, even if we assume that William did indeed hear it during his childhood, the story he writes several decades later cannot under any circumstances be the word-for-word transcription it is purported to be. Second (and erasing any ambiguity over the first), although the monk states that he recounts actual events that occurred during his own lifetime, his claim is utterly compromised by the extremely bookish origin of his material. His narrative is in fact an extended embellishment of information that Augustine provides in the *De civitate Dei:*

> Even I, when in Italy, heard things of this kind about a particular region of that country where women innkeepers, imbued with the evil arts, were reputed often to give something in bits of cheese to travelers, whether ones they wanted or simply the ones they could get. By this means, they were turned into pack animals and would carry whatever was required until the job was finished, and they would then return to their normal selves. Their minds, however, would not be transformed into those of beasts, but would remain rational and human in the way Apuleius, in the books he called *The Golden Ass,* claimed either factually or as pure fiction happened to him when, after being poisoned, he became an ass yet retained his human mind.[54]

At issue, then, is a complex performance of multiple disguises: William makes a story he himself has elaborated from Augustine masquerade as a tale he heard during his childhood; he passes off a voice of his own fabrication as the voice of another; and, within the fiction of orality that results, the delegated narrator falsely presents a rumor committed to writing in the fifth century as a factual account of events that happened during the eleventh or early twelfth.

But the receding frames of narrative transformation do not stop here. The monk's story finally becomes a story of its own previous tellings: it is first told by the young man himself and then retold three times over, first by the servant to his master, then by the master to the pope, and then by the pope to a man of letters. The response of the last of these listeners is revealing:

> The doubting pope was assured by Peter Damian, skilled in the field of writing, who confirmed that it was hardly surprising if things like this should happen. After giving the example of Simon Magus, who made Faustinianus appear in the shape of Simon himself and made him dreaded by his sons, he gave the pope fuller information about the other aspects of such matters.[55] (2.171)

In the *Pseudo-Clementine Recognitions,* the text Peter implicitly cites, the transformation of Faustinianus is a very real act of physical metamorphosis.[56] Simply by deeming it relevant, Peter demonstrates that, in the tale he has heard, the old women did indeed employ magic to turn a man into a beast, just as Simon Magus employed magic to impart his own appearance to another man.

Although the construct of the real author, this narrative prehistory is attributed to the voice of the monk, and it must in the first instance be assessed as a strategic device through which the surrogate narrator draws attention to certain changes he makes in *his* version of the story. For, as he presents them, the old women are not witches, but outrageously successful con artists. At no point does he state that they actually transformed the young man (or any of their victims) into an animal. They simply make people appear to be what they are not—the title of this chapter, "About the old women who made a young man seem an ass" ("De aniculis quae juvenem asinum videri fecerunt"), introduces the verbal causative that is then systematically and exclusively employed in the text itself ("Hae hospitem, si quando solus superveniebat, vel equum, vel suem, vel quodlibet aliud *videri faciebant*"; "ephebum asinum *videri fecerunt*" [2.171]). And a dumb ass the young man certainly was, subscribing to the fiction to the point of losing the ability to articulate words and obligingly following his owners' every command.[57]

The monk therefore alters the story of magic he claims to have inherited to create a story of verbal persuasion, and this emphasis on the power of words in turn illuminates the delegated narrator's own control of a particular type of sorcery. As a fiction of oral performance situated in historical time, the tale implicitly evokes an equally fictive audience, presumably formed of the inmates of Malmesbury Abbey and including in their number the young William himself. The version of the tale this hypothetical group heard was of course in Latin, logically used by the monk as a cenobitic *lingua franca;* and, respecting William's claim to precise transcription, the following is the text of the young man's experiences exactly as it was delivered:

> Multum itaque quaestum conflaverant vetulae, undique confluente multitudine vulgi ad spectandos ludos asini. Rumor vicinum divitem advocavit ut quadrupedem non pauculis nummis in usus suos transferret; admonitus ut, si perpetuum vellet habere histrionem, arceret eum aqua. Custos ergo appositus mandatum severe exequebatur. Praeteriit plurimum tempus: asinus, quando temulentia dominum in gaudium excitasset, convivias jocis suis laetificabat. Sed, sicut rerum omnium fastidium est, dissolutius post haec haberi coepit; quapropter incautiorem nactus custodiam, abrupto loro effugiens, in proximum lacum se projecit, et diutius in aqua volutatus, figuram sibi humanam restituit. Custos ab obviis sciscitatus, illumque vestigiis insecutus, interrogat an vidisset asinum. Refert ille se asinum fuisse, modo hominem, omnemque casum exponit. (2.171)
>
> [In this way, the old women gained quite a golden profit, with huge crowds of commoners gathering from all sides to watch the antics of the ass. Rumor of this prompted a rich man of the area to buy the quadruped for no inconsiderable sum of money. He was warned that, if he wished always to have an entertainer, he should deny it water. So, an appointed guard strictly followed this advice. A long time passed. When its master would grow mirthful with alcohol, the ass would delight the guests with its antics. But, since everything ends up growing tedious, the ass found that it was confined less strictly after times like this. So,

> while inattentively guarded, it broke its bridle, ran off, and threw itself into a nearby lake. After rolling around for a while, it restored its human shape to itself. Its guard questioned people on the way, followed its footprints, and asked him if he had seen an ass. He stated that he himself had been the ass, and was now a man, and explained the whole situation.

From classical times onward, *asinus* carried connotations of stupidity at least as forcefully as its modern English equivalent,[58] and in all of the above the monk is using the word to mean both "donkey" and "idiot." The joke, of course, is on the young man all along, who is an idiot because he accepts the fiction that he is indeed a quadruped beast of burden. Or, with a slightly different emphasis, he shows he is figuratively a dumb ass because he believes himself to be one in a literal sense. This play on *asinus* is reinforced in the Latin by other semantic ambiguities that cannot be adequately rendered in English. Because Latin has no articles and makes no grammatical distinction between masculine things and masculine people, the above translation sustains the illusion of the metamorphosis that dupes the young man himself. Accordingly, any pronoun or possessive referring to *asinus* is rendered by the English neuter "it, its," and a choice is made between "the ass" and "an ass" simply because the choice is inevitable. However, because Latin is without these distinctions, the latter part of the passage I translate above could just as validly be rendered as follows:

> So, an appointed guard strictly followed this advice. A long time passed. When his master would grow mirthful with alcohol, the idiot would delight the guests with his antics. But, since everything ends up growing tedious, the idiot found that he was confined less strictly after times like this. So, while inattentively guarded, he broke his bridle, ran off, and threw himself into a nearby lake. After rolling around for a while, he restored his human shape to himself. His guard questioned people on the way, followed his footprints, and asked him if he had seen an ass. He stated that he himself had been the ass and was now a man again, and explained the whole situation.[59]

The point of this lengthy detour into semantic and syntactic equivocation is simple: the understanding of the tale involves the ability to identify the function of a dominant metaphor and to perceive its relationship with other equivocations. If approached with a sensitivity to the trope, the tale at once yields its ambiguities. Alternatively, it may be interpreted on the entirely literal plane of grammar: *asinus* may be invested with its zoological sense, and "asinum videri facere" taken to be a circumlocution for the physical "transformare/mutare/vertere in asinum." Thus, the listener may always run the risk of being as much of a dumb ass as the young man, may also interpret with a rigid literalness. The young man is an idiot because he believes the fiction that he is an ass. The listener may be an ass for failing to understand that the young man is an ass only because he is an idiot.

If so, the listener would fall victim to a figurative sorcery the monk has surreptitiously woven into his discourse. The most striking amendment he has made to the rumor Augustine reports is his omission of the cheese *(caseum)* the crones use to transform people into animals. Yet he phonically and functionally replaces it with the very story he tells:

> Refert ille se asinum fuisse, modo hominem, omnemque *casum* exponit. Miratus famulus ad dominum detulit; dominus ad apostolicum Leonem, dico, nostro seculo sanctissimum; convictae anus idem fatentur. Dubitantem papam confirmat Petrus Damianus, litteraturae peritus, non mirum si haec fieri possint. (2.171; emphasis added)

> [He stated that he himself had been the ass, and was now a man again, and explained the whole situation. The astonished servant related this to his master; his master to none other than Pope Leo, most blessed in our own century; and, once accused, the old women admitted the same. The doubting pope was assured by Peter Damian, skilled in the field of writing, who confirmed that it was hardly surprising if a thing like this should happen.]

The monk uses the word *casum* to refer to the experiences the young man has undergone. Since these experiences exist for the listener only in and through the monk's immediately preceding words, then the *casum* at issue is functionally equivalent to the first section of the tale. Thus the narrative itself enters a relationship of analogy with the *caseum* it phonically recalls, and the analogous effects it could have are thereby emphasized: just as surely as the cheese used by Augustine's crones, the monk's tale may transform some individuals into dumb asses through the embedded presence of an ostensibly magical device. While Augustine does not specify the nature of the magical preparation his innkeepers put in the cheese, the monk obliquely but unequivocally reveals that the only transformative drug operative in his words is ambiguity, above all that single metaphor bridging diegesis and reception, *asinus*. To emphasize these pharmaceutical properties, William attributes to the monk a particular field of expertise that at first glance seems gratuitous. The storyteller is a doctor by training ("arte medico" [2.170]) and is therefore the master of an art that lexically accommodates no distinction between medicine and poison. For the *medicamentum* he would usually administer to others can both heal or contaminate, may be a remedy to illness or may be *venenum* of the type that transformed Apuleius's Lucius in *The Golden Ass*.[60] At no point does the monk textually display these literal accomplishments in physic, never actually tending to the maladies of those around him. All he does is tell stories, displacing one form of ministration with another. His narrative is the *only* medium for the equivocal art he controls, and, potentially capable of stultifying the minds of its recipients, this verbal *medicamentum* is fully efficacious.[61]

This being so, the monk's discursive manipulations are aggressively mocking in their effects, and it is precisely to distance himself from this mockery that William creates the illusion of quoting someone else. Furthermore, he provides a precise intertextual pointer through which he clarifies this narratological shift and intimates his own ethical remove from the surrogate he has deployed. The pointer in question is the metamorphosis of Faustinianus, perpetrated by Simon Magus in the *Pseudo-Clementine Recognitions*. Simon's principal role in this work is to act as forensic antagonist to Saint Peter, and his hubris, sophistication, and personal idolatry are foils against which the apostle articulates the simplicity of his faith with devastating force. However, three biographical facts are more pertinent to present concerns. First, as his name implies, Simon is a magician.[62] Second, he is a master of rhetoric, dialectic, and sophistry, and he employs these arts of verbal manipulation in concert with his magic to convince the credulous that he speaks the truth even when spreading falsehood (2.5).[63] Third, to gloss the particular *praestigium* that Peter Damian cites, at a turning point in his career Simon transfers his own appearance to another man. Pursued for his crimes by the Roman soldiery, he makes Faustinianus into a decoy, presuming the authorities will arrest and punish his pseudoself while he negotiates his escape. Saint Peter nevertheless turns the situation to his own advantage and has Faustinianus, still bearing Simon's face, speak in public specifically to abjure Simon's teaching. The stratagem is duly successful: Simon's converts now turn to Christ; and Faustinianus has his own form restored. Accordingly, the result of the magician's *praestigium* is exploited to destroy the magician's ungodly influence, and the truth of Christianity is allowed to spread unhindered throughout the Roman populace.

The monk displays certain aspects of Simon's verbal mastery. First, as a variation on Simon's ability to present falsehood as truth, he passes off hearsay reported by Augustine as an account of actual events that happened hundreds of years later. He therefore makes fifth-century rumor masquerade as eleventh-century fact and dresses his own fiction in the guise of history. Second, as a variation on Simon's dazzling control of rhetoric, he uses a set of interdependent equivocations to create the illusion of an asinine metamorphosis when none has in fact occurred. Now of course, although attributed to the monk, both of these Simonic strategies are orchestrated by William, and he is ultimately responsible for their effects. In an effort to sidestep the negative implications of this, William strives to show that he, as author, has also imitated one of Simon's *praestigia:* in adopting the narrative persona of the monk, he has created a grotesque travesty of himself and in effect plays the roles of both Simon and Faustinianus.[64] Like Simon, he is responsible for the transformation. Yet, like Faustinianus, he has his outward self altered to assume the face of malice. The initial result is the same in both cases, with William in his new guise appearing as abhorrent to observers as Faustinianus is to his sons.[65] The final consequences of these two travesties are also congruous: just as Faustinianus eventually speaks to abjure all that he appears to be, William too undoes the negative implications of his stratagem. First, and most obviously, he invites an assimilation between the two crones and the teller of their story: both parties in their different ways make people into asses; and both are equally repellent. Second, he informs the accomplished reader that this repulsive exterior is not his own, using the advice Peter Damian gives Pope Leo as a signal for the textual paradigm that will reveal the nature of the narratological transfer he himself has performed. Third, he employs throughout motifs culled from Augustine, and thereby gestures back to the precepts he has already by this stage circumscribed in his earlier treatment of Gerbert and draws attention to the reality of intent that subtends the masking of appearance. To deploy learning only to make others appear foolish is not simply repellent. It is to turn away from the charitable directives of God himself.

2

Geoffrey of Monmouth and John of Salisbury

Themes of Credulity

By using the *Pseudo-Clementine Recognitions* to help explicate the Anecdote of the Ass, William of course exposes his maneuvers only to the highly literate. Indeed, he himself suggests as much. Peter Damian, who uses an exemplum from the work, is expressly designated as being skilled in *litteratura,* a word that carries a more extended sense than its modern European cognates ("Dubitantem papam confirmat Petrus Damianus, *litteraturae peritus,* non mirum si haec fieri possint"). I have rather clumsily translated "the field of writing" in an effort to render a meaning that embraces not only a written epistemology that tends for us today increasingly toward the abstract, but also everything that is implicated in literacy: a knowledge of letters conceived as mediating symbols for spoken language and, through it, things; an understanding of the displacements of significance that can be achieved through the trope; an acquaintance with a preexisting corpus of written paradigms to be employed in interpretation; a conception, therefore, of the *written* text as a complex means of conveying thought.[1] William implicitly appeals to the *litteraturae periti* of his own era to apply these same talents to his anecdote. As in the story of Gerbert, therefore, a degree of erudition is required to identify intertextual constructs: the *Recognitions,* cited but not named, intimates the self-conscious adoption of a surrogate narrative voice, the disguise of fable as fact, and the subtending presence of magic; and these last two devices can in turn only be understood if the relevant passage from Augustine's *De civitate Dei* is perceived as the unavowed palimpsest that structures the tale's themes.

By inference, all of these intertextual signals were most easily perceived through a close visual analysis of the text, since, within its own internal economy, the monk's tale exposes the deficient responses of listeners only. Although William himself does not explicitly settle this issue, further data from the twelfth century suggest that reading was indeed perceived to be the more productive mode of reception. The following, for example, is how Alain de Lille's Natura describes the sale of naked *falsitas* in the *De planctu Naturae:*

> Don't you know how poets sell falsehood as a naked whore to their listeners, without even having recourse to a garment, and practically enchant the ears of those who listen and intoxicate them with a particular honey-sweet pleasure?[2] (837)

Here Alain has Natura speak exclusively of listening ("poete *auditoribus* nudam falsitatem prostituunt"; "uelut incantatas *audientium aures* inebrient"), and, playing on tensions similar to those already analyzed, he introduces a metaphorical sorcery by conflating the recited poem and the magical spell through the etymological resonances of *incantare.*[3] Thus, through a bizarre but characteristic combination of tropes, Alain projects the poem as a fleshy lie, poets as pimping magicians, and those who would pay for their services as clients in a bordello predicated exclusively on auditory seduction. But what is significant is an implied restriction to the power of these magical manipulators. When moving on to address the *cortex/nucleus,* Alain not only has Natura discard the image of the brothel altogether. He also has her mention *reading* for the first time, as the second and more probing stage in a dual process of hermeneutics. Once again:

> Don't you know how the poetic lyre strikes a false note on the superficial rind of the letter, but on a more profound level communicates to listeners *[auditoribus]* a secret of higher understanding, with the result that, once this shell of falsehood has been discarded, the reader *[lector]* may find secreted inside the sweeter kernel of truth?[4] (837)

Two points are of note. First, the poet is cast as pimp and sorcerer only in a performative context: by implication, his success presupposes the absence of the disabused reader capable of dispelling his verbal enchantments. Second, auditory reception is adequate only for the intimation of a significance that must be subsequently grasped through analysis of the text in its written form. It must again be stated that Alain is not commenting on the *Gesta regum* when he makes these remarks. But he does permit us to maintain the receptive hierarchy outlined in chapter 1: even though some masterful listeners very probably existed, they were exceptions, and, on the whole, complex Latin works required they be read in order to be understood with a full sensitivity to their subtleties.

By its very nature, a close visual analysis of this kind would have been beyond the powers of the illiterate, and it would have severely challenged those of limited *litteratura*. We must, however, display caution when attempting to apply these facts to twelfth-century cultural history. In a manner that may appear thoroughly paradoxical to modern sensibilities, authors did on occasion dedicate their Latin works to the partially literate or analphabetic, with the clear expectation that others would intervene to help clarify obscurities of language and, ultimately, significance.[5] The final intervention of Peter Damian in the Anecdote of the Ass both attests this enlightening role and adumbrates its extradiegetic analogue: by drawing attention to the man of letters in this way, William calls on the accomplished of his own era to unravel the ambiguities of his tale for the less proficient and encourages them to preclude the figurative metamorphosis that may be occasioned by a literal interpretation of the monk's words.

Elsewhere in the *Gesta regum,* William amplifies this appeal and in the process anticipates some of the tensions of patronage and reception that obtained in the latter half of the century. This is his account of the education received by Henry I, the king who was to receive the name Beauclerc among future generations:

> Henry, the youngest son of the great William, was born in England in the third year after his father's arrival. With the unanimous approval of all, he was already as a child receiving an excellent education, because he alone of all William's sons was born to a royal house, and it was to him that the kingdom seemed destined. Therefore, he went through the early, rudimentary stages

> of learning to read, and he so absorbed the honey-sweetness of letters into the thirsting fiber of his being that from then on no tumults in war and no upheavals in administration could banish them from his illustrious mind. Although he himself would read very little in public, and would only recite in a self-effacing manner, nonetheless it is to be truthfully stated that his scholarship, although gained sporadically, provided a great aid to him in the art of government, exemplifying the adage of Plato that says, "The body politic is blessed either if philosophers are its rulers or if kings take to philosophy." And so, in his scholarship, he prepared himself as a child for the possibility of kingship and, even in the hearing of his father, was frequently prone to come out with the saying, "An illiterate king is an ass wearing a crown."[6] (5:390)

William is here employing this unflattering metaphor as an antiphrastic device designed the better to eulogize the enlightened kingship of Henry.[7] But he also uses it to help clarify certain elements of the Anecdote of the Ass. For both ultimately derive circumstantial details from a tale originally told by Ovid in *Metamorphoses* 11. This involves Midas, that potentate of unlimited wealth and dreadful philistinism who is also one of the more celebrated regal buffoons in Western literature.[8]

Midas is guilty of two transgressions. As a result of the first, he learns the appalling consequences of presuming the gods will do as he pleases. Granted a boon by Bacchus, the Phrygian king requests that everything touched by his body be turned to burnished gold (11.102–3).[9] Certainly, this makes Midas immediately and exceedingly rich in the way he had presumably hoped, and he wanders around turning such varied objects as grass, twigs, apples, and pillars into material wealth. But problems arise when he decides to have his first meal and finds himself attempting to bite into slabs of metallic bread and meat, with only liquid gold to make this mineral sustenance more digestible. The starving king is forced to beg Bacchus to reverse his wish and implicitly recognizes the sin of greed (11.132).[10] Bacchus accedes and instructs him to immerse himself in the waters of a river near Sardis, where the spell is broken. But Midas, who seems never to learn, goes on to commit yet another act of hubris, on this occasion disagreeing with the judgment passed by Tmolus to the effect that Apollo is a better musician than Pan. Furious,

Apollo gives Midas the ears of an ass as punishment for this outrageous lack of respectful taste, and the king, excruciatingly embarrassed, takes to wearing commodious headgear in an effort to conceal his divinely bestowed excrescences. But there is one servant of the royal household who perforce has to see what is so assiduously concealed from others, and this of course is the hairdresser:

> The servant saw this. Since he did not dare communicate the shameful sight, yet wanted to bring it out in the open, he went off alone, unable to keep the news to himself. He dug into the ground and, lowering his voice, whisperingly described to the empty earth the kind of ears he had seen on his master. Then he covered over the testimony of his voice by replacing the soil, and, with the hole filled in, he quietly made off.[11] (11.183–89)

If only in the seemingly frivolous context of aural deformity, the ground has become the repository of fact, dug with the specific end to receiving signs. These alter through sequential stages: the voice *(vox)* becomes its own trace or symbol *(indicium vocis)* finally to become words *(verba)*. Although this last term is used to apply to both the spoken and the written word, the median stage of *indicium* unequivocally reveals the buried signs to be scribal. The spatial repository, therefore, contains writing, and the most common enclosed space to which writing is committed is the book.

With slight shifts of emphasis, William employs some of these Ovidian motifs in the Anecdote of the Ass. By having the young man restore his human shape to his own eyes by throwing himself into a pond, William gestures toward Midas immersing himself in the waters of Sardis; and, more obviously, by exploiting the figurative resonances of the word *asinus,* he plays on the trope for stupidity suggested by Midas's ears and anticipates the sense of the unflattering image he later ascribes to the young Henry.[12] Providing his own demonstration of asinine literalness, identifying an analphabetic monarch as an ass wearing a crown, and subtly relating both to the Ovidian paradigm, William draws attention to the historical circumstances of patronage that obtained throughout the twelfth century and points toward the existence of a group of patrons who would potentially be vulnerable to the type of rhetorical poison manipulated by the Aquitanian monk. This is the nobility, formed not only of the king, but also an entire stratum of lesser dignitaries, many of whom, even as William wrote, were beginning to show an increasing interest in works of historiography, and who, within a generation, employed their increasing wealth to patronize the earliest romances.[13] Perhaps, through his oblique and widely scattered deployment of these Ovidian images, William sought to imply that these munificent patrons might display the same literal-mindedness and the same deficiencies in aesthetic judgment as Midas himself. Perhaps, furthermore, he wished to warn against the possibility of there being at least one servant in their employ who would unveil these regrettable inadequacies in writing. If this is so, then he perhaps also warns *litterati,* both present and future, against such facetious maneuvers, tangentially evoking the story of Midas in order to stress the implications of its end. The royal servant may well consign his secret to the ground. But he also creates circumstances in which his own stratagem of concealment will inevitably be undone:

> A clump of trembling reeds quickly started to grow in that place. As soon as they were fully grown at the end of the year, they betrayed the man who had planted them. For, stirring in the gentle south wind, they spoke his buried words and testified to his master's ears.[14] (11.190–93)

Respecting the Ovidian metamorphosis, this process of documentation involves buried words germinating and growing into plants—the servant is said to be the *agricola,* the sower of vocalized seeds that alter and assume vegetal form. Precisely what they become, nevertheless, points subtly toward writing: the spoken word germinates to become the *harundo,* literally the reed, but also the essential tool of the writer, the pen itself. By metonymy, therefore, the story of Midas resolves into a history of glossing, as the words consigned to the book give rise to pens that will disclose its hidden message. Magnates may be covertly mocked. But the cover of writing will be broken by the writing that its secreted sense will generate.

That such warnings subtend William's redeployment of Ovidian motifs is no more than an inference, justified by the monitory tenor of his anecdotes. But, however this may be, a number of writers active in the later twelfth century return to these images. Two Latin authors, John of Salisbury and Gerald of Wales, join William in expressing the view that an illiterate king is to be likened to an ass wearing a crown (and Gerald does so with direct reference to the monarch to whom he dedicated his most famous work).[15] Moreover, a number of contemporary vernacular authors attest what amounts to a positive epidemic of ass's ears and related maladies: the author of the *Roman de Thèbes* declares in his prologue that anyone who is not a cleric or a knight will listen to his work with the same competence as an ass listening to the strains of a harp;[16] the anonymous redactor of *Floire et Blancheflor* attributes to Barbarin the ability to make asses themselves into harpists;[17] and in his version of *Tristan,* Béroul has the malignant dwarf and reputed soothsayer Froncin spread word to the effect that King Mark has the ears of a horse.[18] In all of these cases, asinine imagery is bound up with problems of comprehension, reflecting the epistemological tensions of the later twelfth century. By the 1160s, when Benoît de Sainte-Maure wrote his *Roman de Troie, gramaire* had already become a magical stuff capable of creating gold and the arcane, perhaps threatening, medium for deception designated by the later medieval doublet *grimoire.* It had already come to carry the resonance of the glamour that writing became for the lowland Scots of the late Middle Ages and, divorced from its graphemic origins, still exercises its seductive aura of exclusion and privilege.[19]

To place these later permutations in context, it is necessary to consider briefly certain facts of literary history. During the period roughly corresponding with the Anarchy of Stephen, a new, secularized historiography developed, chiefly fostered by the extraordinary success of Geoffrey of Monmouth's *Historia regum Britanniae.* With it came liberties in historical fabrication and a pronounced emphasis on the writer as an artisan elaborating a cultural construct that was designed to supplement gaps in existing witness and to provide a revisionary past through which contemporary difficulties could be confronted and possible resolutions proposed.[20] This creative freedom brought a new set of receptive problems, difficulties of epistemological perspective that were accurately, if acerbically, intimated by Geoffrey's primary twelfth-century critic, William of Newburgh:

> This man is called Geoffrey and takes Arthur as his second name after the Arthurian fables, which, derived from the ancient fictions of the British and augmented with additions of his own, he conveyed through the highly colored rhetoric of the Latin language and thereby clothed in the honorable name of history.[21]

Although William writes from a partisan position and indulges in misrepresentations of his own,[22] he is the earliest critic to define two aspects of his antagonist's initiative that remain accepted tenets of Galfridian scholarship: that Geoffrey presented material of his own invention as historical fact[23] and that he employed the conventional procedures of historiographic writing to lend his contrivance a veneer of authenticity.[24] Bound up with these two points is a third, less prevalent in twentieth-century criticism but no less important: as William also indicates, Geoffrey's writing of an apocryphal past brought with it a receptive challenge to the contemporary public:

> Only someone ignorant of the histories of ancient peoples would peruse this book of his that he calls the History of the British and fail to see how he shamelessly and impudently lies about practically everything. For anyone who is not apprised of the truth of historical events incautiously admits the vanity of fables.[25] (Proem)

> Since, therefore, the ancient historians make not the slightest mention of any of this, then whatever information that man has spread in writing about Arthur and Merlin to pander to the curiosity of the indiscriminate is patently fabricated by liars.[26] (Proem)

As William implies in his dismissive references to the ignorant ("ignari") and indiscriminate ("minus prudentes") who would be seduced by Geoffrey's contrivance, to identify the *Historia regum* as fabrication requires a relatively advanced degree of *litteratura* in the field of Insular history; and, since he intimates this epistemological challenge in a Latin text and does so in order to disabuse readers or listeners fully capable of understanding the language in which he writes, it would appear that certain *litterati* had failed to apply the requisite discernment in their responses to Geoffrey's work.

Such ostensibly uncritical acceptance on the part of the literate must in turn be evaluated alongside collateral developments in written epistemology. Assessed in the wider context of twelfth-century letters, the *Historia regum* occupies a pivotal position between orthodox Latin historiography and the vernacular romance. In language, style, and genealogical progression, it is an analogue of contemporaneous works such as

Henry of Huntingdon's *Historia Anglorum*.[27] Yet, in its complex interweaving of fact and fabrication, its emphasis on the *ingenium* of its creator, and its superimposition of past and present, it anticipates what have come to be viewed as the fundamental attributes of the *romans antiques* (and, to a lesser extent, the later works of Chrétien de Troyes). When a "fictional factuality"[28] of the type constituted by the *Historia regum* came to be manifested in the romance, it brought with it, in a more pronounced form, the type of hermeneutic challenge rehearsed above. If indeed, according to William's twelfth-century dictum, "anyone who is not apprised of the truth of historical events incautiously admits the vanity of fables," then it is legitimate to speculate to what extent the monolingual and partially literate magnates who formed the greater part of the vernacular audience were adequate to the task of distinguishing between *historia* and *fabula* as they were manipulated by romance authors. Or, rephrased in the light of the material already considered: it is legitimate to speculate to what extent they showed themselves to be discerning listeners or unwittingly proved they were in fact asses wearing minor crowns.

I shall devote this and the next chapter to engaging this issue. Throughout, my aim will not be to retrieve precise evidence that can be adduced to quantify the relative degrees of understanding or misprision that contemporary readers and listeners displayed in negotiating Geoffrey's initiative. In the absence of extensive data, such an enterprise would be impossible. Rather, I shall consider two texts—one Latin, the other vernacular—in order to assess the means their authors employ to alert readers or listeners to the inauthenticity of the past they are constructing. The vernacular text I shall consider in chapter 3 is Benoît de Sainte-Maure's *Roman de Troie*. This begins with a prefatory parable of inscrutable recitation, enacted by a performer wearing a talismanic ring that grants the power of invisibility; it is constituted of an enchanted grapheme that is both *gramaire* and *grimoire* and is sufficient to conjure forth a golden simulacrum of nature; and it is contrived by an author who explores his own potentially mystifying powers of creativity through three diegetic surrogates displaying the talents of architecture ("trei sage engeigneor" [16650]), divination ("trei sage devin" [16729]), and language and necromancy ("trei poëte, sages dotors, / qui mout sorent de nigromance" [14668–69]). None of these vernacular themes, however, can be fully understood without due consideration of the first text I shall address. This is the most successful "magical" narrative of the first half of the century, and it is precisely the alleged tissue of falsehood that William of Newburgh strove to denounce, the *Historia regum* itself.

Geoffrey of Monmouth: A Drama of Reception

As is true of all cases in which pseudepigraphy is unmasked, William's remarks are simply glosses on internal signals of inauthenticity that are already present in the paradigm. This is a matter of some importance. Geoffrey's innovation was not only to disguise fable as history: it was to do so with a degree of self-dismantling candor. Although, as William states, Geoffrey adheres so closely to established historiographic practice in style and structure that he creates a specious truth from the very form he manipulates, he also in one particularly eloquent episode uses Merlin to undo his pretense and to dramatize the challenge of distinguishing fact from fiction that William delineates. To paraphrase briefly: Utherpendragon desires Ingerna, wife of Duke Gorlois of Cornwall; Merlin agrees to help him satisfy his lust and gives Uther the outward appearance of Gorlois (while also transforming himself into one of the duke's retainers);[29] then

> Uther took the drugs given by Merlin and assumed Gorlois's appearance. So the king spent that night with Ingerna and enjoyed the pleasures he had longed for. He had fooled her with the false appearance he had assumed. He had also fooled her with lying words he ornately composed.[30] (137)

As J. S. P. Tatlock has demonstrated, Geoffrey's Merlin is a composite of two figures: one is the classical deity and archetypal *praestigiator* Mercury and the other is Simon Magus of the *Pseudo-Clementine Recognitions*.[31] Elaborating on this insight, I venture still further and state that two other participants in this seduction show powers that derive from Simon's. One is Uther, whose control of a fictitious discourse that convinces through the seductive beauty of form ("deceperat etiam ficticiis sermonibus quos ornate conponebat") closely corresponds with Simon's magisterial deployment of rhetoric to the cause of deceit ("'Simon vehementissimus est orator [et], apud eos qui ignorant eum, falsa allegans put[atur] vera defendere'" [2.5]). The other is Geoffrey himself. The themes of illusion, metamorphosis, and linguistic contrivance that here dominate diegesis so closely gloss the epistemological and stylistic procedures adopted throughout the *Historia regum* that they must be read as self-conscious signals of authorial elucidation. These themes, moreover, are introduced in a context that adumbrates the extradiegetic circumstances in which such signals would or would not be identified by the reader/listener. At issue is a meticulously orchestrated performance, and by its end the combined forces of magic and verbal finesse have assured that falsehood be taken as reality. At issue, in fine, is an internal drama through which Geoffrey anticipates one of the possible scenarios in which the *Historia regum* itself may be received.

To achieve this end, Geoffrey manipulates receding frames of proxy. Following Simon's ability to disguise his likeness and simultaneously bear two faces ("vultum meum commuto, ut non agnoscar, sed et duas facies habere me possum hominibus ostendere" [2.9]), Geoffrey refracts elements of his own authorial procedures through *both* Merlin and Uther. Through the Brythonic soothsayer, he acts out yet another of Simon's shape-shifting talents by altering Uther's appearance. He then exploits the disguised king as a medium through whom to project his own powers of verbal seduction. Two aspects of his writing are thereby sequentially emphasized: his disguise of one thing as another ("falsa species") and his use of discursive constructs that are spurious in their integrity ("fictit[ii] sermon[es]") and ornate in their composition ("ornate conp[ositi]"), both to heighten and defend the travesty he perpetrates.[32] By emphasizing disguise and language in this way, Geoffrey is subtly avowing the procedures that William of Newburgh identified as the defining attributes of the entire *Historia regum:* Geoffrey, William maintains, dressed fables—some British, some of his own invention—in the honorable name of history ("fabulas ex priscis Britonum figmentis sumptas et ex proprio auctas honesto historiae nomine palliavit"), and he did so through the superadded sheen of Latin discourse ("per superductum Latini sermonis colorem"). The "false appearance" that Geoffrey dramatizes as the primary thematic travesty is therefore to be understood as a signal for the transformation of fable into history, the primary epistemological artifice that is constituted by the textuality of the *Historia regum* itself; and the "lying words he ornately composed" gloss the linguistic constructs by which the primary travesty is effected and to which it owes its success. Both of these points are in turn corroborated by the hypotextual presence of the *Recognitions:* Geoffrey, like Simon, is displaying his ability to use language with such persuasion that he makes falsehood pass for the truth: "vehementissimus est orator [et] apud eos qui ignorant eum, falsa allegans put[atur] vera defendere."

While the first of these impostures is found throughout the work, it is particularly obtrusive in the episode under consideration, since the circumstantial props of Arthur's conception are lifted from a paradigm that cannot under any circumstances be considered historiographic. This is Plautus's *Amphitryon,* from which Geoffrey culls the motifs of the admirer who has himself disguised as a husband, the supernatural attendant who is responsible for the metamorphosis, and the prolongation of the night to ensure that the seduction be successfully completed.[33] Not only is this text unadulterated fiction by any postclassical standards; it is also an example of the figments of divine lust that Alain de Lille, articulating the most conservative viewpoint of the twelfth century, went on to vituperate as senseless and pernicious delirium.[34] Yet it is transformed into apparent history nonetheless, and it predicates the most daring of all Geoffrey's affronts to accepted fact, since, in guaranteeing the birth of Arthur, it guarantees the continuation of British dominion beyond the chronology established by Bede. Here too, William of Newburgh was the first to summarize the implications:

> Since the events of the past are sanctioned by the historical truth expounded by the Venerable Bede, then everything that man took upon himself to write about Arthur, or about his successors, or about his predecessors after Vortigern, is proved to be fiction concocted partly by him and partly by others. He makes Aurelius Ambrosius succeed Vortigern. And he then has him succeeded by his brother, Utherpendragon, taking at this point the unbounded license of mendaciously inserting a great deal about that Merlin of his. On Utherpendragon's death, he has his son Arthur succeed to the Kingdom of Britain as the fourth king after Vortigern. But our Bede places Ethelbert, who welcomed Augustine, on the English throne as the fourth king after Hengist. This means the reign of Arthur and the arrival of Augustine must

> have coincided. Now, even the aptitudes of a dull mind can clearly see how in all this the simple truth of history demolishes the contrivances of falsehood.[35] (Proem)

As William points out, the historical veracity of both Utherpendragon and Arthur is severely undermined by the conflicting testimonies of other historians, most notably Bede: both are fabulous because they are otherwise unattested as magnificently energetic kings, and Arthur apparently went on to become the ruler of an international *imperium* that no other historian in the history of Western historiography had ever even so much as mentioned.[36] Yet as William also implicitly attests in the very act of paraphrasing the venerable founder of Insular historiography, these magnificent fictions had gained such credit that "the simple truth of history" had itself been subverted in its historical truth.

This spectacular reversal of epistemological antonyms is the result of the stylistic device that William calls "the superimposed coloration of the Latin language" ("superduct[us] Latini sermonis col[or]") and that Geoffrey himself intimates through his reference to words that are mendacious but ornately composed ("fictic[ii] sermon[es] ornate conp[ositi]"). With vastly different inflections, both authors recognize the *Historia regum* to be a meticulous pastiche of contemporary modes of Latin historical writing, and they both anticipate a point that has been made by a number of twentieth-century critics: although Geoffrey's work is thoroughly specious in its pretense to historical truth, it is thoroughly faithful to the modalities of historiographic prose, mobilizing the conventional principles of rhetorical persuasion *(elocutio)* and topical elaboration *(inventio)* to the cause of the specious history it evokes. In exploiting such conventions, Geoffrey clearly manipulated a "horizon of expectations" of the type that has been so productively analyzed by Jauss, and it must be emphasized that the "horizon" at issue is fundamentally literate, founded on a prior experience of a contextually apposite stylistics.[37] Put simply: Geoffrey contrives to pass fiction off as history because he writes his fiction as history is expected to be written. He himself implies as much by making expectation itself a diegetic concern: Ingerna accepts the imposture because it is formally indistinguishable from the accustomed "reality" it pretends to be, and her acceptance of the ploy internally enacts the extradiegetic reception of the textual imposture that is being dramatized. Or, to switch to the resonant vocabulary that inaugurates these multiple illusions, her acceptance of the ploy anticipates the extradiegetic efficacy of *medicamina* that are functionally indistinguishable from the discourse that Geoffrey so "prestigiously" controls. Once again, this time in the Latin, with emphasis added:

> Uocatus confestim Merlinus, cum in presentia regis astitisset, iussus est consilium dare quo rex desiderium suum in Ingerna expleret. Qui comperta anxietate quam rex patiebatur pro ea commotus est super tanto amore et ait: "Ut uoto tuo potiaris utendum est tibi nouis artibus et tempore tuo inauditis. Scio *medicaminibus* meis dare figuram Gorlois ita ut per omnia ipse uidearis." . . . [Uther] commisit se *medicaminibus* Merlini et in speciem Gorlois transmutatus est. . . . Commansit itaque rex ea nocte cum Ingerna et sese desiderata uenere refecit. Deceperat namque eam falsa specie quam assumpserat. Deceperat etiam ficticiis sermonibus quos ornate componebat. (137)

The *medicamina* at issue is the plural form of precisely the magical drug that William of Malmesbury implicitly manipulates throughout the Anecdote of the Ass. Endowed with an extraordinary variety of meanings, they are at one and the same time the "rhetorical embellishments" of Latin stylistics that Geoffrey has used as a "dye" or "cosmetic" to disguise fable as history, and they are also the "drug" that may potentially dispose the reader/listener to subscribe to the fiction that results.[38]

John of Salisbury: A Court of Magic and Fable

According to the more conservative tenets of contemporary church doctrine, the likes of Merlin are to be assessed as sacrilegious helots of the devil,[39] and clearly Geoffrey's canonization of a diviner bearing an at best ambiguous relationship with Christian orthodoxy marks a daring initiative. This is a fact of some importance, since Geoffrey's precedent was not rejected by later authors. On the contrary, it was followed, producing an entire tradition of demiurgical surrogates who reflect a new conception of written authority and bespeak a profound shift in the epistemological values of the mid to late twelfth century. Merlin and his avatars are symptomatic of a new community of letters that developed at the periphery of ecclesiastical culture and appropriated some of its prerogatives to explore and on occasion criticize the aspirations of an increasingly leisured secular barony. Their distinguishing "demonic" identity was intended to reflect the equally unorthodox activity of creating fictions, of turning language away from what John of Salisbury called "the truth of things" and, ultimately, from the Truthful dispositions of God.

The text in which John considers the poetic perversion of reference is the *Policraticus sive de nugis curialium et vestigiis philosophorum,* which, as its full title suggests, is both a treatise on Christian statesmanship inspired by classical philosophies of government and a commentary on the rituals and pastimes of contemporary courtiers. Although John is nowhere expressly concerned with the Galfridian legacy, he does provide the lengthiest disquisition on magic to have survived from the era; and, writing in the late 1150s, he relates this allegedly demonic activity to a specific culture, which, however negatively portrayed, is recognizably the secular world in which the romance narrative was beginning to flourish. He relates it, moreover, to a communal ethos of frivolity in which the critical faculties of men have so degenerated that falsehood successfully masquerades as the truth.

John addresses the work to the young Becket, at the time chancellor to Henry Plantagenet, and throughout he strives to admonish his chosen ward against worldly seductions and to apply himself to helping regulate the kingdom according to the will of God and the council of his ecclesiastical representatives. He recommends reading and writing as the perfect means to facilitating this end and devotes the entire prologue of book 1 to celebrating their merits. Writing, John states, is a divine gift, and without its services the liberal arts would perish, laws would be forsaken, religion would collapse, and eloquence would disappear. The past would no longer inspire the present to exemplary virtue, the initiatives of the ancients would no longer be followed, any durable claim to glory would be foreclosed, and humanity would lose one of its greatest joys: "When an astute intelligence turns its faculties to reading and writing anything that will prove worthwhile, the mind is released from vice and it is cured of adversity by a subtle and miraculous pleasure. You will not find a more agreeable or useful occupation in human dealings, except of course divinely inspired devotion."[40]

That John should have held letters in such high regard would seem a predictable corollary of biographical factors: at the point at which he expressed these views, he was secretary to Archbishop Theobald of Canterbury and in his later life himself went on to become archbishop of Chartres.[41] However, appraised in the wider context of the *Policraticus,* his remarks are far more than a mere celebration of literacy undertaken by one of the preeminently literate: they identify the principle that John considers the foundation of the truly equitable *res publica,* and they prepare for the pointed stipulations he later makes when first addressing the duties of a king:

> When he has taken up his seat on the throne of his kingdom, he will receive a copy of this law of Deuteronomy from the priests of the tribe of Levi and he will transcribe it for himself into a book. This he will carry with him to read every day of his life, learning how to fear the Lord his God and how to safeguard his words and his ceremonies, which are laid forth in the law.[42] (4.4; 519)

Consistent with the passage from Deuteronomy that he quotes, John conceives of the law as the divine will made manifest in written language and regards the monarch as the obedient and unflinching agent of its directives. Nevertheless, as he recognizes at a slightly later stage, this lawful delegation presupposes rare accomplishments:

> From this it is patently obvious that a skill in letters is necessary to monarchs, since they are commanded to ponder on the law through daily reading. Evidently, an illiterate king would not do this without difficulty. I remember a letter in which the king of the Romans encouraged the king of the Franks to set about having his children instructed in the liberal arts. Among the other points he made, he elegantly observed that an illiterate king is like an ass wearing a crown.[43] (4.6; 524)

To palliate these insufficiencies should they arise, John enjoins all monarchs to surround themselves by *litterati* who will predicate all administrative decisions in accordance with the law and, through it, the commandments of God:

> But if a prince should happen to be illiterate through a dispensation granted in acknowledgment of his egregious merits in virtue, then it is necessary for him to be guided by the advice of the lettered, thereby ensuring that his affairs proceed in the desirable course. Accordingly, let Nathan the Prophet, Zadoc the Priest, and the faithful sons of the prophets stand at his side to prevent any deviation from the law of the Lord, and let the literate use their tongues to open his ears to whatever aspect of the law remains obscure to his eyes and his understanding.[44] (4.6; 524–25)

By divine ordinance, therefore, the *res publica* must be governed by the powers of literacy, represented either by a lettered king or by those he has selected as his lettered advisers.

But John has by this time already demonstrated that government of this kind is a difficult ideal to maintain, hindered in its full realization by an array of social ills. He finds no fault with his king, Henry II Plantagenet, who could certainly read and write and who certainly surrounded himself with educated councilors.[45] But he does direct scathing criticism at Henry's courtiers, who in the best of possible worlds would follow in the learned and literate footsteps of philosophers, but who threaten the very cohesion of the commonwealth by indulging in extravagance and inanity:

> Now the wisdom of nobles is measured by the following criteria: if they know hunting; if they are proficient at that even more damnable evil, the gaming table; if they destroy their natural strength by warbling in effeminate voices; and if they strum out tunes on musical instruments. Oblivious of virtue, they forget how they were born, and this vice is passed on from parents to children. What, after all, would a son do other than what he has seen his father doing?[46] (1.5; 400)

In an effort to warn Becket against such perceived frivolities, John devotes the first part of book 1 to the aristocratic rituals he considers particularly deleterious, fulminating against hunting, gambling, acting, and singing, all of which, he argues, have been carried to excess and have become degenerate affronts to the virile *gravitas* that should be displayed by those in power. The device of rhetorical aggression that John uses throughout is thoroughly consistent with the conservative obloquy of the era: whenever he wishes to criticize anything in men, the sole objects of his concerns, he accuses them of becoming women. Or rather he makes men into what his ecclesiastical education, obligatory chastity, and minimal experience have taught him to imagine women to be — everything that is harmful to reason, and therefore everything that is to be associated with sensual pleasures.[47] John enlists this classic topos to create two visions of society: one is ideal, in essence inhabited exclusively by male paragons of philosophic dignity, moral fortitude, and unwavering Christian conviction; and the other is contemporary reality as John sees it, dominated by an alleged effeminacy that breeds corruption, lust, and superstitious credulity. The first, moreover, is founded on the lettered enlightenment he broaches in the prologue to book I and later associates with divine law, while the second is permeated by a blinkered belief in magic.

John adheres to a rigid view of the social order, arguing that each individual is born to a particular station and must fulfill his prescribed role to the well-being of the *res publica*.[48] Obedience to this stricture is an imperative devolving from two principles — duty, the responsible fulfillment of personal obligation, and nature, the determining law that imposes duty itself.[49] To stray beyond the limits of duty, John contends, is a form of matricide, since it is to impugn the parental directives of nature,[50] and to engage in pursuits that are not consistent with social station is tantamount to unnatural perversion. Since John is solely preoccupied with delineating the duties incumbent on men of noble lineage, the forms of unsuitable behavior he criticizes all resolve into the effeminate degeneration of a rectitude that is conceived as exclusively and hyperbolically male. Examples of this gendered invective are found in early chapters devoted to hunting and music. While conceding that the pursuit and slaughter of wild beasts is justified as a means of providing food, John unconditionally rejects hunting as a blood sport. Stating that this gratuitous indulgence of base appetites was first initiated by the Thebans,[51] he effortlessly aligns its affronts to virile sobriety with parricide, incest, fraud, and perjury; and, describing how this vice was then passed on to the foppish Trojans,[52] he presents hunting as the direct cause of a particular metamorphosis:

> The Greeks relate how the Dardanian hunter [Ganymede] was carried off by an eagle to become a cup bearer and from there progressed to illicit and unnatural embraces. This is indeed appropriate, since levity lends itself to being carried aloft on wings, and since pleasure, ignorant of sobriety, does not blush at being prostituted to any kind of lust.[53] (1.4; 390)

Hunting elides into an inversion of gendered categories: as a capitulation to sensual pleasure, it entails the prostitution of reason to lubricity, and it leads a man to assume a posture John associates exclusively with women. In discussing music at a slightly later stage, he pushes these charges of lewdness still further, arguing that contemporary nobles have displaced the grave joys of social responsibility with scabrous ostentation, ultimately to create what amounts to a transvestite parody:

> Here I am not talking about the pleasure that is born of peace, patience, benevolence, magnanimity, and joy in the Holy Spirit. Rather, I refer to the pleasure that accompanies feasting, drinking, revelry, light music, and gambling—in short, the pleasure that accompanies ingeniously contrived pastimes, fornication, and other variegated depravities, that makes even the more serious of minds effeminate and that by some sick game of nature makes men softer and more corrupt than women.[54] (1.4; 400)

Once introduced, images of sexual transformation come to dominate John's prose: men destroy their natural strength by imitating female voices, they give birth to degenerate heirs and dishonor the manly sex with a womanlike softness, and they defile the sanctuary of God himself by warbling in effeminate strains during church services.[55] In short, the society sketched in book 1 of the *Policraticus* is an exclusive domain of sensual pleasure: the reason and intelligence John associates only with men have been subordinated to vices that are advanced as quintessentially female and feminizing in their effects. This alleged degeneration in turn nurtures a credulousness that is exploited by various magicians who have attained influence and prestige because the forces of virile lucidity have been at best disempowered, at worst turned into their antithesis.

By John's account, the *curiales* of mid-twelfth-century England patronized a multiplicity of diviners, who disclosed arcane truths by scrutinizing such diverse phenomena as swords, basins, ladles, mirrors, stars, hands, dreams, birds, animal carcasses, leaping motions in the limbs, and unexpected movements of the body.[56] Other sorcerers of a more openly malevolent disposition were apparently also consulted. These include *vultivoli,* makers of wax or clay effigies bearing the likenesses of their victims; *imaginarii,* masters of demonically possessed images sent out to probe hidden secrets; *arioli* and *sortilegi,* members of quasi-religious cults; *pythii,* mediums for demonic spirits; and *necromantici,* resurrectors of the dead.[57] It is doubtful that John is strictly accurate in stating that the twelfth-century court was such a fertile haven for magic, since no other writer of the era even suggests anything to this effect. In all likelihood he exaggerates to give added resonance to later developments in his polemical designs. As John presents it, magic is a semiotic fraud, and as such it is a negative pendant to that other form of reading that should ideally guide the body politic. Through divination, its practitioners arrogate a knowledge of the divine will, acting as blasphemous caricatures of the literate administrators who mediate between society and God's lawful, written commandments. In short, they create a demonically inspired inversion of truth, justice, and faith.

The contexts for divination that John discusses can be divided into two categories: the psychic, involving dreams, visions, and oracles;[58] and the phenomenological, involving material signs manifested in God's creation.[59] In both cases, lucid interpretation arises from specific skills, and, in both, the material to be interpreted may derive either directly from God or from manipulative demons who, with his permission, are given freedom to delude sinners, heretics, and infidels.[60] These demonic forces are not limited to disguising devilish falsehood as divine truth: they on occasion give premonitions that are indeed accurate, lulling their victims into credulous acquiescence the better to prepare for their future damnation.[61] In the light of these complexities, John pleads for caution. With few exceptions, he argues, God grants personal clairvoyance only to the highly elect, and it is foolish to presume that professional diviners are anything more than mountebanks who traffic with the devil in an attempt to usurp divine prerogative: to presume to read the future without the direct aid of God is to claim the power of the Almighty, who alone knows all possible resolutions of all phenomena,[62] contemplating in his immutable Providence the mutable vagaries of contingency[63] and periodically intimating the unfolding of his will in earthly time. It is for this reason that John considers astrology to be the most pernicious of all clairvoyant practices. Phenomenological *signa,* he reasons, are indeed furnished by God to be interpreted by the attentive and informed:[64] for example, farmers and sailors call on their acquired knowledge to predict likely changes in the weather;[65] similarly, doctors draw on experience to make valid diagnoses and determine appropriate cures.[66] Yet, by moving from probability to necessity, astrologers grant created phenomena an absolute causality over the future and deny humanity the determining right of free will itself.[67]

At the margins of John's remarks stands the perfect virile world of his own musings in which such devilish chicanery could gain no purchase. But this ideal is disrupted:

> By foisting these signs onto the created world, the father of lies defames the Author of creation himself. It is no less than a madness proper to him to deceive the feeble little souls of the wretched with such fraud, as he hangs them from the tumor of elation that grows from predicting the inevitable course of the future or plunges them into the abyss of despair.[68] (2.26; 459)

In referring to the dupes of these demonic machinations as "feeble little souls" *(animulae),* John exploits a hermeneutic division he has already begun to develop. The true signs of God are lucidly read by those who have already gained experience of their meanings. The false signs of the devil, on the other hand, are seductive snares, deceitfully glossed by his helots and designed to destroy the naively credulous who are incapable of distinguishing divine intimation from demonic fraud. Even though John does not identify the *animulae* exploited by astrologers, he has already by this stage observed that three sectors of society are particularly vulnerable to demonic forces: "From this it is evident that such things happen only to feeble women, to men of a simpler disposition, and to those who are hesitant in the Faith" (2.17; 436).[69] These remarks prove particularly significant because by this time John has rhetorically made practically all the *curiales* of his era into women, in effect to create a nightmarish society inhabited predominantly by those he considers incapable of masculine—and therefore, according to John, rational—judgment.

Although implicitly, this model of interpretation is textual, and the opposition it establishes between the informed and the ignorant is an analogue to the divergence between the accomplished and the deficient in the realm of literary reception. John himself does not directly elaborate on this relationship. Yet, in 2.18, the chapter that immediately follows his identification of those most likely to be seduced by the falsehoods of demons, he provides a disquisition on poetic reference, thereby metonymically associating demonic and poetic delusion, both of which ultimately emerge as equally pernicious affronts to the truth of things and, through them, the Truth of God.

Having stated that the senses are used to perceive things of the material world, John discusses the reason and the intellect as the means of apperceiving the intangible. He ascribes to the second of these conceptual faculties the power of transforming the data that have been apprehended through the senses to create discretions from the conjoined and to make composites out of the discrete,[70] "as is the case when 'it joins the neck of a horse to a human head and adds a variegated plumage to both,' or, as the poet says, when 'it draws a woman who is beautiful at the top but ends in an ugly black fishtail'" (2.18; 437).[71] Here, John is doing more than simply observing the innate human ability to imagine things that do not exist. Through the unstated citation of Horace and the quoted fragments of lines 1–4 from the *Ars poetica*,[72] he advances *poetry* as the quintessential context through which such conceptual figments are externalized and communicated to others. Or, as he would explicitly have it in the next period, "Poets use words to transmit things of this kind to their listeners when they describe the hircocerf, the centaur, or the chimera" (2.18; 437).[73] This, in John's view, is a fact of some import and considerable danger, since such figments, communicated or otherwise, are perversions of created form: "When [the intellect] apprehends things by putting them together otherwise than they are, it engages in a vain undertaking that is unfaithful to the truth of things" (2.18; 437–38).[74]

The poetic activity of communicating unreal forms recalls another type of fraudulence, introduced by John at the very beginning of his excursus on magic: "Mercury is said to have invented conjuring. The word comes from the fact that he could dull clarity of vision. He was the most skilled of magicians, making anything he wanted invisible or transforming things so they appeared in a different shape" (1.9; 407).[75] It must be stressed that John never actually establishes a metaphorical relationship between Latin poetry and magic. But he does present both poets and magicians as manipulators of form, practitioners of untruth, and, in different ways, the antitheses of philosophers. Claiming to control a relatively arcane semiotic system, to disclose hidden truths for the benefit of others, and to possess the gift of prophecy, magicians are devilish pretenders to powers that are analogous to those of the literate philosopher-administrators who should ideally direct the *res publica* and who are characterized as "Nathan the Prophet, Zadoc the Priest, and the faithful sons of the prophets" (4.6; 524). Poets, for their part, indulge in the conjunction of the discrete and, therefore, in the inversion of philosophy itself. Immediately after warning against the poetic *iuncturae* he cites from Horace, John declares:

> When, on the other hand, the intellect individually separates things that are joined together, the idea that results will *not* be vain, since it prepares the most expeditious path to the wisdom of all investigations. For this procedure, exercised in the mind with wonderful subtlety, is the instrument of all philosophy, distinguishing as it does things from one another according to their natural properties. If you took away this intellectual power of abstraction, the practice of the Liberal Arts would perish, since, without its application, none of them could be correctly acquired or taught. Just as it considers form without substance, so too does it consider substance without form. Through an apparent defect of its own, the intellect can apprehend what could not obtain by the force of its own inherent properties, such as seeing darkness without looking and hearing silence without listening.[76] (2.28; 438)

These remarks in themselves, of course, identify the palliative to the dangerous untruth of poetry: since poets impart the conjunction of the disparate, then the philosopher, adept in the logical discipline of separating the conjoined, would effortlessly treat the infidelities of poetic reference with disabused insight. But, by John's unremitting testimony, the men and women of contemporary secular culture are the very opposite of logical, intellectual, and philosophic. They are inane, lubricious, and fundamentally nonliterate in their pastimes. For this last reason, they would obviously run no risk of falling into the literate snares of the Latin poets to subscribe to the reality of the unreal figments that are evoked through Horace and the *Ars poetica*. But they would perhaps be vulnerable to another form of illusion, practiced by entertainers whom John has by this stage mentioned in an earlier chapter bearing the significantly ample title "On actors, mimes, and conjurers" ("De histrionibus, et mimis, et praestigiatoribus"):

> Our age has descended to fables and inanities of all kinds. Not only does it prostitute the ears and the heart to vanity. Through the pleasure of the eye and the ear it caresses its own sloth and heightens dissipation, searching everywhere for the catalysts of vice. Is it not true that the lazy man teaches sloth? He indulges his idleness with the sweet strains of musical instruments, the warblings of the voice, the mirth of singers, the services of storytellers and, to his greater disgrace, with drunkenness and gluttony.[77] (1.8; 405)

While John discusses these *fabulae* with little elaboration and abstains from clarifying their themes, they would seem to correspond at least partially with what we today would understand by the romance: cast into a social context John mercilessly divorces from the literate Latinity of the church, they can only be vernacular narratives; and, characterized as *spectacula* that are delightful to the ear, they are certainly orally delivered and gesturally enhanced.[78] But, however this may be, John introduces them under a rubric that binds together gesture ("de histrionibus, et mimis") and illusion ("et praestigiatoribus"), with the implication that their practitioners are to be assessed as a minor "magical" subcategory.

This last point must not be exaggerated, relying as it does more on inference than evidence. The value of John's testimony is rather to be found in its evocation of all the powers that were self-consciously appropriated by Geoffrey and by the author-magicians of the later twelfth century. He provides the conservative, ecclesiastical standard against which these secular writers constructed themselves, and the opprobrium he casts on magic and—in a more muted fashion—poetry contrastively heightens the daring shown by the modern heirs to the classical poets who figuratively depicted their powers of free creation as a magical prerogative and who, in the process, came close to candidly identifying their venture for what it was. For, by relating their own activity with the demonic and so aggressively flouting the orthodoxy of the church, they ultimately drew attention to the fabricated and fundamentally untruthful nature of their own productions. Their magic is to be assessed as both a paraded power and a vehicle for illusion, potentially dangerous only to those who fail to understand the fiction it generates, its infidelity to the truth of things.

3

Benoît de Sainte-Maure

Magic and Vernacular Fiction

John's caricature of the mid-twelfth-century court is far too polemical to be taken as an accurate portrayal of anything save clerical distrust. This applies in particular to his strident dismissal of the intellectual aptitudes of the secular barony, and it establishes certain boundaries of caution that the twentieth-century critic must respect before attempting to determine how the illiterate and semiliterate responded to works of fiction.

First, under no circumstances must illiteracy be taken to equal stupidity. While we are certainly free to state that the illiterate had no direct access to an existing corpus of texts and therefore could not avail themselves of *litteratura* as a critical device, we have no cause whatsoever to make facile assessments of their critical competence. (By the same token, while the illiterate unquestionably included in their number some highly astute men and women, the literate for their part unquestionably included in theirs individuals displaying inferior judgment.) In fact, we have no unmediated data to permit us to know anything about the unlettered: by the very nature of their disqualification, they left no firsthand testimonies regarding their beliefs, no evidence, therefore, that would allow us to gauge the discernment they brought to bear in engaging works of history and literature. Accordingly, for any insight into monolingual reception in the twelfth century, we are today reliant solely on the potentially biased testimonies of literate authors, and even these are general assessments of competence rather than precise indications of what the unlettered believed given works to mean.

Second, although some midcentury courtiers were indeed analphabetic, others had a familiarity with the functions of written language, in certain cases to the point of being capable of laboriously reading, writing, or both. Henry II, for example, was such a figure. Authors of the era praised his literate skills, and, while their flattering comments are highly exaggerated, there is no reason to believe they are entirely insubstantial.[1] Yet Henry also patronized Old French works intended, however obliquely, to glorify his lineage and his own kingship, and this at least implies that he was more comfortable with his own vernacular than the language of the schools. Consequently, and this despite John's acerbic charges of ignorance, some landed nobles were indeed capable of gaining a firsthand acquaintance with Latin writings. However, except in rare cases over which we can only speculate, they are not to be numbered among those William of Malmesbury categorizes as *litteraturae periti,* the fully proficient who had a far greater facility in reading, whether Latin or the vernacular, and who could also, when necessary, submit texts to a rigorous hermeneutic analysis.[2] This disqualification was not of course the result of any shortcomings in intelligence. It was rather a matter of vocation or opportunity. Clerics had the freedom to devote much of their time to literate pursuits. Members of the landed barony, in contrast, had lands to administer, vassals to contain, and rivals to circumvent; and they had no compelling reason to reject those other pastimes that John found such an affront to sobriety.

Third, while William of Malmesbury warned against the possibility of deception, it would be absurd to argue that all twelfth-century writing (or, indeed, all writing from the Middle Ages) should be reappraised as a potential web of deceit and mockery. My own findings convince me that those authors who did use the written word as a vehicle for purposefully hidden and aggressively disobliging meanings were by far the minority. Most writers of the twelfth century are preoccupied by enlightenment rather than occlusion, motivating all of the topoi I have so far discussed only to temper their more threatening implications. Issues of intelligibility do indeed remain a constant, and "magical" dramatizations of reception continue to enjoy an obtrusive diegetic presence. Yet the very fact that these devices of self-commentary are found with such frequency strongly suggests the development of a critical awareness that was shared in equal measure by both the lettered and unlettered sectors of the contemporary public. Warnings were indeed made. But all evidence suggests they were on the whole heeded.

The topos of enlightenment I mention above finds its exemplary expression in the prologue to the most ambitious vernacular work of the mid–twelfth century, Benoît de Sainte-Maure's *Roman de Troie*. Knowledge must be shared, Benoît declares; if not, people will live like beasts; consequently, the learned have a duty to disseminate what they know.[3] From this Benoît emerges as a responsible mediator, moved to enlighten those who cannot enlighten themselves:

E por ço me vueil travaillier
En une estoire comencier,
Que de latin, ou jo la truis,
Se j'ai le sen e se jo puis,
La voudrai si en romanz metre
Que cil qui n'entendent la letre
Se puissent deduire el romanz.
(33–39)

[For this reason, I wish to undertake the task of beginning a history, which, provided I have the talent and ability, I would like to translate into the vernacular from the Latin in which I find it. This is so that those who cannot understand the written word may enjoy the vernacular version.]

Since Benoît is offering a composite translation of the *Ephemeris belli Troiani* and the *De excidio Troiae historia,* he caters to those who find his paradigms inaccessible. This group would include both the analphabetic and those who, while displaying a rudimentary control of Latin grammar and lexicon, would have been incapable of negotiating the complexities of a Latin text. Under these circumstances, Benoît devotes his bilingualism to the service of the less proficient and sketches a process of mediation whereby the spoken word will convey a message potentially shrouded in two levels of obscurity: Latin will be replaced by Gallo-romance, and the sense encoded in writing will then be liberated through oral performance. But this does not, of course, mean he is excluding the literate from his prospective public. Rather, he accommodates all members of a curial audience, generating discrete levels of meaning for the varied degrees of literate accomplishment they display: he addresses the themes of dynasty, conflict, and individual autonomy; and he realigns an existing written corpus to new literate ends.

Cast in these terms, Benoît's mediating role is in no way exceptional and would emerge as a paradigm applicable to practically any instance of romance authorship. But it is not the only reading that survives from the Middle Ages. While the earliest manuscripts collated by Constans for his diplomatic edition include this assurance of responsible enlightenment,[4] several others cast Benoît's authorial intent in different terms:

> Et por ço me voil travaillier,
> Et une estoire comencier,
> Que de latin où gie la truis,
> Se j'ai lo sen, et se jo puis,
> La voldrai si en romanz metre,
> Que cil qui *entendent* la letre
> Se puissent deduire al romanz.[5] (Emphasis added)

> [For this reason, I wish to apply myself to a history, which, provided I have the talent and ability, I would like to translate into the vernacular from the Latin in which I find it. This is so that those who *can* understand the written word may take pleasure from the vernacular.]

This change of one syllable, altering a negative to a positive verb, alters the cultural significance of the romance and creates something of a contextual paradox—a vernacular translation destined exclusively for a fully literate public. A convenient explanation for this apparent anomaly immediately presents itself. Because the manuscripts that include this variant elsewhere emphasize the responsibilities of the wise to promulgate their knowledge for the benefit of the unenlightened, they in effect make the prologue at best incoherent, at worst contradictory. This could be taken as evidence of negligent transcription, in which case the resultant paradox is no more than an illusion created by scribal error. While this argument can of course never be absolutely disproved, it can be textually interrogated and if necessary rejected. After all, another explanation is perfectly valid. Priority must be given the reading Constans reproduces, since its gesture toward "cil qui n'entendent la letre" is recurrently echoed by similar mediating appeals elsewhere in the prologue of both traditions. Thus, the variants may arise from a deliberate effort on the part of scribes to realign the prologue with what they saw to be the true epistemological function of the ensuing text. We may in fact be dealing with a medieval interpretation that identifies *Troie* as an artifact of such literary density that it fails to enlighten in the manner Benoît envisaged. For this is the only other valid explanation we can adduce. The fact that the variant appears as early as the mid–thirteenth century, and therefore within eighty or so years of *Troie*'s composition, may provisionally permit us to hypothesize the intervening development of a monolingual vernacular readership and to argue that the scribes responsible for this eccentric version offer *Troie* to *litterati* who know no Latin. But this reasoning hardly stands. By the mid–thirteenth century, more people in England and France could certainly read than before;[6] and we may cautiously brook the possibility that, even as early as the twelfth century, some men and women were taught in unusual circumstances to read or write French in isolation from any other language. However, even accepting this last point as tenable, such individuals would not have formed an entire literary public of the type *Troie* is destined to accommodate. On the contrary, they would have been near-negligible exceptions to the cultural norm of the period: in both the twelfth century and the first half of the thirteenth, the initial mastery of Latin remained the founding principle for literacy throughout the francophone world.[7] Consequently, the frames of reception do not change in the intervening years: whether in the mid–thirteenth century or the late twelfth, virtually anyone in England or France who could read *Troie* could also, and necessarily, read its classical sources.

I propose to analyze *Troie* in the light of all that is implied by the alternative prologue, taking the following as my working hypothesis: that the thirteenth-century readers responsible for the later version considered *Troie* quite simply too complex for the understanding of anyone but the highly proficient and accordingly altered their paradigm to point toward what they perceived to be a discrepancy between prefatory statement of intent and eventual literary realization.

The Ring of Gyges

However wide the divergence between the literate skills of the publics they hypothesize, the alternative prologues of *Troie* concur in presenting the ensuing romance as a work of translation, and as a consequence they both draw attention to the Latin paradigms that are to be mediated.[8] The primary object of transfer is of course the history of Troy derived from the *De excidio Troiae historia* and the *Ephemeris belli Troiani,* translations that were respectively ascribed to Cornelius Nepos and Lucius Septimius, themselves respectively working from Greek originals said to be the compositions of Dares Phrygius and Dictys Cretensis. Yet both of these Latin translators include paratextual narratives of their own translations, describing the circumstances in which the Greek source was written, rediscovered, and duly rendered in a new language for the benefit of a new culture. The material Benoît translates is therefore not only Trojan history as it was committed to writing by Dares and Dictys and translated by Cornelius and Septimius. It is also, and just as importantly, the very history of Trojan historiography, and this narrative of past retellings proves to accommodate precisely the problems of interpretative competence, magical manipulation, and specious integrity that I considered in the previous chapter.

In the front matter to the *Ephemeris,* Septimius explains the origin of his paradigm thus: "Dictys of Crete, who fought in the service of Idomeneus, first wrote the diary of the Trojan War in the Phoenician alphabet, which, through the efforts of Cadmus and Agenor, was at the time widely used in all parts of Greece."[9] These remarks provide the distant prehistory to the text Septimius has translated, and they sanction the most eminently authentic of histories. Because it is constituted of observed facts rendered in language, Dictys's journal resists any charge of apocryphal distortion. Because it is written in the primordial script of Greek culture, it is to be venerated in its irreproachable antiquity. However, as Septimius proceeds, he enhances his account of historiographic witness with a veneer of embellishments that point toward a far less reassuring context of origin. While the circumstances in which Dictys wrote are presented with sobriety, those surrounding the rediscovery of his writing border on the anecdotal, involving treasure-hunting shepherds, a tomb, a tin box, and sepulchral books:

> Then after many centuries, his tomb collapsed with age near Cnossos, formerly the seat of the Cretan king. Some shepherds went to investigate and there, among the ruins, they stumbled on a box artfully covered in tin. They quickly opened it up in the belief it was treasure, yet brought to light not gold, or anything

> else of value, but books written on linden bark. With their hopes frustrated, they took their find to Praxis, the owner of that place. Praxis transliterated the books into the Attic alphabet—the language was Greek—and presented them to Nero, the Roman Emperor. Nero rewarded him richly.[10] (Epistle)

The final appearance of Praxis is contextually logical, since he is the mediating figure responsible for the first stage of the text's linguistic disclosure. But this man of letters is introduced only after a colorful but seemingly irrelevant stress on frustrated pastoral venality. The shepherds just appear out of nowhere and, nameless, faceless, and unrewarded, disappear as soon as the literate Praxis intervenes. Nevertheless, however fleeting, their presence is crucial to the implications of the tomb, since their movements have already been anticipated in the realm not of fact, but of fiction. The following tale is from Cicero's treatise on political ethics, the *De officiis:*

> The ground one day collapsed after heavy rains, and Gyges went down into the chasm this revealed. There, so the story goes, he came upon a horse of bronze with a door in its side. He opened it and found the corpse of a giant man, which had a golden ring on one of its fingers. Gyges took the ring and put it on. He then went to a meeting of shepherds (he was a shepherd of the king's employ). There, he discovered that if he turned the bezel of the ring inward toward his palm, he was invisible to everyone while having the ability to see everything. When he turned the ring back to its normal position, he once again became visible. Employing the properties of the ring, he raped the queen and enlisted her aid in the murder of the king. Then, without anyone being able to detect him in his maneuvers, he rid himself of those he thought may stand against him. Using the ring in this way, he quickly rose to become King of Lydia.[11]

Cicero derives this tale from Plato's *Republic* and, like his predecessor, uses Gyges as a negative hypothesis. For both, the Lydian shepherd is an archetype of absolute power, an invisible manipulator who masters the political and economic structure of an entire kingdom by creating for himself a world in which truth and falsehood cease to have any objective value. Maneuvering under the veil of invisibility granted by the talismanic ring, he circumvents the gaze of gods and men, becomes a law unto himself, and controls what is seen and subsequently known by those around him. His rise to tyranny accordingly transcends the merely political and economic and resolves into a mastery over epistemology itself. In the kingdom he usurps, Gyges alone regulates the circulation of knowledge and understanding—unseen and inscrutable, he sees and scrutinizes all.[12]

Through redeploying the established iconography of the tomb, Septimius too writes a parable of epistemological control. The Cretan shepherds act according to the precedent of their prestigious avatar, entering the crypt in the hope of finding the means to rise above their menial status. Nevertheless, they leave not with a talisman granting access to incalculable riches, but with a box containing nothing they can remotely associate with wealth. Yet this is only because they live in a cultural context in which magical rings do not obligingly present themselves as instruments of social and economic promotion. In their world, advancement arises from more down-to-earth considerations of education and literacy. Although not treasure in a literal sense, the books they discover are of value, as Praxis makes clear, offering his transliteration to Nero and receiving gifts in return. By having a man of letters actualize the financial value vested in the tomb, Septimius reveals learning to be as much a transformative talisman as the ring of Gyges. Not only has Praxis the ability to see what remains invisible to others, producing meaning where none is apparent; he can also create wealth, exchange his product against any number of other objects. Through Septimius's anecdote, Gyges' mastery over epistemology loses its mythic proportions and becomes the art of the transliterating scribe.

In the process, the sinister and manipulative implications of Cicero's parable appear to have been erased to create an optimistic tale of enlightenment. The Lydian tyrant has been replaced by the scholar, and the invisible exploitation of others appears to give way to a benign gesture of mediation. But appearances deceive. Following Plato, Cicero employs the tale of the talismanic ring to posit an ethics of truth, prompting his readers to put themselves in the position of Gyges himself:

> You are working to further your interests in finance, power, dominion, or lust, and your maneuvers are destined to remain un-

> known to gods and men. How would you behave in circumstances such as these, with no one knowing, or even suspecting, your actions?[13] (3.9)

This rhetorical question inaugurates a succession of still more exemplary anecdotes, all concerning withheld information and its moral consequences. Throughout, Cicero aims to establish modes of behavior for the philosopher engaged in public life and employs commerce as a figurative paradigm for the circulation of knowledge. The educated must refuse to follow Gyges and must instead be like the tradesman who proclaims the imminent arrival of competitors (3.13), the real estate agent who declares a house to have unstable foundations and bedrooms infested by snakes (3.13), the Roman dignitaries who recognize a will from which they benefit to be forged (3.18), and the buyer who informs a tradesman that the brass he is selling is in fact gold (3.18). Inserted amid these examples is a plea to justice: "since nature is the source of law, then, to be true to our natural proclivities, none of us should exploit in our actions the ignorance of others" (3.17).[14] The wise, then, should never abuse those who are not. But, as Cicero has already indicated, if those who have greater knowledge, whether in philosophy or trade, are to be cautioned against fraud, those who wish to gain learning or material goods must themselves be circumspect in all their transactions:

> We are all moved by the strong promptings of our desire for knowledge and learning, and we consider it praiseworthy to excel in these fields. And, conversely, we consider it unworthy and reprehensible to be wrong, to err, to be ignorant, and to be deceived. In this natural and honorable context, there are two vices that should be avoided. One of these is to take the unknown for the known and blindly agree to everything. Anyone who wants to avoid this vice (and everyone should) ought to give time and careful thought to judging the matter in question beforehand.[15] (1.6)

All men should follow the natural and honest quest for wisdom; to accept the unknown for the known is a vice; therefore, to be natural, honest, and ultimately wise is to subject any purported facts to the widest possible evidential corroboration. Accordingly, the buyer should enter a transaction only after evaluating the commodity for sale. If he does not do so, then he alone is responsible for the consequences. Or, as Cicero would have it at a later stage, scripting words for that shrewd pragmatist of commercial ethics, Diogenes of Babylon: "When the judgment of the buyer has been brought to bear, how can fraud be attributed to the seller?" (3.13).[16]

This injunction always to scrutinize the value and integrity of any object liable to trade is of direct relevance to the *Ephemeris,* since this purported eyewitness account of the Trojan War is a massive hoax, originally written in Greek in the early second century A.D. and translated into Latin by Septimius during the course of the next two hundred years.[17] The oblique paratextual allusions to the Lydian tomb that introduce the translation are signals for caution, designed to admonish the reader that all is not as it seems and to reveal the Greek paradigm to be inauthentic; and, unfolding to dramatize mediation and patronage, the prefatory letter resolves into a parable of receptive naïveté from which Nero emerges as the uncritical buyer of fraud. What renders the subterfuge of Praxis viable is the simple unintelligibility of his alleged paradigm. Since Ionic script—Septimius's Phoenician—is incomprehensible to the dominant polity of the age, Roman *litterati* such as Nero would be incapable of scrutinizing the original. If called upon to defend his transliteration, the likes of Praxis could therefore offer up any arcane scribbling as a prestigious chronicle of the past. His ploy would necessarily remain persuasive, since it is shrouded in the veil of linguistic impenetrability. To control a language or an alphabet unknown to the majority is to inhabit an epistemological domain in which truth and falsehood escape the judgment of others. It is to regulate not only what is known, but also what is not. Because it is limited to the bilingual or to the philologically accomplished and perforce undertaken as a service to those who are not, the transposition of facts from one linguistic or graphemic code to another resists general scrutiny. Because it enacts the passage of meaning from the obscure to the transparent, it may fabricate for itself an origin ratified by the very obscurity it purports to erase. As Septimius warns by recasting Cicero's cautionary fable, the transposed text necessarily escapes the terms of Cicero's own injunction to scrutinize. By its very nature, it presupposes the disempowerment of those for whose benefit it is produced. Its integrity cannot be scrutinized because its putative source cannot be understood.

The story, however, also survives in a different form. In some manuscripts of the *Ephemeris,* Septimius's epistle is replaced by an anonymous third-person prologue that casts the emperor in a somewhat less ingenuous light.[18] This alternative paratext begins in much the same way as Septimius's letter: shepherds come upon Dictys's tomb; they enter, find a box, and discover that it contains linden tablets. But at this point the tale dramatically changes:

> They then took them to their master, who was called Eupraxides. He recognized the letters for what they were and presented them to Rutilius Rufus, at the time governor of the island. Thinking that the texts brought to him contained hidden knowledge, Rutilius sent them along with Eupraxides himself to Nero. When Nero received the texts and noticed that they were written in the Phoenician alphabet, he called for experts in this language, who subsequently explained their meaning. Understanding that they were an account left by a man who had personally been present at Troy in the distant past, Nero ordered them to be translated into the Greek language. In this way, a more reliable version of the Trojan War was made generally accessible. He then sent Eupraxides back to Crete with gifts and Roman citizenship as his reward and placed the history bearing Dictys's authentic signature in the Greek library.[19] (Prologue)

Here, the task of mediation is undertaken not in Crete, but in Rome. Further, Nero is in this instance more than the uncritical patron of the scholarly accomplishments of others; he is the active supervisor of a scriptorium engaged in the recuperation of the past. Subordinated to his institutionalized directives, the scholar loses the autonomy of a Praxis and becomes an anonymous imperial cleric. He is still a mediating presence, negotiating between cultural codes, but his talents are now devoted to a cause that transcends his individual interests. Epistemological control has passed to the ruler of an empire, a ruler, moreover, who is astutely aware of the political function of writing. For Nero supervises the disclosure of a text that is inextricably connected with the hegemonic pretensions of the empire itself. Because devoted to the Trojan War, the journal of Dictys documents the circumstances in which the Trojan people and their culture were originally fragmented; and, because undertaken in the city founded by the Trojan descendants of Aeneas and his followers, it provides the prehistory and pretext for the glorious neo-Trojan hegemony of Rome that is now ruled by Nero himself. Directing the circulation of knowledge and manipulating its relationship with his own political prerogatives, the imperial head of state here plays the role of Gyges, and the transliterating scribe is a mere orderly to his commands.

These tales of epistemological control are relevant to *Troie* for two reasons. First and more obviously, they constitute the prefatory material of one of the texts Benoît translated. Second, they strikingly anticipate a process of historiographic production that obtained in the late-twelfth-century Anglo-Angevin domains. On acceding to the throne in 1154, Henry Plantagenet of Anjou began a program of energetic expansionism, and, by the mid 1170s, he had imposed his overlordship throughout the British Isles and made considerable encroachments into Continental territories theoretically owing direct allegiance to Louis VII of France.[20] It is for reasons such as these that Alain de Lille, a loyal subject of the French Crown, makes pejorative reference to Henry under the transparent guise of a certain tyrannical figure from Roman history when sketching the grotesques of his age early in the *Anticlaudianus:*

> There, Nero strikes the world with a flying thunderbolt, indulging in crime and pushing his madness to want more than madness itself could crave. Any iniquity he refines in his actions then multiplies across the face of the earth.[21]

Mention of this Nero of twelfth-century politics is immediately preceded by equally derogatory allusions to certain contemporary writers:

> There, our Ennius panders to the masses with a song made of rags and extols the fortunes of Priam. There, Maevius, presuming to elevate his dumb mouth up into the heavens, attempts to depict the exploits of Alexander the Great by using the shadow of obscure song, but, scarcely on his way, grinds to a halt and complains that his listless Muse has grown slothful.[22]

Albeit in dismissive terms, Alain here indicates that other distinguishing characteristic of Henry's reign—the production of flattering dynastic narratives explicitly or otherwise intended to glorify the temporal supremacy of the new Angevin line, some of them expressly written at Henry's behest and most of them treating the history of the Trojan people and their modern descendants, the British and the Normans.

As an active patron of the history of Troy, Henry indeed bears analogies to the Nero of the *Ephemeris*. In this he refined cultural and epistemological concerns first manifested some twenty years before his accession. Geoffrey wrote the *Historia regum* in the 1130s, popularizing the story of neo-Trojan Britain established in the ninth-century *Historia Brittonum* and celebrating Arthur as once and future king of the island now ruled by Anglo-Norman monarchs. Geoffrey's text generated sufficient interest to merit at least four French translations. Gaimar produced his now lost *Estorie des Bretuns* in the late 1130s, Wace finished the *Roman de Brut* in 1155, and, in addition, two other anonymous versions survive. By the 1160s, Wace had begun the *Roman de Rou*, his history of Rollo and the successive dukes of Normandy, and, in its early version at least, a vernacular account of the Trojan origins of the Normans. In addition, sometime in the 1150s or early 1160s, three other vernacular texts were produced that complete what is in effect an entire Trojan cycle: the anonymous *Thèbes* relates events that took place one generation before the war; the anonymous *Roman d'Enéas* describes the initial wanderings of the Trojan diaspora; and, finally, Benoît's *Roman de Troie* documents the fall of Troy itself.[23]

This cultural context of patronage appears to evoke a group of pensioned scriveners writing as agents of regal self-fashioning. Whether their names have come down to us or not, these vernacular writers ostensibly fulfill a role fully comparable with that played by the imperial clerics of Nero's employ. They too mediate between past and present, translating texts that supposedly guarantee an access to historical fact. But, to all appearances, their bilingualism is traded into the service of another, supervised by an orchestrating presence that defines the frames of meaning to be disclosed. Thus, with the circulation of knowledge directed from above, the twelfth-century clerics of the Trojan cycle seem to play a subservient role, translating what they are instructed to translate and disseminating meanings to create an imperial past, at best faceless mediators of cultural transmission, at worst lettered tributaries to an egocentric royalty.

With particular regard to Benoît, however, this assumed obeisance is of nuanced validity, since he knew both of his paradigms to be inauthentic and, following the precedent of his antecedents, he too invented the past.[24] Provisionally, this opens vistas for manipulation as expansive as those enjoyed by the classic purveyor of the fraudulent text, Praxis of Crete. Because Benoît is persistently unfaithful to his claim to translate faithfully his Latin sources, then he perforce maneuvers beyond the scrutiny of the unaccomplished audience he ostensibly strives to accommodate: in order to perceive the extent of his deviations, it is necessary to compare translation and paradigm and therefore to indulge in the contextually challenging activity of sustained reading.

A negative interpretation of such creative license would certainly appear to be invited by Benoît himself, who at one point or another introduces into his romance practically every conceivable variation on the theme of magic, thereby gesturing toward all the cultural tensions considered in the previous chapters. In this new written Troy and its surrounding lands, necromancers, soothsayers, diviners, prophets, and sirens are to be encountered practically everywhere, and they are endowed with seemingly limitless powers. There is Medea in Colcis, who can make day into night, fly through the air, and reverse the flow of rivers. There is Helenus at Troy, who sees the future in his dreams. There is his sister Cassandra, who casts lots to know hidden secrets. There is the Trojan dignitary Eüforbius who, during the three hundred and sixty years of his life, probed the ways of providence. There is Calcas, father to Briseïda and master of auguries. There is King Pistropleus, creator of the dreaded Sagittarius who wreaks havoc among the Greeks. And there are Circe and Calypso, who enchant hapless mariners in order to satisfy their lusts. What all of these sorcerers hold in common is a stock of learning that, under other circumstances, would seem remarkably bookish. Medea is "de grant saveir" (1216), "sage e aprise" (1220), "scientose" (1228), and accomplished "ez ars" (1219); Helenus is "sages poëtes" (5391); Cassandra is "merveilles esciëntose / des arz" (5532–33); Eüforbius is an initiate "des arz" (4093) and is of "grant sen e grant clergie" (4092); Calcas is "sages poëtes coneüz" (5820); Pistropleus is "sages des set arz" (6898), "de totes arz fondez" (12346); and Circe and Calypso know "des arz" (28720). Significantly, these attributes reappear in every historicized writer that Benoît mentions: Homer is "clers merveillos / e sages e esciëntos" (45–46); Sallust, "clerc merveillos e sage" (80); Cornelius Nepos, "de letres sages e fondez" (84); Dares, "clerc merveillos / e des set arz esciëntos" (99–100);

and Dictys, "clers sages e bien apris / e sciëntos" (24398). In the romance world of this twelfth-century Troy, sorcerers and writers partake, in equal measure and in identical terms, of the same set of learned accomplishments.

In their most spectacular manifestation, these talents extend to Benoît himself, whose creative control of the grapheme is sufficient to conjure forth a golden simulacrum of nature:

Devant la sale aveit un pin
Dont les branches furent d'or fin
Tresgetees par artimaire,
Par nigromance e par gramaire.
(6265–68)

[In front of the room there was a pine tree, with branches of refined gold cast through magic, enchantment, and writing.]

It is to symbolize this maguslike power over the world to which he lends written substance that Benoît employs the group of three diegetic surrogates I mentioned in chapter 2, those nameless, faceless, and ever mysterious magi who, in displaying the interrelated talents of architecture, divination, and magical rhetoric,[25] are to be assessed as analogues to Geoffrey's Merlin. It may perhaps at first glance seem peculiar that Benoît chooses to dramatize his own control through several surrogates, rather than one. Yet we note that he exploits three as a numerical constant: he is represented by three sages, and these magi show the three interrelated talents. Assessed in terms of the numerological theory that the twelfth century had inherited from late classical Pythagorean thought, this insistence on the triad cannot be gratuitous. Three is the number of Thouth, god of mediation, and the three Trojan sages of three talents must be associated with the most celebrated neophyte of this deity, the demiurgical Mercurius Trismegistes.[26] By selecting this triune master of all magi as his own diegetic emblem, Benoît not only arrogates a control comparable to the necromantic orchestrations Geoffrey performs through Merlin; he also obliquely circumscribes the liberties that literacy may afford in a partially literate culture. For those lacking *litteratura*, the *gramaire* from which Benoît builds the fabric of Troy was always a potential snare through which truth and falsehood could imperceptibly merge into one another.

Benoît himself plays on these inferences by associating *gramaire* with contrivance and therefore with strategies of literate manipulation. The context is the prologue, in which Benoît explains the circumstances in which his other paradigm, the *De excidio Troiae historia,* was discovered by the nephew of the Roman historian Sallust:

> Cornelius ert apelez,
> De letres sages e fondez.
> De lui esteit mout grant parole.
> A Athenes teneit escole.
> Un jor quereit en un aumaire
> Por traire livres de gramaire:
> Tant i a quis e reversé
> Qu'entre les autres a trové
> L'estoire que Daire ot escrite,
> En greque langue faite e dite.
> (83–92)

[His name was Cornelius, and he was wise and thoroughly trained in letters. Much was said about him, and it was in Athens that he was a teacher. One day, he was looking through a book press, trying to bring some grammar books to light. He searched and rummaged for so long that, among the others, he found the history that Dares had written, composed and set down in the Greek language.]

In mentioning a quest for the "livres de gramaire," Benoît has done no less than embellish Cornelius's own first-person narrative of the circumstances in which the lost book of Dares Phrygius was rediscovered.[27] This has two effects. First, Benoît has intervened to change, however minimally, an ostensibly autobiographical account of textual discovery and has therefore misrepresented, however minimally, historical facts sanctioned by his predecessor's first-person witness. Second, this adjustment to literary history entails the first of Benoît's two uses of the word *gramaire,* the second of which we have already considered in the context of his own magical writing. In any other case, this would hardly be a point of interest. But coming from Benoît, an author who systematically conflates the necromantic and literate arts, it is highly significant. However subliminally, Cornelius shares the attributes of both writer and sorcerer, devoting his time to a lexically ambiguous pursuit that may resolve into a quest for a long-forgotten *grimoire.*

To establish what such a "grammar" may be, let us briefly reconsider the analogue that Benoît himself claims to be exploiting. This, we recall, is the third in a list of functional synonyms that convey the magical stuff from which a simulacrum of nature has been molded. Simultaneously creating the formal illusion of an empirical reality yet openly revealing it to be artifice, the *gramaire* in question corresponds to what we today would call fiction. Cited as the force that has produced the fabulous pine, this creative liberty in turn illuminates and enacts its own function, since the object it has fabricated is contextually invented by Benoît himself, finding no precedent in the sources he exploits and inaccurately claims to translate faithfully. Yet this infidelity-through-invention arises from a fidelity of another type. By intervening in the apparent facts of cultural history to suggest that one of his two literate predecessors was also preoccupied with *gramaire* (to the extent, indeed, of engaging in an active quest for books on the subject), Benoît reveals, for the first time, that his paradigm is also a context for free invention. He reveals, in fact, that the *De excidio* too is a fabrication of history, permeating his description of its *inventio* with semantic and syntactic ambiguities. These are at their most densely allusive in the phrase "por traire livres de gramaire," through which Benoît chooses to describe Cornelius's intent. Alongside the more straightforward meaning of "to draw" or "to drag," the verb *traire* carries literary implications and is employed to designate the action of producing one instance of writing from another (as in Chrétien's "et tret d'un conte d'avanture / une molt bele conjointure").[28] Therefore, with a slight change in semantic inflection, "por traire livres de gramaire" would suggest that Cornelius is actively engaged in bibliographical research, that is, looking through a small library *(aumaire),* in order to produce, that is write, "grammar books" of his own. Additionally, if coupled with *traire* in this compositional sense, "de gramaire" may now function as a prepositional rather than adjectival complement, which would create the further reading of "to extract books out of writing," that is, to produce books based on written paradigms. These same syntactic equivocations would still obtain if we lend *gramaire* its figurative sense, Cornelius in this case looking through the library in order to produce books of magic or from magic. In the first instance, the product of his labor would be a handbook on invention itself, subsequently passed to Benoît and translated into the magical cityscape of Troy. In the second, Cornelius's product would be an enchanted invention in its own right, an illusory paradigm conjured into being through the act of pseudotranslation. In all these cases, the compositional lexicon is maintained through the bivalence of *trover,* both "to find" and "to compose": if the latter sense is respected, then what Cornelius derives from the writing/magic in the library is his own written/magical composition, which is none other than the book that Dares wrote in the Greek language.[29]

In translating this freedom of invention into his own text and using magical writing to do so, Benoît establishes what must in context be termed a *translatio nigromantiae,* since the material of his source is *gramaire* itself, that magical stuff through which reality can be invented ex nihilo. But, throughout his adjustments to Cornelius's *inventio,* he indulges in highly literate maneuvers that owe their comprehensibility to a detailed knowledge of Cornelius's own witness. Under these conditions, it would seem that the scribes responsible for the eccentric version of the prologue were indeed justified in reserving the text only for "cil qui entendent la letre": Benoît's vernacular *gramaire* is so rigorously self-reflexive as a device for literate allusion, transposition, and fabrication that only the highly accomplished could have comprehended its fundamentally literary significance.

Later developments in the romance, however, strongly imply that Benoît actively strove to dissolve precisely this veil of literate inscrutability by making the disclosure of fiction itself an obtrusive textual concern. Of course, to what extent he was successful can never be ascertained: as I have already mentioned, we today cannot recuperate the precise responses of the medieval listener. But we can extrapolate elements of the romance that act as commentaries on wider issues of reception and at least delineate how Benoît envisaged his work being understood. In this context it is surely eloquent that the beginning of the text proper is a self-contained narrative devoted to Jason and the Golden Fleece that confronts all of the problems of magical maneuvering I have so far discussed. Although not strictly speaking part of the prologue, this revised version of the Ovidian tale serves a paratextual function: it is positioned at a liminary stage, and its implications inevitably influence our reading of all that follows.

The Quest for the Golden Fleece

Jason's voyage is the result of court intrigue. His renown has made him a threat to the political supremacy of his uncle Peleus, who decides to rid himself of his rival by sending him to Colchis, there to gain the Golden Fleece. But this prize is obviously very difficult to win. Others have tried and all have failed because the fleece is guarded by two fire-breathing bulls and a fire-breathing serpent. Jason's chances of success would therefore appear negligible. But help arrives from an unexpected quarter. Medea falls in love with Jason, and, in return for his attentions, agrees to aid him in his undertaking. On the practical side, she gives him an unguent to protect his skin from heat and glue to seal the noses and mouths of the monstrous guardians. More esoterically, and in the present context more significantly, she also furnishes a number of necromantic devices. First, there is "une figure" (1665–70). Precisely what this may be is unclear, since *figure* can signify any formal design of two or three dimensions and may therefore be a figurine or a picture. But, whatever its form, it is later described as "la figure / ou erent escrit li conjure" (1929–30), and it is accordingly metonymic of a stock of learning that is both written and magical, a *gramaire* that is also *grimoire*.

Once introduced, this stress on arcane, written knowledge is rendered more explicit in the third of the devices Jason receives, which is "un escrit" (1703–14). Here too, the specific nature of the talisman is obscure, since Benoît does not reproduce or paraphrase the text. Yet it proves to be the crucial and final component of a ritual that eventually allows Jason to obtain the prize he seeks:

> La figure a sacrefiiee
> Que Medea li ot bailliee;
> Mist la sor l'eaume e atacha,
> Si come ele li enseigna.
> Après fist as deus sacrefise
> A la maniere e a la guise

Que la pucele li ot dit,
E treis feiees list l'escrit.
(1893–900)

[He offered up as a propitiatory token the design that Medea had given him by placing it on his helmet and securing it there as she had instructed. Then he sacrificed to the gods in the way the girl had told him and read the text three times.]

The ceremony Jason enacts, therefore, proves to involve three stages. He first displays that he is the possessor of the *figure,* that repository of written knowledge that acts a prerequisite to his suitability to perform. Once this credential has been approved and the higher powers appeased, the *escrit* is recited according to precise stipulations. Successfully completed, this textual performance demonstrates the readers' worthiness to appropriate the Golden Fleece and thereby gain what amounts to a stupendous material reward.

Assessed in these terms, Benoît's tale of necromancy yields a very basic economy of exchange: even though presented in a context of pagan ritualism, Jason's recitation is one of the reciprocated terms of a transaction, proffered and accepted according to a precise convention of trade. If only subliminally, therefore, this revised story of the quest resolves into a dramatization of literate performance and remuneration. Central to this exchange is a set of actions designed to appease those who will remunerate. As Medea indicates at an earlier stage, Jason is only to perform the text while making appropriate gestures of submission to the higher powers to which it is ultimately destined:

Jason, quant le mouton verras,
Ne faire ja avant un pas
Desci qu'aies sacrefiié,
Que n'en seient li deu irié:
Crieme sereit, se nel faiseies,
Que chierement le comparreies.
Par iço les apaieras,
E dementres que tul feras,
Cest escrit di tot belement
Treis feiees contre Orient.
(1705–14)

> [Jason, when you see the sheep, do not advance a single step until you have made a sacrifice to ensure that the gods will not be angered. It would be perilous were you not to do so, and you would pay dearly. But this way you will appease them. While you are doing this, you must also recite the text quite clearly three times facing the east.]

The sacrifice, then, is to be made while the actual recitation is taking place. At no point does Benoît reveal what this gift may be. Yet, through Medea's words, he assures that it is lexically absorbed into the trade to be negotiated, since the verb *apaier* ("par iço les apaieras") combines the senses of "to appease" and "to pay." The higher powers, then, will both be mollified into accepting the textual offering and will be paid part of their due in the process. Once again subliminally, the tale introduces yet another aspect of textual recitation: in order to expect a reward, the reader must take pains to accommodate those to whom his performance is destined. To these factors can now be added a third, represented by the enigmatic "figure / ou erent escrit li conjure." As already stated, the open display of this device is the first stage in the ritual Jason performs, and, although its precise nature is never explained, it functions as a token of reassurance that demonstrates possession of a power that is self-reflexively signified by the grapheme. Obliquely, the very prerogatives of literacy itself are here at issue, manifested for the inspection—and ideally also the approval—of the prospective recipients of the text. Without this initial illustration of proprietorship over the written word, the later stages of appeasement, performance, and reward would be impossible.

This takes us very close to a metaphorical reading of the entire episode, with the *figure,* the *sacrefise,* and the *escrit* emerging as tropes for the discrete stages in a twelfth-century textual recitation. Not only is such a reading sanctioned by the otherwise systematic conflation of magic and literacy we have already considered; it is also strongly encouraged by several analogies that Benoît strives to make between Jason's quest and his own undertaking. For, in a metaphorical sense, he too is a mariner, and the linear progress of his composition is a voyage, often arduous, at times exhausting. This he affirms a little before its median point after expressing his wish to lend his material a greater amplitude of description:

> Mais ne m'i leist a demorer:
> Mout par ai ancore a sigler,

Quar ancor sui en haute mer.
Por ço me covient espleitier,
Quar sovent sordent destorbier;
Maintes uevres sont comenciees,
Qui sovent sont entrelaissiees.
Ceste me doint Deus achever,
Qu'a dreit port puisse ancre geter!
(14942–50)

[However, I cannot allow myself to dally any longer because I am still on the high seas and have a great distance yet to sail. Therefore, I must hurry on, to avoid the obstacles that often arise. Many works are begun that are frequently abandoned. May God grant that I finish this one and drop anchor at my port of destination.]

Each discrete episode may always be a detour or an interruption in the trajectory of the work and may excessively withhold arrival at the figurative haven of its ending. Benoît's task is always to maintain a swift pace, to avoid the possibility of never completing the *uevre* that he has begun. By implication, it is only when he has finished that any rewards for his efforts may be forthcoming. Jason, for his part, is fully aware of the need to expedite the journey he undertakes:

Jason a ja tant espleitié
Que en l'isle fu essaivié.
N'i ot puis autre demorance:
Son escu a pris e sa lance,
Eissuz s'en est fors del batel,
Puis est poiez sus en l'islel.
(1877–82)

[Jason has already made such haste that he has arrived at the island. There he delayed no longer, and, taking up his shield and spear, he disembarked and ventured forth.]

The two voyages have more in common than just a vocabulary of nautical speed and dalliance ("espleitier"/"espleitié," "demorer"/"demorance"): by prefacing the story of Troy with this tale of a performer who must demonstrate his proprietorial control over a corpus of written learning, who is prepared to make the apposite propitiatory gestures to the hieratically distant recipients of his text, and who finally receives a golden reward for his endeavors, Benoît is doing no less than offering a tropic rehearsal of the circumstances in which a text such as his own would be performed once the metaphorical voyage of its composition has been completed.

If suspended in these terms, Benoît's rewriting of the quest would be an interesting but somewhat inconsequential exercise in sustained metaphor and metonymy, ostensibly designed to dramatize scholarly obeisance and the material rewards an accommodating disposition will bring. But circumstances are in fact far more nuanced than such a reading would imply, because no reference has so far been made to the most important necromantic device Jason receives. This is a fabulous ring with properties that would enable the performer, if he so chose, to recite his text from beyond the veil of invisibility. Witness Medea's words:

Se tu ne vueus estre veüz,
La pierre met defors ta main:
Adonc puez bien estre certain
Que ja rien d'ueil ne te verra.
E quant ço iert qu'il te plaira
E que tu n'avras d'iço soing,
Clo la pierre dedenz ton poing:
Si te verra l'om come autre home.
(1690–97)

[If you do not want to be seen, turn the stone outward from your hand. Then you can be certain that you will be visible to the eyes of none. And if circumstances have it that you want otherwise, this no longer being your intent, grasp the stone in your fist, and you will be seen just like any other man.]

By making the ring of invisibility the central prop to his tale of recitation, Benoît strongly implies an acquaintance with the Ciceronian tale of Gyges. Whether this means he had firsthand knowledge of the *De officiis* or became familiar with the enchanted talisman from some florilegium or other is thoroughly impertinent to present concerns.[30] Suffice it to say that Benoît, like Cicero before him, inserts the ring into a narrative that binds together invisibility, arcane knowledge, and, albeit in an extremely straightforward sense, economic power. Suffice it to add that these motifs are mobilized at an early stage of a translation that takes none other than the *Ephemeris belli Troiani* as one of its two sources and that in this regard we need show no caution whatsoever in adducing direct transposition. While it is unclear which version of the paratext to the *Ephemeris* Benoît knew, it is also irrelevant to the forces he dramatizes in his romance. Whether inspired by Lucius Septimius's prefatory epistle or by the anonymous third-person prologue, he too investigates the relationship between the translator and monarchic power, and he too works within a context of historical fabrication. Coincidentally or otherwise, he as a result reproduces elements of both paratextual narratives. Inventing the past in order to reflect Henry Plantagenet's suzerainty over a New Troy, he is an analogue of the scribes of the imperial scriptorium depicted in the anonymous prologue. Yet, in the liberties he takes with his material and in his recurrent stress on thresholds of literacy, he both performs and textually objectifies certain attributes of Praxis, the Cretan forger who is rewarded for offering his pseudotranslation to Nero, monarch of yet another New Troy and, in this instance, uncritical buyer of fraud.

It remains to be ascertained, therefore, to what extent Benoît follows his Cretan avatar in attempting to trade apocrypha for financial gain and in deliberately employing his figurative invisibility to mislead the linguistically disadvantaged into accepting fabrication as fact.

This final avenue of inquiry can best be pursued by further considering Jason's recitation, since it is situated between the prologue and the narrative of the war and thereby makes oral communication itself a liminal concern. The questions it raises are first and foremost self-referential (although their import applies also to all ensuing developments): What message would the rewritten quest convey to a curial audience? And, more pertinently, to whom would this message be visible? In an effort to respond, we can of course only speculate. But one point is absolutely clear: the talismanic recitation achieves full significance only through an educated knowledge of classical texts. In his treatment of Jason and Medea, Benoît supplements the laconic information found in the *Ephemeris* with the more fulsome details Ovid provides in *Heroides* XII. He then in turn draws upon the *De officiis* (or a florilegium thereof) to transform the Ovidian tale into a treatment of literate power. In their complexity, these intertextual references could only be intelligible to the bilingual capable of assessing a text in terms of its allusive pointers to antecedents. In this respect, Benoît's allusion to the ring of invisibility is a literate enactment of precisely the recondite literate power that grants it its fundamentally literate meaning. Since an understanding of the ring presupposes an understanding of the paradigm from which it is drawn, its transposed significance remains invisible and unintelligible to those who lack an accomplished *litteratura*. In other words, through remotivating the ring, Benoît is as inscrutable to the majority as Jason is inscrutable to the monstrous guardians of the fleece. However, he differs from Jason in one crucial respect. Unlike Medea's ring, *litteratura* is not a unique attribute. It is shared by others, by a minority for whom, at least theoretically, nothing in writing is invisible, nothing arcane, nothing mysterious. Just as those who possess the ring are impervious to magic ("Soz ciel n'a home qui seit vis, / dès qu'il l'avra en son deit mis, / qui ja puis crienge enchantement" [1681–83]), so also are the literate impervious to the obscurities of the written word. Like the Ring of Gyges, *litteratura* grants its wearer not only invisibility but also the power to see what is invisible to others.

All this appears to set up the cultural scenario of an esoteric club, a virtual freemasonry of letters open only to figuratively invisible men for whom nothing is invisible, including one another. To follow this line of argument a little further, we could say that Benoît here enacts, in the vernacular, the exclusive *praestigium* decried some forty years earlier by William of Malmesbury: he invites his fellow initiates of *gramaire* to exult in their shared prerogatives, to bask in the luxury and privilege of their clear-sighted superiority, and he does so specifically by writing in a manner that only they can understand. Yet the sheer self-consciousness of Benoît's rewriting of the quest, and its liminal position, militate against the effete and hieratic. It would be absurd to suggest that the magical quality of Jason's performance would not have given the listener pause for thought. The use of sorcery as a figure for writing attests a recognized cultural phenomenon, perfectly comprehensible not only to the bilingual, but also, and more importantly, to the less proficient who supposedly made this association in the first place. In short, Benoît offers writing about magical writing to the disadvantaged expressly to warn them that their response to the written word is being addressed. They may not understand the ulterior significance visible to the accomplished, but in this instance they are at least led to see that it is there. By further implication, it is unlikely that, once apprised in this way, the disadvantaged would passively allow that significance to remain hidden. Indeed, by so forcefully emphasizing invisibility, Benoît practically invites his listeners to demand that the obscure veil be dropped and arcane meanings be revealed. It is for this reason that he here addresses the disseminatory function not of writing, but of performance, of the recitation of a text inherited from another. The performer may figuratively possess the ring of invisibility. But he may also if he chooses forsake its powers and be visible to all. In this respect, the advice Medea gives Jason figuratively suggests the advice Benoît offers the hypothetical reciter of his text—"e quant ço iert qu'il te plaira / e que tu n'avras d'iço soing, / clo la pierre dedenz ton poing: / si te verra l'om come autre home."

The active responses I have scripted for a hypothetical unlettered public are of course speculative. But they are nonetheless supported by evidence that Benoît elsewhere provides when considering issues of dissemination. The scene on this occasion is Athens, and the performer is one of Benoît's primary antecedents, Homer:

Quant il en ot son livre fait
E a Athenes l'ot retrait,
Si ot estrange contençon:
Dampner le voustrent par reison,
Por ço qu'ot fait les damedeus
Combatre o les homes charneus.
Tenu li fu a desverie
E a merveillose folie
Que les deus come homes humains
Faiseit combatre as Troïains,
E les deuesses ensement
Faiseit combatre avuec la gent;
E quant son livre reciterent,
Plusor por ço le refuserent.
Mais tant fu Omers de grant pris
E tant fist puis, si com jo truis,
Que sis livres fu receüz
E en autorité tenuz.

(57–74)

[When he had completed his book about [the War] and had recited it in Athens, there was an unusual controversy. They rightly wished to censure him for having made the gods fight with men of flesh and blood. It was taken as pure extravagance and a marvelous act of folly that he had made the gods fight like human beings against the Trojans, and that he likewise had made goddesses fight with people. And when they recited his book, many rejected it for this reason. But Homer was so highly respected, and did so much afterward that, I find, his book was accepted and held in authority.]

Homer's work is published among the Athenians in two stages: first, the author himself performs his text ("a Athenes l'ot retrait"); others then perform it as his surrogates ("son livre reciterent"). Accordingly, the dissemination of Homer's work is entirely an auditive phenomenon, and the responses it elicits are therefore provoked not by close reading, but by attentive listening. Whether they particularly admire what they hear or otherwise, the audiences are clearly sufficiently interested to engage in debate, exchanging their views in what Benoît describes as "estrange contençon." Some listeners consider Homer to be flawed in his handling of the gods; others hold him in authority; still others judge him to be quite simply mad.

This prefatory depiction of delivery and debate helps clarify what has become for us today one of the most obscure aspects of textual reception in the High Middle Ages. The problem is simple: we have no direct Old French testimonies to inform us of precisely the way in which contemporary audiences listened to texts.[31] We have only the oblique evidence of fictive scenes such as Homer's recitation and the autobiographical tale told by Calogrenant early in Chrétien's *Yvain*.[32] But, however displaced, this evidence is of value. Both of these fictive accounts imply that the performative context in which romances were received would invite rather than discourage the audience to engage actively in the work's production of sense.[33] With particular regard to a text of such colossal amplitude as *Troie,* contemporary accounts of Latin delivery are also of value, especially in allowing the modern critic to gauge the length of each performance and the mnemonic requirements for attentive listening. Benoît constantly avails himself of iterative forms that, like their analogues in coeval Latin works (and, indeed, the modern novel), can only be understood through retroactive contrast. On occasion, a given semantic structure is introduced so early in the text that even the medieval listener could hardly have been capable of negotiating the feat of memorization needed to identify its relevance to later permutations. For instance, Jason's voyage anticipates and explicates the nautical metaphors Benoît uses in referring to his own undertaking, and yet they are separated at a distance of some thirteen thousand lines. By modern assessments, this would be the equivalent of approximately six hours of uninterrupted recitation.[34] Under any circumstances, it is scarcely imaginable that memory of Jason could be anything but vague by the time Benoît presents himself as a figurative mariner. But it is very unlikely that such mnemonic acuity would in fact have been required, since it is also scarcely imaginable that *Troie* was ever performed in its entirety at one sitting. If we wish to contemplate this prospect even as a diffident hypothesis, we would first have to accept the extreme implausibility of a recitation beginning (for example) at eight in the morning and only drawing to a close sometime around midnight. This would only have been possible if the text were delivered by several readers, one replacing the other in the inevitable event of fatigue, hunger, or loss of voice. But, however accommodating we make the conditions of delivery, we still have to overcome the difficulty of presuming that any listener could sustain concentration or even interest over a period of sixteen hours. From the evidence of contemporary accounts, lengthy Latin works were performed in discrete units,[35] and it is probable that *Troie* would have been recited under similar circumstances, each audition perhaps devoted to two to four hours of material.[36] In the interests of continuity, each of these readings may conceivably have been preceded by a recapitulation of what had previously been heard, and, since literature inevitably provokes a response of some kind, it is likely that each recitation would also have been followed by discussion, taking the form of either clarifying comments by the reader or an exchange of views among those in the audience. It is also probable that any social assembly would have included at least a few listeners who, independently of the reader himself, could have drawn upon their erudition to help explicate particularly difficult aspects of a work. In a performative context, this explicatory mediation is tantamount to the renunciation of epistemic inscrutability. Or, imagistically transposed, it involves the twelfth-century Jason reading his *escrit* but clarifying his maneuvers.

Within *Troie,* this process of explication is also figuratively enacted as a form of sorcery. Standing against invisibility is yet another power granted by *litteratura,* equally magical but entirely benign. This is divination. Those Trojan soothsayers, Helenus, Eüforbius, Cassandra, and Calcas, all share an acquired skill in decoding "segreiz" inherent in natural phenomena. As already mentioned, their control of the necromantic arts is identical in verbal figuration to the mastery of the liberal arts exhibited by Homer, by his scribal successors, and, indeed, any accomplished recipient of *Troie* itself. Just as the soothsayers use their art to divine the sense encoded in things, the literate use theirs to extrapolate the sense encoded in the written word. For, as Benoît suggests, knowledge can only be apprehended "si com la letre nos *devine*" (4220; my emphasis). The text, therefore, becomes a written space of divination, its graphemes yielding their particular significance to initiates. Under these conditions its *segreiz* would be as inaccessible to "cil qui n'entendent la letre" as, for example, the meaning of a flock of birds would be to anyone lacking the skills of a Calcas. However, just as the unskilled Trojans have meaning revealed to them by their *devin* and *divinere,* so also do the unskilled magnates of the twelfth century benefit from mediating diviners of their own. One is Benoît, who guarantees the information he imparts with the resonant phrase, "de cel vos sui jo bien *devin*" (6767; my emphasis). Others are those who will perform Benoît's text and who will assume the role of mediation.

Indices of the surrogate voice this would presuppose are integral to *Troie,* functioning as semantic markers that supplement and extend the inscribed authorial presence. The first-person verbs of the prologue are evidently signs of a specific act of writing located in historical time: someone obviously wrote *Troie* and, furthermore, wrote about himself writing it. These verbs can legitimately be associated with the name "Beneeiz," which is occasionally introduced in the third person. For example:

Ceste estoire n'est pas usee,
N'en guaires lieus nen est trovee:
Ja retraite ne fust ancore,
Mais Beneeiz de Sainte More
L'a contrové e fait e dit
E o sa main les moz escrit,
Ensi tailliez, ensi curez,

Ensi asis, ensi posez,
Que plus ne meins n'i a mestier.
(129–37)

[This history has not been worn away and it is scarcely to be found in many places. It has not been related before now, but Benoît de Sainte-Maure has adapted it and, with his own hand, has written its words and has so hewn, polished, placed, and positioned them that nothing more and nothing less is now needed.]

All this is fairly straightforward: the author speaks of himself in the third person when he wishes to adopt an aura of authority. Under such circumstances, the authorial "jo" is freed from pragmatic reference to an agent of writing and can now be appropriated by any number of performers, as the reciter assumes the first-person verbs and mimes the words of the absent author. When reading the introductory statement of intent ("e por ço me vueil travaillier / en une estoire commencier," and so on), the reciter would evidently not be claiming that he undertakes, miraculously and implausibly, the extemporized translation of a Latin text physically set before him on the lectern (which he would have to scan and instantly transform into well-wrought octosyllabics). He simply makes himself the medium through which an instance of past writing is once again evoked. However, he also at times switches to the role of secondary mediator that Benoît scripts for him:

Dès or porreiz oïr hui mais
La trezime bataille après:
Beneeiz, qui l'estoire dite,
Oëz queinement l'a escrite.
(19205–8)

[Today, you will be able to hear about the thirteenth battle in what comes next. Now hear how Benoît, who tells the history, put it in writing.]

Under these conditions, any unspecified reference to writing ("la letre," "l'escrit," "l'escriture," "l'estoire," "li livres") is ambiguous, applicable both to the Latin scribally translated and to the vernacular orally performed. The reciter is in equal measure the witness to an act of writing located in the past and the agent of a present interpretative delivery. While Benoît is *devinere* of the Latin letter, the performer is *devinere* of the vernacular divination Benoît has already provided and is equally responsible for disclosing the secrets that come together as the significance of the text. Therefore, mediating assurances such as "de cel vos sui jo bien devin" are both authorial and performative: Benoît derives vernacular sense from the Latin letter; through the spoken word, the reciter mediates between the grapheme and the understanding of his audience.

The Public Space of Romance

Complementing these internal signals of delivery are two diegetic structures through which the textuality of *Troie* is placed *en abyme* and the circumstances of its reception figuratively enacted. The first is a chamber of riotous opulence. The walls of alabaster are liberally adorned with gems (14633–42), which include carbuncles, to which the chamber owes its lighting (14641–46); the windowpanes are panels of precious stone, mounted in Arabian gold (14647–50); the doors are of silver, with hinges of gold (14934–36); the roof is supported by four pillars, one in each corner, respectively of electrum, jasper, onyx, and agate, the least valuable worth two hundred gold marks (14657–64). In addition, the chamber contains a throne hewn out of solid obsidian (14762–63); a mirror mounted in gold (14682–83); a crown of emeralds, rubies, and gold (14771–73); a table made of gold (14720); an eagle made of gold (14817–18); and a topaz censer with chains made of gold (14895–98). Enclosed by these golden and bejeweled walls are four automata, artifacts of inert substance granted a magical life.

Extravagantly decorated with gold, housing moving statues, and illuminated by a carbuncle, Benoît's alabaster chamber closely recalls those vaults of the Campus Martius in which William of Malmesbury projects Gerbert and his attendant attempting to plunder the figurative riches of antiquity. Once again:

> They saw an immense palace, with golden walls, golden windows, with everything made of gold. There were golden soldiers that gave the illusion of life as they played with golden dice. There was a metallic king reclining beside his queen, with a meal set down before them and their ministers standing by.

> There were vessels of great weight and value, displaying workmanship that surpassed nature. Further back in the palace, there was a carbuncle, an eminently precious and rarely found stone, which banished the darkness of night.[37] (2.169)

These analogies are not coincidental: Benoît certainly knew William's work,[38] and the autoreflexive function he lends his vernacular structure leads to a spectacular reversal of the recondite and exclusive privileges evoked by the subterranean chamber in Rome. Benoît's construct is designed not as a hidden, practically inaccessible repository, but as a public space that members of the populace can enter, there to avail themselves of the uncanny powers it encloses. While the golden statues beneath the Campus Martius come to life to prohibit entry, those of the vernacular chamber move to the needs of the populace. The first holds the golden mirror, which is offered to visitors as an unerring device for self-knowledge.[39] The second sits at the golden table, on which are projected moving narratives of birds, beasts, and fish; battles on land and sea; and amorous dalliances.[40] The third, wearing the golden crown, soothes the mind with celestial harmonies[41] and spreads over the floor flowers, which, in their regular oscillation between death and renewal, enact the rhythms of nature.[42] The fourth, holding the golden-chained censer, reveals appropriate courses for future action.[43] Miming self-knowledge, narrativity, harmony, and predication, the automata conflate the varied talents of their makers, those "engeigneor," "devin," "poëte," and "sages dotors" that Benoît employs as his own surrogates, and they do no less than enact the properties of poetic discourse, not to the detriment of those who would enter the chamber, but to their benefit. For their ministrations are a communal possession, metonymically circumscribed by the golden mirror: "A toz iceus ert comunaus / qui onques en la Chambre entroënt" (14690–91).

Thus Benoît imagistically depicts his vernacular as a new form of written necromancy, available to all, beneficent to all; and, to amplify these latter resonances, he also makes his construct into a place of healing. It is here, for example, that Hector is helped to recover from the wounds he sustains in the eighth battle:

> Broz li Puilleis, li plus senez
> Qui de mirgie fust usez

Ne d'oignement freis ne d'emplastre,
Dedenz la Chambre de Labastre,
Tailla Hector si gentement
Que mal ne trait, dolor ne sent.
(14605–10)

[Inside the Alabaster Chamber, Broz the Apulian, the wisest of all practitioners of medicine, fresh ointments and plaster, tended Hector so carefully that he suffered no ill and felt no pain.]

There is of course no direct relationship adduced between this medicinal care and the enchanted ministrations of the four automata. But here, too, the contextual presence of William's magical anecdotes is unmistakable. The chamber mobilizes the benign pendant to the rhetorical *medicamentum* of the Aquitanian monk, whose field of expertise is quite precisely medicine ("arte medico" [2:170]) and who employs language not to enlighten, but to stupefy. These subtle pointers to intertextual filiation and contrast are in turn enriched and explicated by the figure under whose aegis the entire text is written, and whose name is the literal point of origin for this enchanted and healing vernacular:

Salemon nos enseigne e dit,
E sil list om en son escrit,
Que nus ne deit son sen celer,
Ainz le deit om si demostrer
Que l'om i ait pro e honor,
Qu'ensi firent li ancessor.
(1–6)

[In his writing, Solomon teaches and tells us that no man should hide his intelligence. Rather, he should be like the ancients, showing it and gaining respect and honor as a result.]

Benoît presents Solomon as the archetype not of knowledge, but of enlightenment, and he thereby adduces the aphoristic paragon whose practice in predication he himself will follow. In this regard, it is surely significant that Benoît precedes his narrative of Troy with the story of the Golden Fleece, that tale of recitation and invisibility through which the Ring of Gyges is transformed into a symbol for literate mediation. According to William of Malmesbury, Solomon himself had come to be associated with a talisman vested with similar powers: "I believe that it was God who gave Solomon his control over demons, as Josephus testifies, stating that it was so strong that, even in his own time, there were men who expelled malign spirits from the bodies of the possessed by holding up to their noses a ring bearing a seal revealed by Solomon" (2:169).[44] William, we recall, uses this talisman to encourage his peers to banish the demons of illiterate superstition and to erase the popular distrust that can only assimilate education with deviltry. In this he establishes a model that is implicitly respected by his vernacular successor Benoît, through whom the curing properties of literate mediation triumph over the exclusive privileges of literate inscrutability.

The diegetic stress on enlightenment does not, however, resolve certain epistemological difficulties: Benoît is certainly showing that he endeavors to educate members of his curial public; but what is he teaching them? To reply that he illuminates the Trojan past for their benefit simply compounds the problem: under these circumstances, he would be in effect teaching them to believe that his own inventions are historical fact, with the result that he abuses their trust, performs the inscrutable deception he seems so anxious to erase, and thereby indeed follows the precedent of Praxis.

But, at a slightly later stage in his writing, Benoît himself confronts precisely these problems. Sequentially replacing the alabaster chamber is an analogous architectural space, designed to preserve the dead rather than the living. This is the tomb of Hector, in which are placed the warrior's corpse, voided of internal organs and embalmed,[45] alongside two forms of commemorative representation:

Si ont une image levee
Qu'a merveille fu esguardee:
De fin or fu resplendissant
E a Hector si resemblant
Que nule chose n'i failleit.
Un brant d'acier tot nu teneit,
Grezeis par signe manaçot:
Ço voleit dire e ço mostrot
Qu'ancor sereit vengiez un jor.
E si fu il al chief del tor

Si faitement com vos dirons,
Anceis qu'a la fin parveignons.
(16787–98)

[They erected a statue that was looked at with wonder, since it shone with refined gold, and so resembled Hector that nothing was lacking. In a gesture of defiance toward the Greeks, it held a drawn sword of steel. This signified and demonstrated that he would still someday be avenged—and so he was by the end of the war, as I shall tell you before I finish.]

Chier refu mout le pavement,
Quar toz esteit de fin argent.
E s'i ot d'or plus de set listes,
Ou en greu ot letres escrites,
Que diseient, qui les liseit,
Que toz entiers iluec giseit
Hector, qui tant fu proz de sei,
Qu'Achillès ocist al tornei.
(16807–14)

[The paving too was of costly materials, for it was entirely of refined silver. And inlaid into it were more than seven lines of gold, formed of letters written in Greek, which told those who read them that there lay Hector, whole and entire, who was of such personal prowess, and whom Achilles killed in battle.]

This extravagant receptacle for historiographic signifiers is a reconstruction of a specific antecedent, and it displays in the liberty of its writing a disregard for the empirical foundation from which it should purportedly be built.[46] The tomb of Hector is none other than the tomb of Dictys rewritten with a lucid awareness of the conventions it encloses. It is "invented" in the Latinate sense from the reading of its source, and this "invention" leads to a reaffirmation of the fictive origin and the original fiction of the tomb, the corpse, and the text. Through the sepulcher, Benoît reveals his Latin paradigm to be a pseudepigraphy, and, like Septimius before him, he employs the sepulchral construct directly to address issues of mediation. For the vernacular tomb is built not simply to preserve historiographic signifiers; it is periodically opened and its message disclosed to the general populace:

Quant icil anz fu acompliz
Qu'Ector fu morz e seveliz,
Si vos puet hom por veir retraire
Qu'onques si riche aniversaire
Ne fu el siecle celebrez
Com li a fait ses parentez
E toz li pueples comunaus.
Mout fu festivez li anvaus:
Mout par i chanta li clergiez,
Mout fu icil jorz essauciez.
Mout par i despendi li reis.
N'i ot chevalier ne borgeis
Qui icel jor ne festivast
E qui a son voleir n'entrast
Dedenz la riche sepouture,
Ou li cors est senz porreture.
Le jor le virent bel e freis
Chevalier, dames e borgeis.
(17489–506)

[When that year had passed since Hector's death and burial, you can be assured in all truth that never in the history of the world was an anniversary celebrated with such splendor as it was by his relatives and by all the common people. The anniversary occasioned many acts of commemoration. Through the many songs of the priests, the day was widely glorified, and the king spent lavishly. There was no knight nor burgher who did not commemorate that day or enter of his own accord the rich tomb where the body remains against putrefaction. That day knights, women, and burghers saw it beautiful and fresh.]

The anniversary of Hector's death serves as a regal festivity, in which the urban populace participates alongside the chivalric magnates and the royal family. This celebration in essence takes the form of a communal witness to history: on entering the tomb, the people of Troy perforce contemplate the corpse, the statue, and the writing it contains. The first two of these would be comprehensible as signs to everyone: Hector's death is a recent occurrence, and the Trojans would still be in a position to identify the embalmed cadaver and its sculpted representation. Yet the writing inlaid into the silver paving is of more restricted accessibility, since, as Benoît pointedly observes, to understand its import presupposes the ability to read ("en greu ot letres escrites, / que diseient, *qui les liseit,* / que toz entiers iluec giseit / Hector").

It will be noted, however, that Benoît also pointedly stresses the duties of the clerics who "sing" the past ("mout par i chanta li clergiez"). There is no relationship of cause and effect here between the commemorative words of the "clergiez" and the entombed revelations granted to others. Yet the presence of *litterati* cannot be coincidental to wider preoccupations with the disclosure of the past: the arcane sense of the "letres escrites" would have to be glossed for the benefit of those incapable of reading them for themselves, and it is precisely the "clergiez" who are contextually mentioned as the agents of verbal commemoration.[47] Here, time of theme is reflexive of time of writing: in the twelfth century, the general populace could only acquire knowledge through the performances of clerics such as Benoît himself, an elite group capable of disclosing the otherwise hidden messages of books. The most frequent occasion for such performances, moreover, was the court festivity, as Benoît's contemporary Wace affirms in the prologue to the "Troisième partie" of the *Roman de Rou:*

Pur remembrer des ancesurs
les feiz e les diz e les murs,
les felunies des feluns
e les barnages des baruns,
deit l'um les livres e les gestes
e les estoires lire a festes.
Si escripture ne fust feite
e puis par clers litte e retraite,
mult fussent choses ublïees
ki de viez tens sunt trespassees.[48]

[In order to remember the deeds, the words, and the customs of the ancients, the felonies of the felons and the valor of the valorous, we must read books, commemorative songs, and histories at festivities. If writing was not made, and then by clerics read aloud and performed, things would certainly be forgotten that happened long ago.]

Like those contained in Hector's tomb, the historiographical signifiers latent in *Troie* will also gain generalized circulation once they pass to the mediating *clergiez* capable of activating them as signs.

What the knights, women, and burghers of the twelfth century are made to contemplate through the opening of *Troie* is the relationship between this particular instance of vernacular writing and the past it purports to evoke. Through being embalmed to resist the depredations of time, Hector has in effect become the representation of himself: he is dead, but, as an everlasting sign, he projects reference to a now absent life into a potentially unending future. The immortal corpse is accompanied by the first of its interpretants in the form of the golden statue, the dead Hector-as-representation giving way to sculpted representation-as-Hector. The statue marks one stage further back in the receding frames of semiotic coincidence, as artifice now molds the Trojan warrior into an icon for a reality that is of course irrevocably absent. But this recourse to the supplement is to some degree palliated, as representation now accommodates a measure of narrativity. The statue, unlike the corpse, may no longer be physically consubstantial with its signified, but it is also free to recreate the illusion of the life that the corpse has absolutely lost, since it is wrought in a gesture of vital energy that bears a relationship of synecdoche to the events from which that life was made. This illusion of life is further enhanced by the third stage in the widening arc of representational modes, which is, of course, writing. The narrative gesture of the golden statue finds full epiphany in the golden letters inlaid into the silver paving, which come together as the words forming the first, albeit minimal, narrative of the Trojan War. Transformed into sculpted gold, Hector is no more than a static narrative fragment. But, transformed into words, he can once again enjoy the dimension of time, function within sequence.

Yet, as Benoît reveals to his public, this dependence on writing creates a spectacular illusion. Not only is Hector committed to a narrative; to borrow Alain de Lille's vocabulary, he is also a *nucleus* surrounded by a golden *cortex*.[49] For the remaining component of the tomb is a fabric that is administered to Hector's corpse as a supplement explicitly intended to refabricate the exterior ("e si refirent il defors / d'un drap"

[16517–18]) and to sustain the illusion of life ("semblant vos fust que toz fust vis" [16527]). In this, the textile mirrors in function the equally golden letters entombed alongside: the text too is a fabulous death shroud, both displacing and supplementing a referent devoid of autonomous significance, breathing life into death through a grammatical process of resuscitation. Like Hector's corpse, things that once existed have become empty hypotheses, fully compensated by the fullness of their covering. Accordingly, *Troie* itself is liberated from any myth of referential fidelity to fact and enabled to fabricate a signified of its own. Benoît has taken the liberty to create ex nihilo because he knows that his material has lost any *direct* relationship to the experiential truth of the past. As a narrative of the empirically enacted events of history, it is as empty as Hector's corpse. But this loss is covered through the supplement of a new text, through an illusion that is both magisterially performed and lucidly dismantled. In fine, through the tomb of Hector, Benoît makes fiction itself the primary object of disclosure, figuratively dramatizing the circumstances in which the audience of *Troie* will be led to contemplate the loss of the Trojan past and understand the function of the "magical" writing by which it is palliated. Accordingly, he makes his *gramaire* into a supple medium for pedagogy that unveils, among other things, its infidelity to historical reference.

Militating against inscrutability and disenchanting the privileges of education for the benefit of the public, Benoît must be assessed as a vernacular disciple of William of Malmesbury. Yet, as I shall demonstrate in the next chapter, he radically differs from his Latin predecessor in his systematic exploration of the material rewards he considers should be offered to those willing to devote their learned services to others. In this he activates that other property of the mythic Ring of Gyges and explores a potential that is intimated early in words he scripts for Medea:

Se tu ne vueus estre veüz,
La pierre met defors ta main:
Adonc puez bien estre certain
Que ja rien d'ueil ne te verra.
E quant ço iert qu'il te plaira
E que tu n'avras d'iço soing,
Clo la pierre dedenz ton poing:
Si te verra l'om come autre home.

Onques Oteviens de Rome
Ne pot conquerre cel aveir
Qui cest poüst contrevaleir.
(1690–700)

> [If you do not want to be seen, turn the stone outward from your hand. Then you can be certain that you will be visible to the eyes of none. And if circumstances have it that you want otherwise, this no longer being your intent, grasp the stone in your fist, and you will be seen just like any other man. Never could Octavian of Rome amass the sum of money that could equal the value of this [ring].]

Through this reference to the fabulous wealth of Octavian, the talisman for illuminating literacy is once again aligned with the themes of William's anecdote of the Campus Martius: the ring not only confers the ability to see what is invisible to others and to transform the invisible into the intelligible; it also permits access to a sum of knowledge that can itself be transformed into material profit. Vested with its figurative magic, Benoît employs his vernacular to create a veritable exposition on the financial value of writing, finally to conflate the learning it conveys with that most treasured of all commodities, gold itself. As it is now affirmed, *saveir* is more than simply a sum of knowledge that the wise should share with others. It is a power that is to be rendered visible and intelligible as a matrix for those concepts it is frequently made to rhyme—*aveir, valeir, poëir.*[50]

4

William FitzStephen, Richard FitzNigel, Benoît de Sainte-Maure

Bureaucratic Power and Fantasies of Literate Control

As William of Malmesbury's tale of the Campus Martius demonstrates, an awareness of the financial value of learning had come to exist even in monastic circles as early as the 1120s, and, although in context energetically resisted as a satanic compromise, it does nonetheless adumbrate the increasingly secular function that writing was to assume in late-twelfth-century England. However negative in its implications, William's biography of Gerbert suggests the possibility of a single cleric assuming almost unlimited temporal power, transforming the metaphorical gold of Augustinian knowledge into the literal wealth of the terrestrial city and affording the papacy a regal opulence. The anecdotal Gerbert is, of course, an extreme example, and, respecting William's hyperbole, the Insular clerics of the latter half of the century are far less spectacular and successful figures. Yet they did control a metaphorical necromancy that partially corresponds with Gerbert's alchemical talent of changing learning to gold. In their case, however, sublimation was realized through far more pedestrian means: they became professional bureaucrats and exchanged their literate talents for financial reward. In this they were facilitated by the wealth that accrued to the kingdom during the reign of Henry II and the alterations in administrative policy it occasioned: the complexities of coordinating the finances of England and the expansive Angevin domains on the Continent necessitated refinements in calculation and accountancy, which were themselves accompanied by an ever-increasing recourse to the written word as a device for promulgating and recording information.[1] Most of those who provided the requisite numerate and literate talents were of the lesser nobility, and some were of mercantile origin.[2] Raised to positions of often considerable influence, the members of this new social stratum rapidly attracted the resentment of landed magnates[3] and were dismissed by certain *litterati* as virtual parodies of true intellectualism, mere opportunists willing to prostitute learning to the service of vanity and extravagance.[4]

I shall now consider some of these figures. At this early stage, I stress that I shall not be proceeding as a historian. The material I consider is written by literate clerics to celebrate the prerogatives of literacy, and it is nuanced by inherent degrees of partisanship and prejudice. My intent is not to gauge the historical accuracy of these often patently exaggerated—and, on occasion, whimsically fantastical—perspectives. It is rather to present such distortions as an eloquent symptom of a developing self-consciousness. English *litterati* were among the first in Europe to recognize in writing their role in coordinating the fortunes of the landed barony, and thus analysis of their views becomes the virtue of investigating the dispositions of those who began to exert an ever-increasing influence at a critical juncture in the cultural history of the West and who claimed, in however biased a fashion, a constitutive control over a variety of social functions. Simply by drawing attention to themselves and their peers with such persistence, these new magi of the written word become a sociological phenomenon in their own right, and their literate fantasies of literate power are as historically significant as the codes of chivalry that were nurtured among their baronial contemporaries.

The license and hyperbole I shall be considering emerge to particularly striking effect from the following description of late-twelfth-century London, which by metonymy represents the new domain of social and creative freedom that had by this time been opened to young men of mercantile families:

> Among the noble and celebrated cities of the world, the metropolis of London, the center of the English realm, spreads its fame particularly wide, sends its goods and merchandise particularly far, and holds its head particularly high. To the west it is pro-

> tected by two robust strongholds, and its city walls are lofty and expansive, connecting seven portals with double gates. Further westward, two miles from the city in a busy suburb, the Royal Palace rises from the river. According to the chroniclers, London is considerably older than Rome. Both owe their origins to the same group of Trojan forefathers. But London was founded by Brutus before Rome was founded by Romulus and Remus. The metropolis of London has produced several men who have subjugated many kingdoms to their will, including the Roman Empire, and a number of others whose dominion over the world Virtue has lauded to the gods, as was promised to Brutus by the Oracle of Apollo: "Brutus, where the sun sets, beyond the realm of Gaul is an island in the ocean, enclosed on all sides by the waters. Seek it out, for it will forever be your home. It is there that another Troy will be established for your descendants. It is there that kings will be born of your lineage, and the entire world will be subordinate to them."[5]

These are the words of William FitzStephen, one of Becket's biographers, and they ostensibly celebrate a destiny gloriously realized. The London of the 1180s is the New Troy, its foundation sanctioned by the Latin verse of Geoffrey of Monmouth; it is older than Rome and enjoys the greater prestige of antiquity; and it is without peer among modern cities, its temporal supremacy aggressively asserted in the crenellations of the palace of Westminster and the seven portals of its city walls. However, the banalities of this set piece of Galfridian propaganda suddenly swerve off into unexplored Trojan territory. For all its magnificence, the palace of the discreetly nameless king is peripheral to the city itself and is located in the suburban margins. The central edifice of this particular New Troy is somewhat less hieratic:

> In London, there is also a public kitchen, situated on the bank of the river, among the stalls selling wine that has arrived by boat or been stored in cellars. There, every day you can turn up when you choose and find food and provisions, roast, baked, fried, or boiled. They have fish, large and small, and the less choice cuts of meat for the poor and delicacies for the rich, such as game and various types of fowl. This kitchen is public — it is

> a service to many inhabitants of the city and it belongs to the citizenry.[6] (Prologue, 10)

The mythic city of the past is resurrected as an urban polity of *civilitas,* gathered around the counters of a public cookhouse catering for rich and poor and at any hour of the day or night. Emblematic of the city it sustains, the refectory denies any hierarchy except that of money, offering delicacies to those who can afford them and whatever is left to those who cannot. Within this developing mercantile economy, a new class was beginning to recognize its immunity to the feudal structures existing beyond the confines of the city.

London is particularly remarkable in this context because it is birthplace to several monarchs who are emphatically not to be confused with Henry II: "In modern times, London has produced illustrious and magnificent kings: Empress Matilda, King Henry III, and the blessed Archbishop Thomas, glorious martyr of Christ" (Prologue, 19).[7] Although of some magnitude, the implications of this statement should not be exaggerated: by equating a woman and a commoner with a crowned prince, FitzStephen is not making the contextually unprecedented move of challenging the essentialist doctrine of kingship; rather, he invests the term *rex* with a wider meaning than it habitually enjoys and presents the New Troy as an arena through which a new line of rulers can achieve an active role in governance.

Within twelfth-century English politics, Matilda occupies the unique position of being the only woman ever decreed rightful successor to the throne; moreover, in an effort to enforce this decree, Henry I was rumored to have obliged his feudal vassals to swear an oath ratifying his daughter as legitimate heir. But, if this was the case, then many of these dignitaries clearly found the prospect of being ruled by a woman inadmissible and, immediately on Henry's death, lent their support to the rival claim of Matilda's cousin Stephen, count of Boulogne.[8] While Matilda, for a short time at least, was monarch in theory but not practice, Becket enjoyed the immeasurable privileges of his gender and was seen by supporters such as FitzStephen to have been effective regent of the kingdom, and this despite the theoretical disqualification of mercantile origins. Obviously, there is a great deal of partisanship in this perspective, and yet this in itself is exemplary of a more general trend. Some authors clearly adored Becket and transformed him shortly after his death into an immortal icon for the social mobility granted by education; others found him loathsome and created of his biography an exemplary tale of hubris (even though few sought to defend the circumstances of his murder).[9] The antagonistic parties hold little in common except the hyperbole of their respective positions and the extensive corpus of works they produced to articulate their views. And herein lies Becket's extraordinary literary and historiographic importance: whether adulated or detested, he was considered to be as worthy of written documentation as any king of the era.[10]

This fashioning in words is in itself an extension of the prerogatives that Becket seems to have arrogated during his lifetime. As chancellor, Becket indulged in an opulence of self-production that no monarch of the time appears to have equaled. Take, for example, his ambassadorial assignment to France, undertaken to negotiate the marriage of Henry the Younger and Margaret, daughter of Louis VII and Constance of Castile (*Vita,* 19). According to FitzStephen, Becket's train was preceded by two hundred and fifty men on foot, singing in various languages. Behind them came a procession of greyhounds and other sporting dogs, each led on a leash by a retainer. Then followed eight carts, each drawn by five horses of similar markings, each horse accompanied by its own page. For added effect, a mastiff was chained to each vehicle. Two of the carts contained nothing but beer (which, specially prepared to have the color of wine and a superior taste, appears, perhaps with a degree of facetiousness, to have been intended as an accommodating gesture to the discerning French palate). There were also twelve packhorses, each ridden by a monkey. Some bore chests of silver, gold, and minted coins; others, the twenty-four changes of costume that Becket brought along for his own use; and the leading horse carried the sacred plate and documents of the Royal Chapel. These were followed by two hundred members of the chancellor's household, all dressed in magnificent raiments. And, surrounded by a few companions, finally came Becket himself.[11]

The response that FitzStephen scripts for the French is predictable, but more complex than it seems: "This King of the English is truly a cause for wonder, if his Chancellor can ride around like this" (*Vita,* 19).[12] The French are so aghast at the reflected wonders of Henry because they lack crucial information that FitzStephen himself has already provided: the effective "rex Anglorum" of the time was none other than Becket himself. While some writers such as William of Newburgh attribute the restoration from anarchy to the political acumen of Henry,[13] FitzStephen has other ideas:

> By the compassion of God and on the advice of the Chancellor and the clerics and barons of the king, all castles were demolished throughout England except the ancient strongholds and fortified towns necessary to uphold the peace. The English Crown, once its alienated rights had been restored, was made whole once again. Patrimonies were returned to the disinherited. Thieves left their forest lairs for the villages and, moved by the gentle peace that was of benefit to all, melted down their swords into plowshares and their pikes into scythes. It was through the industry and counsel of this Chancellor, supported by the decrees of God and aided by count and baron, that the noble Kingdom of England was renewed as though a new spring, and the Holy Church honored.[14] (*Vita,* 10)

Becket's particular role in the restoration of kingship is nowhere more clearly manifested than in the suburbs of London: "The Chancellor Thomas saw to the rebuilding of the king's residence, the Palace of London, which was previously almost a ruin" (*Vita,* 10).[15] The hieratic edifice of royalty has become so secondary to the forms of power circulating in the New Troy that it becomes a mere construct supervised by others. As chancellor, Becket adopts certain prerogatives of kingship itself, possessing an icon of royal prestige that in theory represents Henry and in practice allows him to be displaced altogether:

> It is the dignity of the Chancellor of England to be held throughout the realm as second only to the king. He is empowered to sign his own mandates with the Royal Seal that it is his duty to safeguard. He is responsible for the organization and maintenance of the Royal Chapel. He must uphold and protect any archbishoprics, bishoprics, abbacies, and baronies that fall vacant and pass into the king's hands. He must attend all the king's councils and must be present even when not invited. He must assure that all documents are signed by the hand of the Royal Seal-Bearer, his secretary, and that all affairs of the Chancellery are decided by council.[16] (*Vita,* 9)

This semiotic transfer of regency is also attested by another of the bureaucrats of Henry's reign, Richard FitzNigel, treasurer to the Crown and author of the *Dialogus de Scaccario* (c. 1176–79).[17] FitzNigel was clearly no admirer of Becket, never deigning even to mention the former chancellor. But his work shows precisely the insistence on delegated government that characterizes the early sections of FitzStephen's biography. In many ways FitzNigel and FitzStephen (and perhaps also Becket in his calculated performances) indulge in a fantasy as precarious as those of the Arthurian knight and the Trojan prince. But they attest the prerogative to write themselves into the present, a prerogative beyond king and baron, who rely on others to write flattering fictions of the past. Significantly, in the work of FitzNigel, this power is physically symbolized by the Exchequer itself, the rectangular and hierarchical table that, occupied by clerics in London and designed to regulate the finances of the kingdom and to coordinate the Royal Treasury of Winchester, contrastively evokes that analogue celebrated elsewhere in twelfth-century letters, the Round Table seating king and barons in the Arthurian fiction of equality.[18]

The Dialogue of the Exchequer

FitzNigel's treatise takes the form of a dialogue between a Magister and an obligingly curious Discipulus, and it is mainly concerned with the factual matters of who sits at the table and why. However, it is marked throughout by a tension between the Exchequer and its overlord, King Henry himself. In theory, the first simply serves the second, and FitzNigel is no exception among writers of his time in the expansive praise he lavishes on his monarch. In the dedicatory prologue, he addresses Henry as "illustrious King" ("rex illustris" [2]), "Excellency" ("excellentia" [2]), and "the greatest of all worldly princes" ("mundanorum principum maximus" [2]); later we learn that the king's accomplishments defy human belief (1.5; 27), that he has extended his empire ("imperium") over vast stretches of the globe (1.5; 27), that he is like Maecenas (1.5; 27), and that he is even a modern avatar of Hercules (2.2; 76). But he has also delegated to others the responsibility of supervising the finances to which he owes not simply his military successes, but also his ability to function as king. For, as the Discipulus wryly observes with reference to the Chief Justiciar: "He is certainly a great man, since he is entrusted with responsibility for the entire kingdom. After all, it is written: 'Where your treasure is, so too is your heart'" (1.5; 16).[19] This ambiguous relationship between a bureaucratic delegation and the monarch it is theoretically committed to serve is introduced at the beginning of the text proper, in which the Magister explains that the Exchequer is both the raised abacus for calculation and the clerical curia that supervises its functions:

> The table itself is called the Exchequer, but this name has been transferred to refer also to the court in session.... The power of this court unquestionably devolves from the authority of the great men by which it is formed, and its statutes are so binding that no man would attempt to break them, or even show the temerity to resist. And this is what it holds in common with the royal court in which the Lord King himself administers justice—its records and sentences may never be contradicted by anyone.[20] (1.1; 6–7 and 1.4; 14)

The king administers secular justice elsewhere, and, in his absence, the Exchequer enjoys plenipotentiary powers to regulate finances as it sees fit, evaluating administrative regions, preparing the writs of assessment, and issuing the summonses of attendance through which payment will be legally binding. These powers are ratified by two things: "The court of the Exchequer owes its signal authority to the preeminence of the royal image that is imprinted on the king's seal and preserved in the treasury by legal stipulation, and, as already stated, to the men who attend, by whose care the entire realm is preserved in indemnity" (1.4; 14–15).[21]

As even these introductory comments make clear, FitzNigel is elaborating not simply an alternative court, but an alternative barony to which he explicitly transfers the true preservation of the realm. Still more contextually remarkable is the social extraction of these *maiores*. As his own patronymic surname suggests, FitzNigel was not a noble. Nor were several other preeminent men associated with this financial curia. FitzNigel provides a striking example in the figure of Thomas Brown, who, despite his obscure origins, attends in session with his own scribe and "wields no lowly authority in the Exchequer" ("huius ad scaccarium non uilis est auctoritas" [1.6; 35]). FitzNigel complements this biographical fact of social mobility by lending the abacus itself a symbolical meaning. He has the Discipulus note that the pennies used as counters may be invested with whatever value the Exchequer decrees, variously representing a penny, a shilling, a pound, a hundred pounds, or a thousand, depending on their convened function in calculation (1.5; 25).[22] Obviously, this subliminally accommodates a recognition of the conventionalized semiotics of money, as the Magister goes some way to confirm, observing that the Accountant may attribute to each coin whatever value he wishes, appreciating or depreciating the signified as he sees fit (1.5; 25).[23] But it also serves as the pretext for a commentary on the possible semiotic changes of men:

> This too could apply to any man born in the lower orders of society. He is a man and can be nothing else, but, through the contingencies of experience sanctioned by the will of God, he may rise from the bottom to the top, and then, as the wheel of fortune revolves, return to where he started. Throughout, he would remain the same, however much his dignity and status may be seen to have altered.[24] (1.5; 25–26)

The reference to the wheel of fortune is conventional and in itself relatively anodyne. Yet it is here employed as a gloss on Providence and applied to the social advancement available to men of explicitly plebeian origin ("quiuis de plebe"). This too would be of little consequence were it not for the context in which such mobility is symbolized, since those who form the curial Exchequer exemplify precisely the appreciation enacted in the semiotics of the abacus. They are men and nothing less, and by the will of God they have risen.[25]

FitzNigel, therefore, views rank as a fundamentally semiotic phenomenon, an external integument that is categorically not consubstantial with the individual beneath: just as the penny remains a penny despite the value convened by the Accountant, so too does a man remain a man despite the dignity and status he has achieved by divine decree. Rank is also contingent on circumstances ultimately beyond the control of the individual: it is bestowed by God and, as the Magister proceeds to point out, it is not bestowed in equal measure to all (1.5; 26).[26] However, this last restriction notwithstanding, the symbolism of the abacus retains its coherence within the Exchequer itself, and it prompts the Magister immediately to elaborate on the recondite, exclusive, and divinely ordained duties of the new barony God has created:

> However it should seem to others, it gives me some pleasure to see you derive ulterior meanings from this. For it is praiseworthy to seek out the flowers of mystic understanding from among the thorns of this world. And it is not only from the context you have broached that holy truths *[sacramentorum quedam]* are to be retrieved, but from the entire description of the Exchequer.[27] (1.5; 26)

At first glance, the term *sacramenta* is curious. Close examination of the specific procedures observed within the Exchequer nevertheless reveals that it does have a certain validity. For the members of this financial curia are indeed participants in a quasi-sacred ritual. Its final aim, however, is not the transubstantiation of Body and Host, but the consubstantiation of king and *thesaurus*. As already mentioned in passing, FitzNigel states that two things grant the Exchequer its prestige. The second in order is the authority of those present in assize. And the first is a particular icon, variously designated as the "regia ymago" and the "regie imaginis impressio." Its primary function is quite utilitarian: the king is personally absent and through his seal he delegates a regally sanctioned power. But FitzNigel employs the royal icon as the nexus for a wide-ranging (at times provocative) semiology, ultimately disclosing the true prerogative of his alternative barony: the members of the Exchequer are men of such great authority because they are the protectors and makers of signs. He systematically avoids a genitive when referring to the image imprinted onto the seal: it is royal ("regia ymago"), rather than the king's ("regis ymago"),[28] and it is served and preserved ("servatur") according to a specific and unique law of its own ("individua lege"). Through this displacement of the referent and the attendant insistence on the legal indemnity of the sign, FitzNigel contrives to make Henry himself a corollary to the power the Exchequer wields. The subordination this implies has already been touched on briefly in the maxim FitzNigel scripts for the Discipulus: "Where your treasure is, so too is your heart" ("ubi est thesaurus tuus ibi est et cor tuum"). Through metaphor, the heart of the king, and therefore his very existence, has become dependent on a set of governmental procedures; and, through extension, Henry loses human attributes and becomes one with his wealth. Ultimately, the Exchequer derives its authority in part from a sign signifying an *abstraction* of kingship, and Henry circulates as a secondary representation owing its significance to a clerical elite.

The conflation of the living monarch and the finances coordinated by the Exchequer is made quite literal in the Magister's lengthy exposition on coinage, since, in the silver penny, Henry and wealth are juxtaposed as mutually signifying interpretants. As such, they also circulate in a public domain in which the authority of the Exchequer is at its most vulnerable. For these representations are susceptible to a variety of abuses: "This can result from the work of forgers or those who cut and clip coins. Take note, then, that English money can be false in three ways, since the weight, the alloy, and the imprinted image are all liable to falsification" (1.3; 12).[29] To avoid perversions of this type, the Exchequer employs its own metallurgist, who regularly tests the wealth that constitutes the heart of the king by melting down samples of the coinage in which it circulates.[30] The constant regularization of the king's value in silver is further refined by another medium, itself governed by its own laws of checks and balances. This is writing, undertaken by the three scribes who sit at the Exchequer. The risk of written falsification is avoided in two ways. Because the conclusions of each session are written in triplicate, an error in transcription by any of the three scribes can be corrected through collation with the other copies (1.5; 18).[31] Moreover, any mistake must then be kept clearly visible, the relevant Roll becoming a palimpsest displaying the corrected scribal deviations (1.5; 31).[32] To enhance these measures further, the medium used for the Rolls is exclusively sheepskin, since sheets of such parchment "do not easily allow erasures that leave no trace of the emendation made" (1.5; 31).[33] Precautions are also taken in the preparation of the summonses. Although these missives are sent to the Sheriff unsealed, no one would deem it worthwhile to intercept and falsify them, since the Exchequer also keeps a record of the amount each demands from the appropriate administrative region (2.2; 74).[34]

This brief commentary on the *Dialogus* has yielded two points. First, FitzNigel attests the existence of a professional, secular clergy formed of men who by divine decree have risen above their initially humble status. Second, he is concerned throughout with the maintenance of authority, achieved by systematic procedures intended to circumvent the perversion of signs and thus to safeguard the Exchequer's monopolized and quasi-religious privilege to signify. In unexpected but striking ways, Benoît addresses similar issues. His manner is obviously far more oblique than FitzNigel's, since he superficially writes not of the present, but of the past. Yet he also attests the existence of a median social stratum, a clerical elite inextricably associated with the circulation of wealth. Moreover, he too is concerned with the power to signify and, like FitzNigel, recognizes the dangers of written falsification. In citing these similarities, my aim is not to argue that there is any direct relationship between the royal treasurer and the vernacular author. It is rather to point out that, by showing such similar preoccupations, they both reflect an ambient social ethos in which literacy, finance, and mobility were inextricably bound together in contradistinction to the established feudal prerogatives of the landed barony. Furthermore, my own stricture notwithstanding, I shall demonstrate that Benoît certainly knew of the Royal Treasury and may quite possibly have employed this knowledge to create a vernacular *thesaurus* that can be helpfully explicated through certain aspects of FitzNigel's later treatise.

Written Gold

Benoît's alabaster chamber is more than simply a specular device employed to dramatize the power of vernacular *mirgie*. It is also a construct of staggering wealth through which writing and gold are collapsed, ultimately to reflect a mercantile economy of textual production. After providing his extraordinary set of variations on the theme of the golden artifact, Benoît predictably estimates the room to be worth more than one hundred thousand pounds (14958). Less predictable is the fact that he does so in order to assess the value of another material artifact—the book that will someday become the repository for the text that is here placed *en abyme*. So stupendous are the marvelous talents responsible for the chamber that Benoît is obliged to pause in order to proclaim laconically:

> Bien met son aveir e empleie
> Qui en tel uevre le despent.
>
> (14932–33)

[Whoever spends his wealth on such a work puts it to a worthy cause and uses it well.]

Money has been put to good use by whoever commissioned the building of the chamber. But the polysemy of *uevre* also embraces the work of Benoît, the modern artificer who has created out of his own magical words not only the chamber itself, but also its fictive diegetic architects. Therefore, with a degree of self-indulgent and self-mocking fantasy, Benoît contemplates the value of his own undertaking and proceeds to round off his calculations with a resonant homophony:

Quant Paris ot pris dame Heleine,
Si li dona tote en demeine
Ceste chambre li reis Prianz,
Par le voleir de ses enfanz:
Onques a dame n'a pucele
Ne fu donee autresi bele
Ne si riche, ço dit li livres:
Plus valeit de cent mile livres.
(14951–58)

[When Paris abducted Lady Helen, King Priam, on the bidding of his children, gave her this room as her own personal possession. The book tells us that no room matching this one in beauty or wealth was ever given to another woman or girl. It was worth more than one hundred thousand pounds.]

Since the chamber exists in neither of the Latin works translated, the only book that will ever make this statement of value is the book that will contain *Troie* itself, the material guarantor of the written word from which the text will be read aloud in performance. As this twelfth-century book affirms, the chamber is certainly worth a great deal. But so too is that other *uevre* upon which money has been so well spent—once consigned to the material space of parchment and binding, *Troie* also achieves the prodigious market value of over a hundred thousand pounds.

But of course, as Benoît is well aware, his work will be worthless until he finishes it: before it can circulate as the material commodity of a book and have its immense value declared, it has to be carried through to completion. It is for this reason that, having documented in lingering detail so many of the chamber's opulent furnishings, Benoît declines to say anything about the bed and abruptly begins to employ the nautical metaphors briefly considered in chapter 3 in their relevance to Jason's quest for the Golden Fleece:

Del lit par sereit trop grant chose,
Se j'en comenceie a parler;
Mais ne m'i leist a demorer:
Mout par ai ancore a sigler,
Quar ancor sui en haute mer.
Por ço me covient espleitier,
Quar sovent sordent destorbier;
Maintes uevres sont comenciees,
Qui sovent sont entrelaissiees.
Ceste me doint Deus achever,
Qu'a dreit port puisse ancre geter!
(14940–50)

[I would be taking on far too much if I began talking about the bed. I cannot allow myself to dwell on it because I am still on the high seas and have a great distance yet to sail. Therefore, I must hurry on, to avoid the obstacles that often arise. Many works are begun that are frequently abandoned. May God grant that I finish this one and drop anchor at my port of destination.]

Metaphorically projected in these terms, Benoît's written enterprise assumes the qualities of a mercantile voyage, a journey through precise coordinates that accrues in value but will only actualize its worth once completed: just as the merchant cannot sell his wares until he drops anchor at his final destination, the writer cannot negotiate a profit for his efforts until he has created a well-wrought and finished artifact.

All of these considerations are obliquely introduced in the prologue, which reads as something of an open-ended admonition to profit from learning and the rewards it may bring. At this early stage, Benoît's handling of finance is deft, a subliminal resonance to his outward grammar of responsible enlightenment. Nevertheless, it raises the issues of social mobility and material advancement that Benoît develops as his literary journey proceeds. In this context, it is significant that the prologue begins with an emphasis not only on learning, but also on the intellectual eminence of individuals who have assured that they are still remembered. Once again:

Salemon nos enseigne e dit,
E sil list om en son escrit,
Que nus ne deit son sen celer,
Ainz le deit om si demostrer
Que l'om i ait pro e honor,
Qu'ensi firent li ancessor.
(1–6)

[In his writing, Solomon teaches and tells us that no man should hide his intelligence. Rather, he should be like the ancients, showing it and gaining respect and honor as a result.]

As projected in these early couplets, writing is an opportunistic medium for self-promotion, and, if literary works are of value, it is in part because they convey the talents of their writers. Consequently, Benoît advocates what is in effect a *sciënce* of *sens,* and he promotes the teacher as an object of knowledge and perpetuation as important as the material he teaches. To disseminate learning is to create a performative autobiography, to define oneself in the present; and, because textually enacted, this self-definition will in turn contribute to the sum of knowledge passed down to future generations. Fully consistent with the terms of his own appeal, Benoît later in the prologue inscribes his own authorial signature into his *escrit,* consigning himself to the future through a material object bearing his personal sign of exclusive authority and actualizing the eloquent, if only fleeting, vistas of worldly fame he has already sketched:

Remembré seront a toz tens
E coneü par lor granz sens,
Quar sciënce que est teüe
Est tost obliëe e perdue.
Qui set e n'enseigne o ne dit
Ne puet muër ne s'entroblit.
(17–22)

> [These writers will always be remembered and known for their great intelligence, since knowledge that is withheld is soon forgotten and lost. A man who is wise but does not teach or proclaim his wisdom will inevitably pass into oblivion.]

The elliptical couplet "qui set e n'enseigne o ne dit / ne puet muër ne s'entroblit" militates against clarity of meaning; nonetheless, for this very reason, it is richly suggestive. Its straightforward first element ("whoever knows and does not teach or does not say") leads to a statement of effect apparently formed of balanced verbs introduced by the negative particle: "ne puet muër ne s'entroblit." Read aloud, this seems to suggest, as its first concluding proposition, that, by being delinquent, the scholar fails to seize the opportunity to change, alter, or transform himself (*muër,* which is both transitive and intransitive, carries all of these meanings). However, these implications of personal mutation and their attendant resonances of economic advancement are denied as soon as we try to make sense of the second verb, "ne s'entroblit." Not only is it illogical following "ne puet muër," since this would force the incoherent "cannot change, and is not forgotten"; it is also subjunctive, and must therefore be subordinate to the phrase "ne puet muër"—"cannot prevent himself from being forgotten." However, although of only momentary grammatical validity, the first reading cannot be easily jettisoned. It may be bracketed as untenable as soon as made. But it has briefly helped constitute a path for understanding and, even when discounted, still acts as a semantic vector inflecting all that follows:

> E sciënce qu'est bien oïe
> Germe e florist e frutefie.
> Qui vueut saveir e qui entent,
> Sacheiz de mieuz l'en est sovent.
> De bien ne puet nus trop oïr
> Ne trop saveir ne retenir;
> Ne nus ne se deit atargier
> De bien faire ne d'enseignier;
> E qui plus set, e plus deit faire:
> De ço ne se deit nus retraire.
>
> (23–32)

[Knowledge that is heard germinates, flowers, and bears fruit. Let it be known that a man is often better off who wants to know and is prepared to listen. We cannot hear, know, and retain too much that is good. Therefore, no one should hesitate to do good and teach others; and who knows more should do more. No one should retreat from this duty.]

The first of these hortative couplets rhetorically transfers learning into the realms of autonomous proliferation, where it assumes the power to produce more of its own kind when distributed. In its tropic attributes, learning here remarkably resembles wealth, that indefinable thing that can constantly and exponentially multiply itself through its judicious expenditure. Within the allied domains of knowledge and finance, the more one has, the more one has the power to have more. Hence Benoît's tangential play on the fruits that intellectual labor may bring: learning not only reproduces itself when disseminated; it also brings rewards of a material nature to the learned who devote themselves to the enlightenment of others. Reinforcing this point, Benoît shifts attention from learning that is attentively heeded ("sciënce qu'est bien oïe") to the dissemination, knowledge, and retention of *biens:* "De *bien* ne puet nus trop oïr, / ne trop saveir ne retenir." The substantive *biens* marks a semantic shift from the purely abstract *(sciënce)* to a thing of sufficient substance to accommodate the verb *faire,* with its ambiguous elisions between doing and making: "ne nus ne se deit atargier / de *bien faire* ne d'enseignier." Therefore, teaching well gradually assumes the attributes of making a good thing. As a further move, Benoît then replaces this *biens* with the unequivocally quantitative *plus*—the thing that is good disappears in favor of more, which is in turn revealed to be the object of its own multiplication: "e qui *plus set,* e *plus deit faire.*" As *biens* becomes *plus,* we return once again to the earlier theme of germination, flowering, and fruition, although now expressed in far more concrete terms: the more you know, the more you must do, and, indeed, the more you must make. Already in these semantic shifts we observe a movement away from an abstract concept of learning to a more tangible commodification: *sciënce* is sequentially displaced by *biens* as the product of labor, which is then in turn subsumed into a grammar of quantification and accretion. Profoundly implicated in this production of an accumulating thing is the parallel emphasis on the producer, the individual who will be remembered for his *sens*. Cast into a context mobilizing *biens,* the intellect veers toward an aptitude in the accumulation of the material.

Since it is expressed purely through verbal equivocation, the financial value of these prefatory remarks can hardly be taken to constitute a literary economy of production and profit. However, all of these ideas reappear in the epilogue, there to achieve an unambiguously acquisitive and proprietorial meaning:

> Ci ferons fin, bien est mesure:
> Auques tient nostre livre e dure.
> Ço que dist Daires et Ditis
> I avons si retrait e mis
> Que, s'il plaiseit as jangleors,
> Qui de ço sont encuseors,
> Qu'as autrui faiz sont reprenant
> E a trestoz biens enviant,
> Ne que ja rien n'avra honor
> Qu'il n'en aient vie et dolor,
> Cil se porreient mout bien taire
> De l'uevre blasmer e retraire;
> Quar teus i voudreit afaitier,
> Qui tost i porreit empeirier.
> Celui guart Deus e tienge en veie,
> Qui bien essauce e montepleie.
> (30301–16)

[I shall end my work here, as is only right. My book is sufficiently filled and has lasted long enough. I have described and put in it what Dares and Dictys say. Therefore, I ask one favor of those performers who criticize works such as this and reproach the deeds of others, always envious of anything good, always plunged into grief and pain by things that are held in honor. They should refrain from criticizing this work of mine. They should also refrain from performing it, because anyone who tries to improve it will only make it worse. May God protect and guide my book and grant that it productively grow and multiply.]

The end of the text, that maritime journey across an inhospitable sea, is marked by a subtle tone of mercantile assessment: the information conveyed by antecedent authors is here conceived as a physical stuff, as a weight and value that Benoît has accumulated through his translation in order to produce a satisfactory sum ("*auques tient* nostre livre e dure / Ço que dist Daires et Ditis / i avons si retrait e mis"). Reinforcing this catachresis of the material, Benoît claims the resulting product to be his exclusive property ("*nostre* livre") and finally employs *biens* with a meaning that contextually tends toward the tangible. Through the bivalence of *reprendre,* Benoît first reveals that *jangleors* appropriate what others have produced and disparage the deeds others have perpetrated ("as autrui faiz sont reprenant"); through another equivocation, he then accuses them of envying anything good and any item of wealth ("trestoz biens enviant"). This anathema is an absolute interdiction. The *jangleors* are not merely disqualified from criticizing the present work—they have no right to perform it: "cil se porreient mout bien taire / de l'uevre blasmer e *retraire.*" Through the polysemy of *retraire,* both "to recite" and "to censure," Benoît suggests that his *uevre* would be vilified simply by being read aloud by the mercenary and would, furthermore, be ruined by their woeful efforts to improve what has already been revealed to be the just and rightful measure. By way of final envoi, Benoît calls upon God to parry these envious depredations, and in so doing he associates author and text, equivocally linking them together as objects of linear transmission ("*celui* guart Deus e *tienge en veie*") and as subjects of prestigious proliferation ("qui bien essauce et montepleie"). Under divine protection the book will multiply in an intransitive sense, will enjoy ample copying and diffusion; and the author will transitively multiply his understood rewards and gain honor and respect for and through the *sens* he has demonstrated in his writing.

Benoît's claim to textual proprietorship is a vernacular manifestation of a self-consciousness that was already by this date an established norm in Insular Latin letters. In the final period of the *Gesta regum,* for instance, William of Malmesbury gives pointed advice to another historian, most probably Henry of Huntingdon: "If anyone should undertake to write on the subject I have covered (and I have already heard it rumored that someone has), then I grant him leave to select whatever material he wishes from my work, provided he recognize that I was responsible for the research" (5.445).[35] This claim to authorship, which gained its most articulate voice later in the century through Gerald of Wales, is often obtrusively present in some of the more ambitious and protracted Old French translations of the era, most probably as a direct consequence of the very Latinity of the material from which the vernacular derived. The most pertinent example is found at the end of Wace's *Roman de Rou:*

> Die en avant qui dire en deit;
> j'ai dit por Maistre Beneeit,
> qui cest'ovre a dire a emprise
> com li reis l'a desor lui mise;
> quant li reis li a rové faire
> laissier la dei, si m'en dei taire.
> Li reis jadis maint bien me fist,
> mult me dona, plus me pramist,
> e se il tot doné m'eüst
> ço qu'il me pramist, mielz me fust;
> nel poi aveir, ne plout al rei,
> mais n'est mie remés en mei.
> ("Troisième partie," 11419–30)

> [From now on, let anyone say on these matters what he has to. What I have said will be of profit to Master Benoît, who, at the king's bidding, has undertaken to put this work into his own words. Since the king has asked him to do this, I am obliged to stop and say no more. In the past, the king treated me very well, giving me many things and promising me even more. And if he had given me everything he promised, I would have been better off. However, for reasons completely beyond my control, I was unable to benefit this way, since it did not please the king.]

At issue here is more than simply the bilious resentment of a writer embittered by Henry's failure to remunerate and envious of the successful rival for whose benefit he has been dismissed. Wace not only knows that he will receive nothing for his unfinished *Roman de Rou*. He also is keenly aware that this work, over which he has toiled for some fourteen years, will now be appropriated by his rival, rewritten and offered up as an entirely new text. As he himself points out, he has been working for the profit of another author; and the author in question happens to be none other than Benoît himself, who at Henry's bidding did indeed undertake his own vernacular history of the Normans to create the text today known as the *Chronique des ducs de Normandie.*

It is with some irony, therefore, that we encounter Benoît inscribing his proprietorial signature into *Troie* during the 1160s, only to be characterized some ten years later as a displacing upstart given to the expropriation of another author's work.[36] Yet there is in fact no contradiction: Benoît's efforts to assure the authorial integrity of *Troie* is a symptom of precisely the spirit that leads him later to treat Wace's work with such opportunism—he attempts to offset a tendency that he recognizes not only in others, but also in himself. Viewed in a wider cultural context, Benoît's claim to proprietorship acknowledges a system of dissemination and performance that militates against the finite text and enables the mercenary to exploit the initiative of others for their own gain. As Benoît is well aware, his text will be subject to a multiplicity of emendations, additions, and erasures as soon as he allows it to circulate. Hence his attempts to proscribe any effort to improve, and inevitably impoverish, his completed and signed artifact:

Ceste estoire n'est pas usee,
N'en guaires lieus nen est trovee:
Ja retraite ne fust ancore,
Mais Beneeiz de Sainte More
L'a controvê e fait e dit
E o sa main les moz escrit,
Ensi tailliez, ensi curez,
Ensi asis, ensi posez,
Que plus ne meins n'i a mestier.
(129–37)

[This history has not been worn away and it is scarcely to be found in many places. It has not been related before now, but Benoît de Sainte-Maure has adapted it and, with his own hand, has written its words and has so hewn, polished, placed, and positioned them that nothing more and nothing less is now needed.]

The narrative of the war is conceived as a substance that has not been worn away with the passage of time. It is an inchoate mass, preexisting, but not yet crafted to the contours that Benoît provides. That no mention is made of literary antecedents is not at all a mark of strategic omission. Since *l'estoire* is entirely made from *gramaire,* then it is susceptible to any number of reworkings: as a sum of information, it exists independently of "Daires," "Ditis," and "Beneeiz"; however, through the disparate formal attributes that it achieves in their crafting hands, it circulates as three paradigmatic modulations bearing disparate signatures. It is not therefore the idea that is the possession of anyone, but its treatment—in this case, the artifact that Benoît claims to have created from words with such magisterial finesse that nothing should be added or subtracted from its harmonious design.

This concern with the authorial signature and with the text that is to remain integral and inviolate is analogous to FitzNigel's preoccupations with the unique authority of the Exchequer, that financial curia which both preserves signs and constantly regulates the integrity of the numismatic and graphemic symbols through which its power is made manifest. As I have already mentioned, these analogies cannot be attributed to intertextual filiation: FitzNigel was the later of the two authors, and there is no evidence and no compelling reason to argue that he depicted the functions of the Exchequer with a fidelity to imagistic motifs employed by a vernacular predecessor. Yet, as I have also pointed out, Benoît certainly knew of the Royal Treasury, creating conditions in which it is legitimate to suggest that certain of his concerns may have been influenced by its functions. The point at which Benoît makes this acquaintance explicit is a passage from the *Chronique des ducs de Normandie* in which he describes William the Conqueror giving instructions to prepare for his investiture at York:

E il conmanda aporter
De Guincestre ses ornemenz,
Sa chapele, ses garnemenz,
Sa coronne e sa grant vaissele,
Que reis n'aveit sos cel plus bele.[37]

[He ordered brought from Winchester his regalia—the icons from his chapel, his robes, his crown, and the great quantity of (silver and gold) plate that he possessed and that no king in the entire world could match in its beauty.]

Left to itself, this reference would be devoid of interest. It achieves significance, however, because it is chronologically preceded in *Troie* by a minute description of an edifice that proves to have a remarkably similar function. This is the tomb of Hector, constructed as a stupendous display of imperial wealth. It is demarcated by a wall of colored marble extending twenty feet into the air and surmounted by a vault constructed entirely of gold ("voute i ot faite d'or vousee" [16719]). Beneath is a secondary canopy taking the form of a baldachin. Its roof too is of gold, enhanced with an incrustation of jewels ("ainz fu de fin or e de pierres / mout precioses e mout chieres" [16709–10]). This is supported by four columns hewn from single gemstones of staggering value (16665–94), which are themselves held by golden statues standing on golden pedestals ("eschameaus orent soz lor piez / d'or esmeré bien entailliez / les images, d'or ensement" [16655–57]). The paving is of silver ("chier refu mout le pavement, / quar toz esteit de fin argent" [16807–8]), and it is here that the golden epitaph is inlaid ("e si ot d'or plus de set listes / ou en greu ot letres escrites" [16809–10]). The furnishings are completed by the golden statue of Hector ("de fin or fu resplendissant" [16789]) and the warrior's corpse, itself clad in its raiment of golden thread ("de fil d'or fu tote cosue" [16525]) and seated on a throne of magnificent opulence (16737–44). But the most unusual—and, potentially also, valuable—of these artifacts is the sarcophagus:

S'ont un sarcueil dedenz asis,
E si n'est hom ne nez ne vis
Qui de si riche oïst parler.
Quar pierres orent fait tribler,
Esmeraudes, alemandines,
Saphirs, topaces e sardines:
En or d'Araibe sont fondues
E trestotes a un venues.
Li trei sage devin ont fait
Un molle entaillié e portrait
De la plus riche uevre qui fust
Ne que nus hom veeir poüst.
L'or e les pierres i geterent,
D'estrange chose s'apenserent.
(16721–34)

> [Inside, [the three sages] placed a sarcophagus. No man who ever lived or is still living ever heard of one so rich. For they ground precious stones into powder—emeralds, rubies, sapphires, topaz, and agate—and melted them all into refined Arabian gold, thereby creating of the whole a single substance. The three wise diviners made an incised mold, decorated with the richest work there ever was and that any man could ever see. With uncanny intent, they poured the gold and the gems into it.]

This is the reading offered by Constans. But it is not the only one. Whatever the paradigm may have been, this process of metal casting was evidently perceived by certain scribes to merit a very suggestive interpretation. For example, line 16721 has the variants "s'ont un seel dedanz asis" (MS *K*) and "si y ont un seel asis" (MS *M*). In these two cases, it is not a sarcophagus that is cast, but a seal. A similar idea is expressed in MS M^1, although as a variant of line 16730; here, in place of the incised and sculpted mold of the Constans reading ("un molle entaillié e portrait"), we find the mold of a man finely wrought, "un molle d'ome bien portrait." This stress on the representation of a human form carries over into the subsequent lines. These, in the Constans edition, abruptly switch attention to Hector's throne with the phrase "de la chaeire que direie?" (16787). In MS *J*, an almost identical question is asked, but with a significant vocalic change, "chaeire" becoming "chiere." In this case, what resists identification and displays such wealth is not a throne, but a face.

These variants may or may not directly correspond with the words written or dictated by Benoît at some unspecified moment in the second half of the twelfth century. Let us assume, simply for expediency, that they do not. This is by far the easiest course, and in any case it changes little. Even if they are later modifications to the original paradigm that now exists only as a hypothesis, these readings retain an absolute validity, rendering explicit a significance that was perceived to be already latent in the fabric of the tomb. This significance is a numismatics of authority that resists any stable identification. Perhaps this *seel* and the image of individual power it displays are intended to reflect Hector himself. But this obvious inference is weakened by the curious terms in which the three sages are described pouring the fused gems and gold into the incised recess. This is no ordinary maneuver, and if these necromancers go to such lengths to perpetuate a numismatic image, it is with an intent that is wondrous: "d'estrange chose s'apenserent." This marvelous design can be cogently read as a self-perpetuating gesture on the part of the original *sages* who orchestrated the actions of his diegetic analogues, Benoît de Sainte-Maure himself. Under these circumstances, the tomb becomes the repository for two images of power: the first is the Trojan prince, dead yet resuscitated through the "magical" properties of *gramaire;* and the other is the agent of this miraculous resuscitation, the "Beneeiz de Sainte More" who inscribes his signature of personal propriety into his work and casts his own image into the figuratively metallurgical properties of the written gold his work represents.

5

Gerald of Wales

Writing for the Crowned Ass of England

During the half century of his prolific career, Gerald of Wales produced works revealing a prodigious range of interests, including Neoplatonic philosophy, ethnography, political ethics, secular history, and ecclesiastical reform.[1] He was also something of a historical anomaly in the extent of his autobiographical writing. Gerald not only liberally inserted personal anecdotes into contexts only marginally related to himself;[2] he also wrote his own life history, collated the passages he most admired in his own works to create an authorized florilegium, and wrote two short tracts of unabashed literary self-endorsement,[3] both evidently designed to prompt others to share his own belief in the excellence he had achieved in the domain of contemporary letters.[4] Perhaps even more unusually, the end of his career was marked by a set of retractions,[5] among which was a response to an unstated but contextually clear charge of plagiarism[6] and an acknowledgment that he had on one occasion deliberately misrepresented his sources and as a result potentially written fiction in the guise of history.[7]

This extreme authorial self-consciousness was intimately bound up with perceptions of personal influence and power. Gerald aggressively promoted learning as the true sign of authority and disdainfully disclosed the inadequate education displayed by several dignitaries of the era,[8] thereby sanctioning his own literate prerogatives and, however impressionistically, affirming his superiority over those to whom he was in theory subordinate.[9] He too employed magic as a trope for his erudite powers, although to an extent that far exceeds anything attempted earlier in the century. The primary domain of these enchanting manipulations is Gerald's written landscape of Ireland, the *Topographia Hibernica,* which was first promulgated in 1188 and, within as few as three years, expanded to almost twice its length through additions to its many anecdotes describing metamorphoses of form and gender.[10] From the first redaction onward, these tales were intended to constitute a receptive challenge, issued by a belligerent *litteratus* and negotiable only to those displaying a *litteratura* comparable to his own.

It is with this topic of literate competence that I shall begin, since certain of Gerald's own literate misrepresentations must be clarified before his written magic can be engaged in its relevance to the late-twelfth-century reading public. My point of departure is the proem to the second redaction of the *Expugnatio Hibernica,* which probably appeared a little before 1210[11] and which shows Gerald providing a fulsome commentary upon how his own works had by this date been received:

> If a written record of events has to be explained by an interpreter, it has neither the same flavor nor the same hold on the memory as it would if conveyed to listeners in their own familiar idiom. I recommend, therefore, that this not insignificant book of mine be committed to someone skilled in language and letters and translated as quickly as possible into French. Perhaps the translator will receive some reward for his labor, since, after all, he will be able to make himself understood. So far, I have received nothing, barely understood by barely literate princes.[12] (Proem to the second redaction)

It seems, then, that the *Expugnatio* had met with bewildered incomprehension and had owed its intelligibility only to extemporized performative commentaries in the vernacular. It also seems that certain regal presences were numbered among the receptively disqualified. Although Gerald leaves these *principes* in discreet anonymity, he suggests the identity of one of them by quoting some observations once made by Walter Map:

> Master Gerald, you have written a great deal, and you still have a great deal to write. I, on the other hand, have spoken a great deal. You have devoted yourself to writing, and I to speaking. And, although your writing is far more deserving of praise and will last much longer than my words, I have received some re-

> ward for what I have said because I have made myself clear by using the language of the people. But your writing is in Latin and accessible to far fewer. And so, because genuinely literate and generous princes have for some time now been a dead breed, banished from the face of the earth, the reward you have managed to gain is far below the merits of your outstanding writing.[13] (Proem to the second redaction)

Gerald fails to specify when this conversation took place. But he precedes it with a reference to Walter's death,[14] making his quoted comments refer to an already anterior period and implying that the state of pitiful philistinism they evoke has been the norm for some time. Under these circumstances, John, the contemporary king of England, is obviously a signal example of the ignorance and parsimony that Gerald and, through him, Walter lament.

But, if this is so, then Gerald's lamentation can only appear somewhat impolitic, since it is to John himself that he dedicated this revised version of the *Expugnatio*. Perhaps Gerald wished to suggest that his Right Honored Sovereign was an exception, flattering his regal sensibilities as a result. But no exceptions are brooked by his uncompromising tone and unequivocal vocabulary: Gerald bemoans the incompetence of insufficiently lettered princes ("principes minus literati"), and he has Walter banish the truly literate monarch to some idealized point in the past ("princip[es] literat[i] nimirum et larg[i] obsolet[i] olim et ab orbe sublat[i] [sunt]"). We accordingly discover Gerald late in his career addressing his king in Latin only to explain that his king cannot understand what is being addressed to him. We discover, moreover, that the language of the literate has achieved such a level of unintelligibility to regal ears that it is now a medium through which regal monolingualism is facetiously mocked in words that parade their own obscurity—in order to understand Gerald's observations, John would have to call on a vernacular interpreter and by so doing would confirm their truth.[15]

This liberty could be explained away in biographical terms. By this date, Gerald had personally known John for over twenty years, and it could be argued that familiarity permitted him this unflattering license. Furthermore, since the second redaction of the *Expugnatio* appeared between John's widespread loss of Continental domains to Philip Augustus and the signing of the Magna Carta, it could also be suggested that

Gerald felt free to disparage because he knew the king was preoccupied by far graver concerns than a single cleric's estimation of his literate skills. However, if we consider the works Gerald produced before the turn of the century, it becomes clear that his view of the literacy displayed by John's two predecessors was at best nuanced, at worst highly pejorative. It becomes clear, in fine, that such cavalier liberties had always marked Gerald's relationship with the House of Anjou, and this erases the need to rationalize his facetious attitude toward John exclusively in terms of personal familiarity and contemporary political upheavals.

In evoking a golden age of letters supervised by the benevolent and the literate, Walter appears to be speaking of the reign of John's father, Henry II. This assumption is not only strongly supported by the many works that were written with Henry as their inscribed patron;[16] it is also endorsed by remarks that both Gerald and Walter make elsewhere. In his *De nugis curialium,* Walter extols Henry's literacy and asserts that he had a knowledge of all the languages from the Atlantic to the river Jordan,[17] and Gerald in the first redaction of the *Expugnatio* cites his monarch as something of an anachronism, the modern king who is literate and learned in letters.[18] Nevertheless, the statements of both authors must be treated with caution. To be sure, Walter's praise of Henry's polylingualism is extremely flattering. But it is also extremely absurd. Henry could certainly understand French, which was his native vernacular, and Occitan, which had a high degree of intelligibility to speakers of *oïl.* He probably also had a rough understanding of English.[19] But it is somewhat unlikely that he showed any skill whatsoever in any of the other languages spoken across the expansive territory that Walter mentions (which would include the contemporaneous manifestations of German, Rheto-Romance, Italian, Dalmatian, Serbo-Croat, Bulgarian, Greek, Turkish, Armenian, Arabic, and Hebrew). This of course leaves Latin, the international language of the western European *litteratus.* However, even in this regard, Gerald considerably complicates matters in the *Itinerarium Kambriae.* He addresses the dedicatory preface to Bishop Hugh of Lincoln and there lauds the enlightened and ideally munificent disposition of the ecclesiastic. The *Itinerarium* will receive the attention it merits because Hugh is exemplary for both *religio* and *litteratura*[20] and will therefore be an exception to what has apparently become something of a frustrating rule of ignorant indifference. Or, as Gerald would have it: "Undertaken for princes who were insufficiently lettered and extremely busy, my efforts have so far been vain and unrewarding" (first preface).[21] The deficient magnates in question prove to be Henry II and Richard the Lionheart, to whom the *Topographia* and the first redaction of the *Expugnatio* were respectively dedicated.[22]

There are obviously two ways of approaching these comments. Since they are accompanied by a hyperbolic celebration of a new patron, they could be no more than instances of manipulative antiphrasis, with Gerald exaggerating the ignorance of Henry and Richard the better to flatter Hugh. Alternatively, they could be genuine, with Gerald speaking from one of two positions. Perhaps his reference to regal philistinism is the result of a newly acquired insight: previously he labored under the false impression that the first two Angevins were sufficiently erudite to appreciate fine writing, but now, enlightened by bitter experience, he acknowledges the extent of his error. Or perhaps he is merely attesting a fact he knew all along. The second of these two possibilities certainly appears the less compelling, since it would mean that Gerald undertook the idiosyncratic course of dedicating works to patrons he knew to be incapable of understanding them. It would also mean that he still expected reward for his unintelligible endeavors. But it is a possibility nevertheless, and it cannot at this stage be rejected without further evidence.

This is provided by Gerald's treatise on political ethics, the *De principis instructione*. Announced as a treatise designed to admonish kings how to behave, the *De principis* is one of the most extraordinarily erudite works to be found in Insular letters of the period, and the prodigious bibliographical resources that Gerald brings to bear throughout are intended as an open exhibition of literate prerogative and learned didacticism. The preface of the first redaction makes the reasons for this pedagogical design patently clear:

> For my sins, I was summoned from my studies to attend the court, summoned by a king whose mind was predisposed to lying, whose principal pleasure consisted in deception and deferral, and who took delight in torturing the minds of both retainers and toadies by indefinitely neglecting to recognize their services.[23] (First preface)

The tone is bilious and resentful. But it does betray genuine frustration with a system of control that imposed obedient service through the vague and potentially empty promise of future reward and, as often as not, ended up benefiting sycophants who employed self-abasing flattery as a means to preferment. Gerald's response to what he considers ten wasted years of enforced curial labor is simply to document the corruption of privilege and its primary cause:

> I find myself compelled to write a treatise on the education of a prince primarily because it is specifically in monarchs and prelates that I see the type of behavior that is above all others worthy of condemnation, and this despite the reputed duty of such people to regulate and influence others by example and by the authority they wield. Which modern prince does not nonchalantly abuse his prerogatives, indulging each and every capricious thought, each and every license and luxury of the flesh, each and every atrocity of depraved tyranny? Which modern prince, confident that his every whim will be obeyed, does not proceed with the serene knowledge that the only limits to his power are his own wishes? Which modern prince respects the responsibilities imposed by the sacrament of royal unction, by the crown, by the scepter, and by the insignia of kingship? It is in response to questions such as these that in the writings of previous generations illiterate princes are likened to asses wearing crowns.[24] (Second preface)

Not only does Gerald emphasize that kingship is a semiological investiture of responsibility and not self-interest; he also unveils the cause of such petty abuses of power. In his view, the perversion of duty is a direct result of ignorance. Those who are entrusted with the task of leading by example but who dictate through intimidation, dishonesty, and greed are to all intents and purposes stupid asses who are thoroughly unworthy of the privileged positions they occupy.

Two points are to be noted. First, the image of the crowned ass is intended to refer to Henry II, the apparently tyrannical monarch who summoned Gerald to court and whose behavior prompted the composition of this particular work. Second, one of the antecedent authors Gerald mentions as authorities on such ignorant kings is unquestionably William of Malmesbury. Not only does William, we recall, depict Henry Plantagenet's grandfather, Henry I, employing the same unflattering image of the *asinus coronatus*.[25] He also wrote a particular tale of an ass that finds its striking analogue in book 2 of the *Topographia*, the written landscape of Ireland that Gerald dedicated to Henry II in 1188.

THE WEREWOLF OF ULSTER: *TOPOGRAPHIA HIBERNICA* 2.19

While traveling through Ulster, a priest and his servant pitched camp and were preparing to settle down for the night. Then, much to their consternation, they were accosted by a wolf. The animal proved to be highly unusual, unwittingly contriving to terrify the travelers all the more by availing itself of a human voice to reassure them of its good intentions. At length, the priest recovered from his shock and invited the creature to tell its story. The wolf obliged, and as part of his tale revealed that its female companion had suffered a similar metamorphosis and, now dying, required the ministrations of the church. Anxious to help, the priest followed the wolf to its den and there administered the Last Rites.

Gerald is well aware that this tale may seem preposterous, and to allay any doubts he calls on the authority of Augustine, who addresses the phenomenon of lycanthropy in book 18 of the *De civitate Dei*. After quoting some of the church patriarch's remarks verbatim, Gerald observes:

> After moving on to discuss various cases in which men have been turned into wolves, Augustine adds: "Even I, when in Italy, heard things of this kind about a particular region of that country where women innkeepers, imbued with the evil arts, were reputed often to give something in bits of cheese to travelers. By this means, they were turned into pack animals and would carry whatever was required until the job was finished, and they would then return to their normal selves. Their minds, however, would not be transformed into those of beasts, but would remain rational and human in the way Apuleius, in the books he called *The Golden Ass*, claimed happened to him when, after being poisoned, he became an ass yet retained his human mind."[26] (2.19)

This, of course, is precisely the passage from the *De civitate Dei* that William of Malmesbury transforms into the Anecdote of the Ass, and its presence may be interpreted in one of two ways. First, it may be pure accident that the two authors allude to this same paradigm. If so, then it would be unjustifiable to attribute to Gerald the same motives as his predecessor. Second, it may be calculated and functional. If so, Gerald would not only be following William's precedent, but would also, presumably, provide additional signals to make this clear.

Scrutiny of the tale fully substantiates the second of these hypotheses. It will be recalled that William's anecdote was originally a minimal autobiography first told by the idiot to one of his master's servants, and then passed up a literate hierarchy from servant to master to pope and finally to Peter Damian, the *litteraturae peritus* who proceeds to gloss the metamorphosis for the benefit of the pontiff. A similar process of narrative delegation marks Gerald's tale. The werewolf tells his story to the priest, who in turn apprises the local bishop, who convenes a synod to discuss the matter and invites Gerald to attend. Even though he cannot be present in person, Gerald expounds his judgment on the matter in writing and sways the Irish bishops to send the priest to Rome to inform the pope himself of this extraordinary event. Complementing these circumstantial analogies is the nature of the metamorphosis itself, which proves identical in both cases. William takes pains to stress that no physical transformation actually took place, systematically using a verbal causative to emphasize appearance over reality.[27] Gerald does likewise, but to more explicit effect. Having observed that the Irish couple were transformed into wolves as the result of a curse leveled against the people of Osraige, he provides a few comments on such powers of verbal damnation:

> I agree with Augustine that demons or evil men can neither create things nor truly change their essential nature. But they can alter outward appearances, with the permission of the True God who created them. By these means, they can make things seem to be what they are not. Observers, meanwhile, have their senses enthralled and stupefied by some wondrous illusion and do not see things as they are. Rather, they are miraculously led to see false and contrived shapes through the power of a deceptive or magical incantation.[28] (2.19)

If we apply these remarks to the tale they are intended to gloss, then the Irish couple remain a man and a woman in their essential nature ("natura"), but they exist beneath an enchanted and enchanting integument ("falsa et fictitia forma") originally imposed by words ("incantatio"). This collapse of the verbal and magical invites analogies between the art of the demon and the particular scribal talent that Gerald is displaying throughout. Of course, there are differences. While the shifter of shapes is a conjurer who employs words with magical effects, Gerald is merely an author with no ostensibly enchanting powers. Furthermore, whereas the first is explicitly malign, the second ostensibly is not.

However, if we turn to the "Introitus" of his next work, the *Expugnatio,* we discover Gerald making a number of stylistic remarks that considerably complicate these distinctions. Imagining the nostrils of the fastidious reader contracting in nauseated contempt at the transparent and plain Latinity he will use for this, his second work on Ireland, Gerald enjoins the potential critic to show sensitivity toward the public he is now attempting to accommodate: "Let him first and foremost bear in mind that this material has been prepared for laymen and princes who have an inferior control of letters, and that it requires this plain and easy style simply to be accessible to their understanding."[29] A straightforward register, he goes on to declare, is a pressing necessity for any writer who wishes to reach the modestly literate *(parum litterati),* and this because anything more elaborate would militate against intelligibility itself, the obvious goal of writing:

> What could be more thoughtless than to use unfamiliar ambiguities of diction and intricate convolutions of words and, as a result, conceal and veil the sense of what we set out to make clear? Or to use what we should make comprehensible as a pretext for appearing the unique and scholarly masters of an arcane knowledge? This would have two effects: we would be unintelligible; and we would leave others convinced they see and understand when in reality they remain blind and uncomprehending.[30]

Gerald, then, claims to write as the proponent of clarity and sense. But he does so with a sublime disingenuousness, since these charges of obscurantism inevitably apply to the style he employed for his earlier

Topographia, which he proceeds in the next paragraph to praise as an outstanding example of scholastic elegance ("scholastici stili elegantiae omnium unica laus est et uniformis"). Thus, by the very logic of his paraded decision to change registers for his latest work in an effort to reach a wider but less accomplished readership, Gerald implicitly recognizes that the *Topographia* was indeed an exercise in rhetorical convolution, that it did remain unintelligible to the majority in all of the ways he apparently seeks to criticize.

All of this is deliberate, however, and it works to illuminate the particular *scientia* that Gerald is flaunting by antiphrasis. In acknowledging that a particular style may leave others believing they see and understand when in fact they are blind and uncomprehending ("aliis videndo non videntibus, et intelligendo non intelligentibus"), Gerald is providing a variation on the power of the demon ("sensibus hominum mira illusione capitis et sopitis, quatinus res non videant sicut se habent, sed ad falsas quasdam et fictitias videndum formas, vi phantasmatis seu magicae incantationis, mirabiliter abstrahantur") and establishing an intertextual paradigm through which such powers are to be interpreted. For these stylistic remarks lexically recall Christ's parable of the sower and his seed. This is recorded in similar terms in the Gospels of Matthew, Mark, and Luke, and its grammatical import requires little rehearsal here: some of the seeds are eaten by birds, some germinate among rocks and soon perish, some are starved of sustenance by thorns, and some take root in fertile ground and fruitfully multiply. More pertinent to present concerns is the ulterior significance Christ lends his words:

> And when he was alone, those who were about him with the twelve asked him concerning the parables. And he said to them: "To you has been given the secret of the kingdom of God, but for those outside everything is in parables; so that they may indeed see but not perceive, and may indeed hear but not understand."[31]

For those who have not received the love of God, the world is a parabolic texture of displaced senses—obscure, opaque, and awaiting the epiphany. By transposing Christ's reference to this hermeneutic disqualification into his comments on his own style ("ut videntes videant et non videant, et audientes audiant et non intelligant" > "aliis tanquam videndo non videntibus, et intelligendo non intelligentibus"), Gerald promotes the *Topographia* itself as a parable of displacement, an expansive territory of writing that has been contrived to yield its subterranean meanings only to those who share the *singularis scientia* displayed by the author.

The arcane knowledge at issue is to be culled from Alain de Lille's treatise on stylistic and sexual vices, the *De planctu Naturae,* which Gerald uses as the paradigm for both the rhetorical excess he shows in his own writing and, interreflexively, the sexual excess he describes. The result is an Irish topography that is populated with fictions of sexual and generic extravagance, which include bearded ladies (2.20), ox-men (2.21), and women who show perverse lusts for beasts (2.23–24), all of them imposed by the "unnatural" writing lamented in Alain's treatise and all of them unfaithful to their natural Irish referents.[32] The talking wolf is the first of these unnatural hybrids; and the gloss on demonic misrepresentation that draws its story to a close is to be assessed as an open signal to the accomplished reader that appearances will be resolutely deceptive in the immediately following chapters. The ensuing exercise in deliberate misrepresentation serves two political functions: it offers a distorted image of the Irish to members of the Anglo-Norman public, most notably their leader, Henry Plantagenet, the inscribed recipient of the work and, according to Gerald's retrospective testimony, an *asinus coronatus;* and it sanctions the prior territorial rights that supposedly fell to the author's Cambro-Norman brethren, who had first intervened in Irish affairs in the late 1160s only later to be dispossessed by administrators representing the Angevin *imperium.*[33]

In engaging the significance of these enchanting manipulations, however, we must show a degree of caution. Most notably, we cannot assume that Gerald intends to suggest Henry will read the tale of the werewolf and the depictions of venereal depravity it inaugurates, take them to be true, and, in his credulity, reveal himself to be a dumb ass incapable of distinguishing fact from fiction. This would be a ridiculous assumption. By the appearance of the *Topographia* in 1188, Henry himself had spent almost a year in Ireland, and during this time he would have had ample opportunity to know that it was not populated by talking wolves, bearded ladies, women in love with goats, and kings copulating with mares. In short, Henry's personal experience would eloquently convince him that Gerald's spectacular revelations were fantasy. But this in turn prompts us to question the logic of Gerald's every move. Since

Henry was perfectly positioned to know that book 2 of the *Topographia* was a tissue of misrepresentations, it is curious indeed that Gerald should have so eccentrically offered it up to him as unimpeachably veracious fact. In order to negotiate such an apparently illogical maneuver, let us consider the circumstances in which Gerald claims the *Topographia* was received by its first generation of readers.

Critical Asses

In the "Introitus" to the *Expugnatio,* Gerald explains that the general public had shown little liking for his earlier treatise, apparently alienated by such prodigious monstrosities as the talking wolf and the bearded lady.[34] Yet there is something decidedly suspect in this, since these critical grievances prove strangely congruous with a series of warnings that Gerald himself makes as a prelude to book 2 of the *Topographia* itself:

> Of course, I know with absolute certainty that I am about to write some things that will strike the reader as either utterly impossible or even ridiculous. But may the gods bear witness to my amiable disposition and attest that I did not place anything in this little book that I with the utmost diligence did not determine to be true, either by submitting it to personal observation or to the testimony of the most upright and veracious men living in the appropriate regions.[35] (2, incipit)

Despite their apparent antagonism, therefore, Gerald and his critics ultimately show a remarkable interdependence. The author proclaims that he will document phenomena that will seem preposterous; and, with admirable fidelity, his readers go on to relegate the marvels in question to the lunatic fringes. But these readers in turn owe the unique record of their criticism to the obliging intervention of the author they criticize, who proceeds to reproduce their grievances in writing and as a consequence attests their obliging obedience to his own written prescriptions. Further, Gerald does more than simply acknowledge that what he describes may seem unreasonably outlandish. As he progresses, he adopts a hortative tone to wish upon himself all of the opprobrium he starts out ostensibly trying to parry:

> In sum, let this book of mine be torn to shreds by the present and praised by posterity. Let it be censured now but read in the future. Let it be condemned only eventually to be appreciated. Let it be met with disapproval only the better in due course to be approved.[36] (2, incipit)

Because they are so extraordinarily faithful to this appeal for vituperation, the otherwise unattested and demonstrably predictable voices of censure can only be assessed as written figments in their own right; and, evaluated accordingly, they prove to be as integral to the message of the *Topographia* as the talking wolf they reputedly reject as absurd delirium. Most important, they furnish a pretext for the introduction of an ass.

By aiming their outrage at the marvels documented in book 2, these critics provoke Gerald to an immediate rejoinder: "Let anyone who so vehemently rejects such things as these read about the ass who talks to Balaam in the Book of Numbers and roundly criticizes the prophet" (*Expugnatio,* "Introitus in recitationem").[37] To all appearances, the ass is cited as an authoritative paradigm for empirically witnessed prodigies, and Gerald therefore seems to be doing no more than informing his readers that such marvels as he describes do in reality exist, with the implication that they should hardly be rejected as absurd figments because they are hardly in any way exceptional. But these appearances are unfounded, since Gerald ends his defense with the following paraphrase: "Let the reader be more sensibly advised and attentively bear in mind that, as Jerome says in his apothegm, there are many incredible things that are found in writing that are not plausible but are nonetheless true" (*Expugnatio,* "Introitus in recitationem").[38] Writing, then, is the arena of the veraciously incredible; but the experiential world itself is passed over in discreet silence. The implications of this can hardly be exaggerated. Obviously, Gerald is admitting that the prodigies he documents are written phenomena corresponding with no empirical reality, and he is therefore avowing the fabulous nature of his Irish landscape. But he is also—and in context precociously—affirming a belief in fiction: to be sure, he has wildly misrepresented, but his misrepresentations in and of themselves carry a truth of their own, and this despite their clear infidelity to the Irish referents they purportedly convey. Furthermore, in mentioning the talking ass, Gerald purposefully selects a written example of a beast that accedes to voice in circumstances that reflect the very reason for its selection. The ass he mentions, after all, speaks only to criticize and consequently follows the precedent of the critical reader. Under these circumstances, Gerald is certainly constructing an ass of his own from any who would reject his work, and, by the same token, he is advancing himself as a voice of prescience, since the critical ass speaks quite precisely to upbraid a prophet ("legat in libro Numeri asinam Balee locutam, et prophetam increpantem").

Before proceeding, let us pause to take stock of four points. First, the voice of the critical reader is a purely literary construct created as a foil against which Gerald articulates crucial mechanisms of his writing. Second, this voice is asinine, and it therefore must be assessed in its relevance to the anecdote of the werewolf, throughout which William of Malmesbury's Anecdote of the Ass functions as a clear hypotext. Third, this talking ass bespeaks a critical blindness to the truth of fiction. Fourth, this fictive truth is bound up with the vatic tenor of the work. Remaining to be determined, therefore, are the following points: (1) the relationship between the voice of the critical reader and Henry Plantagenet, the Crowned Ass to whom the *Topographia* is dedicated; (2) the aspect of the text that sets in motion the asinine metamorphosis announced by Gerald's reference to the talking ass; and (3) the prophetic tenor of the work as a whole.

PREDICTIONS OF CHANGE

As already stated, the werewolf of Ulster is the first of the "hermaphroditic" monstrosities that Gerald creates in his purposeful adhesion to the depraved poetics of the *De planctu*. It also predicts that a specific group of foreigners will perhaps be afflicted by a similar transformation:

> As long as this alien race fulfills the mandates of the Lord and walks the path he has defined, it will be safe and uncontaminated. But, because their inclinations tend to pleasures and their nature to vice, they will perhaps by contagion descend to our customs, in which case they too will inevitably attract divine retribution.[39] (2.19)

The werewolf itself has by this stage already glossed the meaning of these customs, alluding in the immediately preceding period to the *vitiorum enormitates* and the *generatio prava* of the Irish. Since these depravities are entirely the product of the vicious writing Gerald deploys, then the werewolf is predicting that certain aliens will fall victim to the same stylistic transformation and become hermaphroditic prodigies displaying, like itself, both human and bestial attributes. The alien race in question is formed of the Anglo-Norman emissaries of Henry II, who, by this date, were in effective control of Ireland. As such, they are also representatives of an imperialistic hegemony that Gerald himself virulently resisted for avowedly personal reasons. When Henry arrived in Ireland in 1171, it was to curtail the expansionist ambitions of a number of his subjects and to impose his own overlordship of the land. Those he thwarted were by majority marcher barons from South Wales, led by Gerald's uncle, Robert FitzStephen, and including in their ranks his brother, Robert of Barry. This created conditions in which Gerald was prejudiced against Henry's Irish policy,[40] and it explains his motives both for occluding Ireland beneath the veils of the rhetoric and for exacting an idiosyncratic vengeance of his own. Like the werewolf itself, the prediction of change is entirely Gerald's invention, and it must be viewed as a prophecy to be fulfilled through the agency of writing. Since the natural phenomena of Ireland become hermaphroditic monstrosities in fidelity to the depraved poetics through which they are conveyed, the forms of signification altering the signified in accordance with its own perceived vices, then, by the logic of Gerald's prophecy, the Anglo-Normans will now by contagion suffer this same fate, metamorphosed into beast-men by venereal rhetoric itself. Yet, in textual terms, no such transformation is ever realized, since at no point does Gerald interrupt his description of Irish prodigies to state that the new Anglo-Norman masters of the island have recently begun to participate in this same hermaphroditic deviance. Their alteration must therefore be achieved by other means.

It is in this context that Gerald's hypothesized critical ass gains its full significance. Evidently, the reader denoted by this unflattering metaphor has failed to grasp adequately the serious import of hermaphroditism itself: he or she is cited as inveighing against the prodigious depravities documented, and he or she is duly identified as an ass for doing so.[41] A transformation, therefore, has been achieved, and it has been realized through the agency of the venereal rhetoric employed. But in this case, the change of man into beast is effected entirely in the realm of reception: while the metamorphosis of the Irish is a semiotic phenomenon, that of the reader is provoked by the very inability to understand the semiotic nature of the referential metamorphosis in question. In fine, those who reject book 2 of the *Topographia* as arrant nonsense reveal themselves to be asses who are simply too ignorant in a specific field of poetics to perceive the significance of form itself. Fully in accord with Gerald's transposition of the parable of the sower and his seed, they do indeed believe that they see and understand. But they in reality remain blind and uncomprehending quite precisely because they believe they see all too clearly, understand all too well, that such phenomena as talking wolves and ladies with bristly backs are absurdities.

Now of course this charge is partially justified, since the prodigies at issue are unquestionably delirious. But it is also flawed, arising as it does from an inability to see and understand that the very absurdity of the phenomena documented is the result of a stylistic choice that carries a significance of its own. And herein lies the sense of Gerald's demonic illusions and the identity of those he wishes to transform. It will be remembered that Gerald states that demons or evil men can neither create things nor change their essential nature. But they are able, with God's permission ("Deo permittente"), to create false appearances ("falsae et fictitiae formas"). This last term perfectly glosses Gerald's own venereal misrepresentations, and the divine authority by which they are obliquely shown to be endorsed must be read as an amplification of the werewolf's prophecy, which precedes by only a couple of hundred words and which itself includes a reference to God's retribution ("divina vindicta"). Consequently, the excursus on demonic fabrication is in fact an announcement of the divinely sanctioned vengeance that Gerald himself will exact against the invasive aliens to which he, via the werewolf, alludes. This being so, the readers he proposes to turn into asses are revealed to be exclusively Anglo-Norman, representatives of the same imperialist hegemony that is now in control of Ireland and that takes Henry Plantagenet as its crowned head. At hand, therefore, is an act of transformation that is directed at an entire ethnic polity, but that singles out Henry, as both synecdoche and ruler, as its primary victim.

By this I do not of course mean that Gerald intended that none of his contemporaries should appreciate the work in all its complexity. Indeed, the very nature of the facetious stratagem he orchestrates implies the existence of a select group who would understand what he was doing and why he was doing it. In his autobiographical "Ad capitulum Herefordense de libris a se scriptis," Gerald reveals the identity of three such readers. These are Baldwin, archbishop of Canterbury; Robert, canon of Salisbury; and Walter Map, archdeacon of Oxford, who were all accomplished in *litteratura*,[42] who were all sufficiently impressed with the *Topographia* to submit it to attentive personal reading,[43] and who emphatically did not greet the unbounded depravities it discloses with the scorn Gerald claims they elsewhere received. Or, to switch to Gerald's own terms, Baldwin, John, and Walter were competent enough in the *singularis scientia* of Neoplatonism to read with approval and to avoid becoming asses who spoke to upbraid the prophet.

Gerald, then, writes fiction, flaunts the fact he does so, and invents an inscribed group of readers who reject his work as implausible nonsense and thereby reveal themselves to be oafs who have quite simply missed the point. He has therefore spectacularly adjusted the terms of the metamorphosis dramatized in William of Malmesbury's Anecdote of the Ass. While William hypothesizes the transformation of the credulous reader, Gerald chooses to victimize exclusively the *in*credulous. It is in the light of this fact that we must assess his apparently illogical decision to dedicate the text to Henry. Of course the king had sufficient personal experience of Ireland to know that Gerald's purported representations were signally unrepresentative, and he could therefore never have read the *Topographia* and assumed it to be a valid documentation of fact. But this is the very opposite of what Gerald intends. By proclaiming he will write the impossible and the ridiculous, by announcing that his work will not be understood by the present, by inventing detractors to heap scorn on his endeavors, Gerald is purposefully inviting Henry himself to dismiss the work as the demented ravings of an addled mind, purposefully constructing circumstances in which Henry will show his asinine disposition, and purposefully creating a climate of reception in which a message of political gravity will pass unnoticed to all save those capable of applying the requisite *litteratura*.

But Gerald also does more. As I shall now demonstrate, he not only manipulates style and textual antecedents to conceal truth beneath the depravity of unnatural rhetoric. He also attests a higher mode of communication that is analogous to verbal semiotics but superior in its primeval ties with nature itself. In this case also, issues of comprehension and exclusion are raised, but in a context that far transcends literacy.

POISONED PLENTY

Gerald prepares his revelation of this alternative code in the latter chapters of book 1, in which he depicts the East in extremely pejorative terms the better to laud the simplicity of the West. The Orient abounds in plenty, he concedes, but, in his view, the enjoyment of such abundance is deleterious in the extreme: "The East indeed has silken fabric obtained from worms and dyed in many colors. It has various precious metals; it has brilliant gems and fragrant spices. But what are these worth, accompanied as they are by the loss of life and health?" ("Habet quidem, vermiculorum beneficio, lanuginem sericam vario colore fucatam. Habet pretiosa metallorum genera: habet gemmas perlucidas, et species odoriferas. Sed quid haec cum vitae sanitatisque dispendio?" [1.34]). This last comment leads to an extraordinary set of variations on the theme of physical decay. Gerald first lists the dangers posed by the environmental phenomena he believes characteristic of the East, including the fetid water (1.35); the ground, too hot to be walked on barefoot (1.35); the air, by turns torrid and frigid (1.35); and marble furnishings, by implication excessively cold to anyone who has been exposed to the Eastern sun (1.35).[44] Then, as he progresses, he begins to advance opulence itself as a direct cause of death: oriental food, he states, must under no circumstances be eaten in quantity (1.35); similarly, oriental wine must not be imbibed undiluted (1.35). These admonitions in turn lead to a metonymy through which Gerald claims that poison is ubiquitous in the East, not only administered in food and drink, but also insinuated into clothing and furniture (1.36).[45] Finally, this metonymy is resolved into metaphor, as Gerald, taking leave of Eastern civilization, identifies opulence itself as a poisonous category ("Habeat igitur oriens *venenosas,* habeat *toxicatas opulentias suas*" [1.37; emphasis added]).

So all-infecting is this venom and so ungodly the effects of sumptuous plenty that the entire East emerges as the modern domain of the Serpent, the original harbinger of pride and artifice. In the Orient, men and women enjoy the fruits of the illusory divinity promised at the primordial moment of temptation: they are rich, they bask in opulence, and they apply their minds to technology; but, surrounded by these literally poisoned luxuries, they compromise with the gifts of the Devil and ultimately trade life against an illusory empowerment. As a consequence,

Eastern civilization bears the heaviest burden of lapsarian supplementarity, its rich fabrics and perfumes acting only as a gorgeous veil that covers disease-ridden bodies and the stench of putrefaction. It is a culture of deceit predicated on the disjuncture of inside and outside and dominated by the Beast whose descendants inhabit the oriental countryside:

> Asps and vipers infest the place. So too do dragons, and the basilisk that is to be dreaded simply for its glance and to be feared simply for its appearance. The seps also abounds, a tiny snake that makes up for its modest size with its deadly effects, consuming with its venom not just the flesh, but also the bones.[46] (1.36)

It is with these slithering infestations that Gerald brings his disquisition on *toxicatae opulentiae* full circle: the gorgeous wrappings developed to deceive the eye "with the help of worms" ("vermiculorum beneficio" [1.34]) are resolved into the gnawing venom of the wormlike seps. The East may be closer to the site of the original Eden, but it bears the imprint of the Fall far more deeply.

At first glance, none of this would seem to be in any way offensive to Gerald's prospective regal patron, Henry II. After all, the domain of poisoned plenty is the Eastern Mediterranean, and it therefore bears no connection with the Western isle now ruled by the House of Anjou:

> Let the East have its venomous and poisoned opulence. We make up for all those oriental riches just by breathing the air of our temperate climate, benefiting as we do from a golden mean that enables us to make use of what is appropriate and to satisfy our natural needs. What a gift from God we enjoy, a gift that has no equal anywhere else in the world! What an inestimable sign of Grace, bestowed on mortals from on high and not yet sufficiently recognized![47] (1.37)

Proffered as a gift of God, these attributes of health, simplicity, and security are signs of a primordial communion with the Divine that circumvents the most deleterious effects of the Fall, and they are enjoyed by all the inhabitants of the Western hemisphere, including the Anglo-Normans.

Closer perusal of the global excursus nevertheless reveals that Gerald is in fact making subtle distinctions within the West itself, to the final detriment of the populace that has recently brought Ireland under its dominion. The Anglo-Normans may not have attained Byzantine extravagances of plenty and poison, but, compared with the Irish, they are nonetheless resolutely Eastern in a number of respects:

> This [Irish] people does not nurture its newborn infants in the usual careful way. Other than for food, which is given to them by their harsh parents to prevent them from completely perishing, Irish children are left to nature for practically all their needs. They are not looked after in cradles and they are not swaddled in cloths. Their soft limbs are neither tended by frequent bathing nor shaped by artificial means. There are no wet nurses using hot water to raise the nostrils, flatten the face, or elongate the legs. Without recourse to artifice of any type and solely as she sees fit, Nature alone composes and disposes the limbs she has created. As though to demonstrate what she is capable of if left to herself, she does not cease to mold and shape, finally to produce these men and to reveal them in their adult strength, with admirably tall bodies and fine, healthily complexioned faces.[48] (3.10)

That Gerald makes this contrast for the benefit of Anglo-Norman readers presupposes the centrality of physical deformation to their own cultural practices. This being so, the foreign invaders are isolated from the salubriousness that is here so forcefully celebrated: whereas the Irish are perfect exemplars of natural growth, the Anglo-Normans attempt to improve the work of nature itself, restructuring the bodies of their infants to produce upturned nostrils, flattened faces, and longer legs. They accordingly surpass even the cult of the exterior practiced in the East, seemingly finding gorgeous integuments insufficient and moving beyond textile coverings to reinflect the body to a culturally determined and thereby artificial set of aesthetic paradigms.

Here, too, external fashioning takes as its corollary a corresponding internal decay, in this instance suggested by a second implicit contrast. Not only are the Irish of perfect physical proportions; they also have no need for medicinal supplements to the health: "The island has hardly any need for the work of doctors. You find few sick people, except for those who are on the point of dying. They scarcely ever pass through a median stage separating their continuity of health from the finality of death" (1.33).[49] Again, this statement of Irish alterity is comprehensible only through the contrastive presupposition of an Anglo-Norman standard, and, revealing as much about the invader as the invaded, it amplifies the resonances of an earlier passage in which Gerald discusses the relative salubrity of western air in terms that anticipate and determine the reading of his later global excursus:

> As is true of France in relation to Britain, Britain itself far excels Ireland in the serenity and clarity of its air. The farther you move to the east, the more you will find a pure and bright air illuminating the heavens, but, the milder you find the climate, the more you will find it deleterious and inclement.[50] (1.3)

This westward progression from France to Britain and thence to Ireland maps out the sequential stages of territorial expansion undertaken by the Normans and their Angevin heirs over the previous one hundred and twenty years, and it serves to align the soteriological paradigm with contemporary movements of Insular politics. For the country from which the Anglo-Normans have launched their invasion is inferior to Ireland in one other respect, although this distinction would perhaps at first sight appear frivolous in the extreme. Britain, it transpires, is not only afflicted by a relatively insalubrious climate and is not simply home to such unnatural evils as doctors and physically deforming wet nurses. It also accommodates a remarkably Eastern population of venomous beasts. Certainly, the invasive foreigners are not obliged to encounter such monstrosities as the basilisk, the seps, the asp, and the dragon slithering about their native countryside; but they must nonetheless compromise with the viper, the frog, and the toad. If judged by modern criteria, this hardly seems cause for concern: frogs and toads just hop around, and, except perhaps in a visual sense, they are not particularly noxious; vipers, for their part, are indeed deadly, but they are not particularly common. However, Gerald views frogs, toads, and snakes as related species, and he considers all three to be poisonous.

This preoccupation with venomous creatures is relevant to Angevin expansionism simply because, as Gerald informs us, unwonted creatures of this variety have begun to appear on Irish shores. For instance, Gerald has heard that a group of toads arrived aboard a merchant ship, subsequently to be let loose onto Irish soil (1.29), and he records the discovery of a portentous alien near Waterford in the chapter bearing the self-explanatory title "About the Frog Recently Found in Ireland" (1.32; "De rana in Hibernia nuper inventa"). It is while elaborating on the amazement and despond this particular specimen of exotic fauna provoked that Gerald begins to unveil the seriousness of intent that subtends his ostensibly excessive concern over snakes, toads, and frogs:

> The English were astonished as they inspected it, and the Irish much more so. Domnall, King of Osraige, a man versed in the lore of his people and loyal to them, was by chance present at the time. He emphatically shook his head and, with great sorrow in his heart, suddenly exclaimed, "This creature has brought to Ireland the worst possible news." Taking it as a true portent, he explained that this signaled the coming of the English and the imminent defeat and subjugation of his people.[51] (1.32)

From collateral information that Gerald provides in the *Expugnatio,* this fabulous discovery can be attributed to the late 1170s.[52] It is therefore made between Henry's visit to Ireland in 1171 and the more definitive imposition of Angevin power that was to be occasioned by the arrival of Prince John in 1185. This explains the apparent illogicality of Englishmen being already present to witness the prodigy and to hear Domnall announce the arrival of the English and the imminent defeat of his compatriots. It also helps illuminate the significance of certain details that Gerald weaves into his description of Anglo-Norman cultural practices. It will be recalled that, unlike the Irish, the readers for whom Gerald apparently writes are accustomed to inflecting the limbs of their infants. What has so far been left unspecified is the logical result of the inflections he describes, which, left to themselves, appear ludicrously extravagant and by any aesthetic standards highly unflattering. Since the Anglo-Normans raise the nostrils ("nares erigunt"), flatten the faces ("faciem deprimunt"), and elongate the legs ("tibias extendunt") of their children, then they curiously—but in context significantly—go out of their way to fashion the physiognomy to reproduce the somewhat uncomely aspect of the frog or the toad. Subtly, Gerald establishes a physiological analogy between the wondrous frog of Waterford and the invasive foreigners whose arrival and victory it is read to portend.

In scripting Domnall's predictions, however, Gerald is in fact doing no more than contemplating a future that can never be realized. Contrary to the view expressed by the King of Osraige, the Anglo-Normans will never be masters of Ireland, since, as Gerald has already by this stage observed,

> Ireland is fortunate in being home only to creatures that cause no harm. In fact, it lacks poisonous ones entirely. It has no serpents or snakes. It has no toads or frogs. It has no tortoises or scorpions. And it has no dragons. It does not strike me as surprising that this land is naturally deficient in creatures of this type, along with harmful fish, birds, and animals. But what is truly cause for astonishment is the fact that it cannot tolerate anything poisonous that is brought in from the outside, and never has.[53] (1.28; 1.29)

By implication, like anything else that is by nature poisonous, the ranamorphic foreigners will inevitably be repelled by the natural salubrity of Ireland. At no point does Gerald actually state as much. But he does accumulate anecdotes dramatizing the agonies suffered by imported toads, frogs, and snakes. For example, the toads he mentions arriving as stowaways may well have come into contact with Irish soil. But they emphatically did not find the experience a happy one, since "with many people looking on in amazement, they immediately rolled over on their backs, split down the middle, and died" (1.29).[54] Gerald then proceeds to provide ample information to show that these astonishing death throes were in reality quite predictable: it was discovered long ago, he observes, that snakes captured abroad drop dead halfway across the Irish Sea (1.29), that Irish dust can be used to devastating effect when sprinkled over foreign parts populous in noxious beasts (1.30), and that the hide of Irish animals, cut into pieces and quaffed with water, proves an efficacious antidote to snake and toad bites (1.31).[55] Hardly prone to credulity, he lends these observations the support of firsthand experience, having seen with his own eyes an imported toad repeatedly fall backward as though struck about the head while desperately attempting to clamber over a thong of Irish leather (I.31).[56] Thus convinced, Gerald confidently cites the Venerable Bede, who personally witnessed how Irish codex leaves soaked in water assuage the swelling caused by snake venom (I.31).[57]

The Irish antipathy toward poison is significant in the paradigmatic relationship it bears to the imposition of all signs of Angevin power. The Anglo-Normans are the harbingers of Eastern corruption, and their cultural practices, their bodily sickness, their reliance on doctors, and their isolation from the pristine harmony of nature are all symptoms of their radical alienation to the land they now presume to possess. Because all of these phenomena are associated with poison in the global disquisition, then they all display the same incompatibility with Ireland that Gerald deftly suggests through his conceit of cultural ranamorphia. For this same reason, they will also inevitably be erased by the salubriousness that naturally repels such toxins. Or, to use Gerald's expression, they will evaporate in the land that "cannot tolerate anything poisonous that is brought in from the outside, and never has."

Since this is so, Gerald would appear to be making an extraordinarily unfortunate avowal, recognizing that he and his fellow Cambro-Normans are themselves, to all intents and purposes, carriers of a venomous culture who have arrived on the salubrious shores of Ireland in woeful disregard of the inevitable fate that awaits them. After all, even though they take Wales as their homeland, they come from the same poisoned terrain of Britain as their Anglo-Norman neighbors. Fortunately, however, Gerald and his regional compatriots do not have to fear the dire consequences of incompatibility. Since the venom of the East becomes progressively weaker toward the western perimeter of the known world,[58] then, by Gerald's own logic, the part of Britain least tainted by Eastern corruption is its most western coordinate, which happens to be Wales. Furthermore, one particular area of its seaboard, Manorbier in Pembroke, proves to be especially significant:

> It is an area with plentiful provisions of wheat, sea fish, and imported wine. And, most remarkable of all, it is tempered by air that owes its salubriousness to the proximity of Ireland. It should be no cause for astonishment—in fact, it is entirely excusable—that I, the author, heap such lavish praise on this re-

> gion, since this is where I was born and where my family originated.[59] (*Itinerarium Kambriae,* 1.12)

By a happy coincidence, Irish salubrity is just extensive enough in radius to embrace the westernmost regions of Wales, including the birthplace of Gerald and those members of his extended Cambro-Norman family who were the first to intervene in Irish affairs and to whom—Gerald maintains—Ireland rightfully belongs. Therefore, although they are natives of British soil that is elsewhere infected by Eastern toxins, Gerald and his relatives enjoy the distinction of being born to the salutary atmosphere that radiates from Ireland, and they share with the Irish the incomparable boon of a divinely bestowed and ever immanent purity that is lacking in the venomous Anglo-Normans to the East.

Now, it must at this point be stressed that, in vaunting the purity of Ireland, Gerald is in no way moved by a desire to glorify its inhabitants in their political practices. Although he states that the Irish are superb exemplars of physical growth, he elsewhere reveals them to be no more than colonists to the land[60] and, by implication, adventitious recipients of the natural gifts it bestows. In their internecine conflicts and their moral laxities,[61] they have proven themselves unworthy beneficiaries of such purity, and for this reason they are rightfully to be supplanted by a new Cambro-Norman *imperium,* itself born to the natural fullness of Ireland but obedient to the stipulations of law and religion. Gerald is therefore preoccupied by the land and its natural properties and not by its inhabitants, and his global anthropology in part serves to define Ireland as the privileged space that is to be transferred from the dominion of its slothful and disorganized tenants to the enlightened governance of new but eminently qualified masters.

MUSIC AND THE PERPETUATION OF MEMORY

Gerald discloses the full implications of this political transfer in book 3 when negotiating the apparently insoluble problems of logic that beset the history of Irish settlement. The difficulty in question is first intimated in the detailed account Gerald provides to document the arrival and disappearance of the earliest group of colonists:

> According to the most ancient histories of the Irish, Caesara, Noah's granddaughter, hearing that the Flood would come in the near future, set sail with a number of followers to find refuge in the most remote of the so far uninhabited islands of the West. She hoped that a place where no sin had yet been committed would be spared the vengeance of the Flood. The entire fleet she assembled was shipwrecked, except for one boat carrying three men and fifty women, which, a year before the Flood, did by chance reach the Irish coast. But, even though Caesara attempted to avoid death through this shrewd—and, for a woman, laudable—ploy, she was finally unable to escape the end that awaited practically everyone everywhere. The part of the coast on which her ship first came ashore is called the Coast of the Ships, and the place in which this Caesara was buried is today still called Caesara's Grave.[62] (3.1)

The urgency of self-perpetuation is forcefully determined: both the history of inhabited Ireland and the history of Irish historiography begin at precisely the moment at which all human survival was threatened by divine stricture. Since no one lives on to speak to future visitors, then Caesara and her followers must have left a written record of their deeds that was discovered by later colonists and committed to canonical Irish history:

> With practically everything destroyed by the Flood, one seems justified in doubting how any memory of things such as the circumstances of Caesara's arrival could have been preserved afterward. But whoever first wrote these histories would have seen for themselves. I present myself as an expounder of histories, and not as their critic. It could perhaps be that memory of these people was safeguarded by being written onto some material or other, such as stone or brick, in the same way we read of music, invented before the Flood, being preserved.[63] (3.1)

Predicating writing on seeing ("qui historias istas primo scripserunt, ipsi viderint"), Gerald suggests that the earliest version of the story was written by eyewitnesses and therefore by the first settlers themselves, since they were the only people present at the time to have witnessed anything. Graphemic historiography would seem to be at issue, the verb *scribere* taking *historias* as its object. But, provisionally promising as it may be, this hypothesis is rapidly compromised. According to the chronology of biblical history that Gerald is following, the earliest written graphies were Syrian/Chaldean, introduced by Abraham, and Hebrew, first manifested in the Torah received by Moses on Mount Sinai.[64] Since both of these scripts first appeared several generations after the Flood, then any text written by the primordial inhabitants of Ireland predates the initiatives of Abraham and Moses, and the biblically inspired history of writing is contradicted.

Aside from the difficulties inherent in this revision of accepted sacred truth, there is also a more localized problem. Even if taken to be chronologically prior to Syrian and Hebrew, the writing employed by Caesara and her retinue would by necessity signify the ante-Babelic tongue. Perhaps, therefore, the Gaelic of the later settlers retained sufficient affinities with this primeval language to enable its speakers to unravel the written memory left by their predecessors. This, however, proves not to be the case, Gerald elsewhere furnishing a history of precisely the Gaelic language in terms that deny any such purity:

> According to some, the Irish [Hibernians] derived their name from the aforementioned Heberus. But it is more likely that, following another tradition, they got it from the Ebro, a river in Spain, where they came from originally. They are also called the Gaels and the Scots. The ancient histories have it that a certain Gaidelus, a descendant of Phenius, was an extremely accomplished scholar of various languages during the period of linguistic fragmentation caused by the Tower of Babel. It was in recognition of these accomplishments that King Pharaoh had him marry his daughter, Scotia. Since, as it is said, the Irish trace their origins back to this couple, then it is after their primordial ancestors, Gaidelus and Scotia, that they are called Gaels and Scots. This Gaidelus is reputed to have invented the Irish language, which is called Gaelic, and which was almost exclusively formed from elements of all the others.[65] (3.7)

"Quasi ex omnibus linguis collecta," Gaelic was synthetically invented by a master linguist in the wake of Babel, and at its origin it brought together aspects of all other languages. But this does not imply a pre-Babelic plenitude. Gaelic is merely a primeval Esperanto. Under such circumstances, its speakers, like anyone else, would be unable to understand and be understood across linguistic frontiers. In fact, rather than affirming anything particularly positive about Gaelic, these remarks rather serve to stress fragmentation. All tongues, Gaelic included, are the consequences of Babel, and, with language irrevocably fallen, originary unity can only be mimed in philological gestures, such as that of Gaidelus, that finally signal nothing more than the absence they attempt to palliate. Gerald demonstrates this problem in the contradictory etymologies he offers. Brought into direct conflict, the two derivations for *Hiberniensis* work to efface the recuperability of linguistic origin. The word has become convention, adrift from any perceptible relationship with an originary referent, anchored one way "secundum quosdam," another way "secundum alios." It has fragmented, furthermore, into derivations from incompatible sources. If the Irish are in truth the offspring of Gaidelus and Scotia, then they did not originate in Spain, have no relationship with either Heberus or Hiberus, and therefore cannot be *Hibernienses*. Language is now so removed from unity that the same signified can accommodate mutually effacing signifiers competing with one another across the boundary of different linguistic codes: Latin *(Hibernienses)* and Gaelic *(Gaideli, Scoti)* cancel one another as derivative traces and in the origins they are said to convey. Etymology is here a symptom and a performance of *linguarum confusio* itself.

Consequently, the later Gaelic speakers of Ireland could not have understood the type of pre-Babelic language that would have been used by Caesara and her followers. Rather, they would have been faced by an unreadable nexus of petroglyphs, perhaps analogically recognizable as a text, but thoroughly arcane in significance. Even a conjectured philological intervention by Gaidelus, that master linguist and future ruler, would not foreclose this problem: he became skilled in a variety of languages only after Babel and, since he controlled the discrete fragments of a lost unity, but not that unity in itself, he too would have found the antediluvian text indecipherable. Therefore, even if we accept that the first visitors preceded Abraham and Moses themselves in consigning language to a written semiotics, then we must also concede that what they wrote became a tangled knot of scribblings to future generations. Only one possible explanation accordingly remains: that Caesara and her followers preserved an account of their arrival through a graphy that signifies something other than language and is comprehensible to initiates across the boundaries of ethnic and regional difference.

The sole script that fulfills this criterion has already been mentioned. This is musical notation, cited by Gerald in his conjecture over the means the first settlers employed to perpetuate memory. It must be conceded that Gerald himself does not state that this nonlinguistic graphy was used to this end by Caesara and her retinue, still less explain how such an extraordinary feat would be realized. He does, however, return to musical notation at a later stage, yet again to stress its primeval origin:

> As can be read in Genesis, the inventor of musical consonance was Jubal, a descendant of Cain, who lived before the Flood. To him applies the title "The father of those who play the cithern and the organ." Because he heard Adam's prophecy of the two judgments, he contrived to prevent the art he had invented from perishing. He therefore wrote it in its entirety onto two columns, one of marble and one of brick. One of these would never crumble in the Flood, and the other would never disintegrate in a fire.[66] (3.13)

Antediluvian and invented generations before the earliest graphemes signifying spoken language, musical notation is the *only* historically pertinent system of writing that could have been employed by the first settlers, who must accordingly have first consigned their narrative not to words, but to rhythm and harmony, and then in turn consigned this music to written symbols that could be read by later colonists and transformed back into sound and significance.

To have any validity, of course, the above reasoning entails two presuppositions: first, that musical notation remained unchanged throughout the centuries separating the first and most recent groups of settlers; second, that music itself must potentially be endowed with the capacity to convey subtleties of narrative meaning that are usually associated with spoken linguistic codes.

Gerald provides no information directly to elucidate the first of these points. Yet, throughout his diffident comments on the perpetuation of memory, he takes the future intelligibility of the primordial narrative as an unimpugnable fact, directing his skepticism only toward the likelihood of any human artifact surviving the cataclysmic effects of the Flood. Like musical notation itself, the story of the earliest settlers perhaps owed its survival to the brick or stone upon which it was written. But it incontrovertibly did survive, and the written script used for its preservation must have remained comprehensible, simply because the account of Caesara and her followers was subsequently incorporated into the canonical history of Ireland, and this despite the differences in spoken idiom displayed by the later settlers and their earliest antecedents.

While Gerald leaves the intelligibility of the earliest script as an unstated but unassailable inference, he devotes extended space to affirming that music can indeed convey complexities of significance and to identifying the contemporary inhabitants of Ireland as preeminently qualified to understand and perform the narrative-in-sound this would imply. For, as the heirs to the discipline elaborated over time by Jubal, David, Pythagoras, the brothers Zetus and Amphion, and Orpheus's mentor, Linus of Thebes (3.13–14), the Irish are the supreme musicians of the modern world:

> It is only in their skill with musical instruments that I find this people shows commendable talents. In this they have reached an incomparable level of mastery, far surpassing any other population that I have encountered. The modulations they produce from these instruments is not slow and morose, as is the Welsh practice to which I am accustomed. Their sound is rapid and energetic, while also pleasant and joyful. It is amazing that they can sustain musical proportion while moving their fingers at such astonishing speed.[67] (3.11; "On this People's Incomparable Skill with Musical Instruments")

Later in this same chapter, Gerald states that this consummate mastery has been achieved on the only two instruments that are played in Ireland, the harp and the drum.[68] This is an extraordinary assertion, since it denies any indigenous use of the flute and, more remarkably, the bagpipe. It is, nonetheless, eloquent. Gerald in effect banishes from Irish culture any instrument that requires the agency of the breath to produce sounds. Under these conditions, the harp supersedes all devices that could be viewed as an extension or enhancement of the human voice, and, as Gerald observes, it assumes unto itself the communicative attributes of signifying utterance: "the harp cries out through the hands and without a voice it speaks" (3.12).[69]

The relationship of displacing analogy that Gerald creates between the harp and the voice leads to a series of ulterior contrasts and comparisons between the sounds the two produce. Like human discourse, the music the Irish perform with such unrivaled dexterity can signify on different levels:

> It transpires that it can either bring ineffable delight and speak internally to those who are capable of understanding its finer points and of perceptively discerning its arcane properties, or it can afflict rather than delight the ears of those who lack insight and who therefore see without seeing and hear without understanding.[70] (3.11)

Under usual circumstances, these remarks could be assessed as no more than an anodyne flourish, a recognition that some people appreciate music while others do not. In the present context, however, circumstances are highly unusual: book 3 of the *Topographia* is inaugurated by an epistemological enigma that can only be solved by positing music as a system of complex signification; and, as this same book progresses, the modern Irish are advanced as the most accomplished practitioners of this art and therefore as those who would have the requisite proficiency to read, perform, and perpetuate the antediluvian and ante-Babelic narrative left by the primordial settlers. Finally, and most pertinently of all, by commenting on music in terms of hermeneutic disqualification ("quasi videndo non vident[es] et audiendo non intelligent[es]"), Gerald here makes his earliest reference to Christ's parable of the sower and his seed and thereby anticipates the discussion of arcane stylistics he provides in the "Introitus" to the *Expugnatio*. Because it is related to a parable of interpretation that is itself later related to the difficulties of perceiving the ulterior meanings of written language, music is here drawn into a topical field elsewhere associated with verbal semiotics, and its capacity to signification is forcefully underscored: just as Christ employed the parable as the medium through which to convey an ulterior narrative, the Irish employ music to recount the past in all its narrative subtlety, still practicing an antediluvian art that has been lost to all other cultures.

Although Gerald at no point explains how this prodigious control of a supralinguistic code operates, he clearly intends to relate its implications to the global excursus that brings book 1 to closure. As already observed, he makes an explicit analogy between the preservation of music and the commemorative act of the first settlers: not only were both performed before the Flood; both were perhaps achieved through the medium of stone or brick ("Sed forte in aliqua materia inscripta, lapidea scilicet vel lateritia, sicut de arte musica legitur ante diluvium inventa, istorum memoria fuerat reservata"). Through these remarks, Gerald suggests that memory was inscribed onto the mineral substance of the Irish landscape, which in turn came to function as a topographical parchment guaranteeing continuity of witness. Inserted into a treatise that in its very name purports to constitute the topography of Ireland and that in its style and themes constantly plays on the dichotomy of nature and artifice, the hypothesis of writing inscribed into a medium derived from the natural terrain is of extraordinary resonance. Certainly, the graphy employed for the primeval narrative is the product of human ingenuity and as conventional as any of the notations developed to signify spoken language. But, as Gerald himself emphatically affirms elsewhere in book 3, music, the sound it signifies, is the very song of nature itself: it is the compositional principle of planetary bodies, including the earth (3.12), and it is the guiding force for the revolution of the heavens (3.12); to master its properties is to participate in a universal accord, to gain the power to move beasts, birds, and snakes (3.12), and to control the founding principles for all human intellection (3.12).[71] Accordingly, Ireland itself is fully consonant with the music that is retained in its landscape and activated by its inhabitants as an indigenous history: both are located at the furthest remove from the poisoned artifice that is cultivated in the East, and both are the unadulterated manifestations of a mankind's harmony with nature and, through it, God. Assessed in terms of Gerald's soteriological commentary, Irish music is the ultimate system of signification still available to mankind, as much a gift that devolves from the Almighty as the physical perfection and robust health enjoyed by the modern Irish: it partakes of nature and not of artifice, it transcends the accidentals of national language, and it functions as the bond through which men and women may communicate both with one another and with God's created world.

The modern Irish, nevertheless, bear only a tenuous relationship with this transcendence. As already noted in passing, Gerald considers music to be the only Irish achievement that is in any way remarkable, and he elsewhere emphatically decries the woeful degeneracy that the Gaelic population displays in every other field of cultural endeavor.[72] Indeed, since superiority in music is the sole signal attribute of a people that is otherwise presented as rigorously inferior, it would appear to be far more the product of the environment itself than the consequence of any innate and distinctive talent. This inference is strongly supported by the extent to which music and the Irish landscape complement one another as categories that have circumvented the most deleterious effects of human artifice: Ireland, the *locus amoenus* of a natural purity that has been bestowed as a gift of God, is also the most apposite domain in which mankind would be able to commune harmoniously with and through the song of Creation. In searching for a haven that had so far been left unsullied by sin, Caesara and her followers coincidentally found a land that was preeminently suited to preserving not men and women, but the natural art that had been developed before the sins of mortal hubris were punished, first by the Flood and subsequently through Babel. And all subsequent colonists have benefited from this concord with nature, partaking of a discipline that resonates from the very topography of Ireland.

Gerald implies that control of this harmony is integral to the political suzerainty that he considers to fall rightfully to his own regional brethren. In gaining dominion over Ireland, the Cambro-Normans will also appropriate and perpetuate the cultural legacy that has been mastered by the Gaelic populace and that by implication will remain inaccessible to the emissaries of the Angevin *imperium*. In the *Topographia* itself, Gerald arrogates for Wales precisely the incipient skills that this transfer of power would presuppose:

> It is nevertheless to be noted that Scotland and Wales are striving to imitate Ireland in music and are beginning to rival her in the discipline. The first has been moved to this by exchange and affinity, and the second by cultural diffusion.[73] (3.11)

Despite the glorious implications of its musical acumen, Scotland is peripheral to Gerald's political interests. Wales, on the other hand, quite emphatically is not: it is the homeland of Gerald and his extended family and therefore of those to whom dominion over Ireland should rightfully pass, and it is the object of Gerald's two later treatises, the *Itinerarium Kambriae* and the *Descriptio Kambriae*. Throughout these two works Gerald is as concerned with the fate of Ireland as that of Wales,[74] and, in the later of the two, the *Descriptio,* he attests the fulfillment of the cultural appropriation anticipated in book 3 of the *Topographia*. In a chapter devoted to the incisive yet subtle intelligence of the Welsh (1.12; "De ingenii acumine et subtilitate"), Gerald extols supreme musicianship in terms that are explicitly lifted from his work on Ireland ("Hibernica Topographia nostra declarat in haec verba") yet are now applied to the inhabitants of his Brythonic homeland. Contrary to the slow and morose practice he earlier attributed to the Welsh, he now ascribes to them a manual dexterity identical to that of the Irish,[75] and, in commenting on the effects of this revised Welsh proficiency, he observes:

> It transpires that [their music] can either bring ineffable delight and speak internally to those who are capable of understanding its finer points and of perceptively discerning its arcane properties, or it can afflict rather than delight the ears of those who lack insight and who therefore see without seeing and hear without understanding.[76] (1.12)

Not only, therefore, has the technical skill previously unique to the Irish now been mastered by the Welsh. So too has the ability to employ music as the medium through which to impart nuances of meaning that remain inaccessible to those who are not initiates to the recondite art of harmonic communication.

By the logic of the political concerns that inform all of Gerald's ethnographic writing, this newly acquired skill applies not only to the Brythonic Welsh, but also to the Cambro-Normans, who trace one side of their genealogy back to the ancient British and who are elsewhere attributed with the outstanding virtues of both the Celtic and Gallic populations.[77] As a result, the epistemological supremacy adumbrated in the *Topographia* is finally achieved: now masters of the highest art of the fallen world, the Cambro-Normans are elevated to an immediacy of communion with all of Creation, and their Anglo-Norman rivals will remain forever deficient, isolated from the pristine harmonies of nature by their poisoned artifice and excluded from the history that resonates in accord with the Irish landscape. They may well believe themselves heirs to the past, present, and future of Ireland. But, in their relationship with the historical truth of the antipodean domain they claim to possess, they in reality "see without seeing and hear without understanding."

Conclusion

By way of closure I shall first reiterate a point I made in the introduction: my analyses are not intended to define how particular sectors of the twelfth-century public responded to given works; they are rather commentaries on literary devices through which authors envisaged how and by whom their writing could be understood. All of the admonitions I consider are directed first and foremost toward those William of Malmesbury calls *litteraturae periti,* and they are designed to exhort such sophisticated readers to clarify obscurities for the benefit of those who cannot do so for themselves. By its very nature this delegated duty of explication leaves open the possibility of negligence and misunderstanding. Those who are "skilled in letters" may fail to heed these authorial directives and may therefore omit to aid the disadvantaged in interpreting points of rhetorical and intertextual difficulty. In such cases, and this despite the author's internal pleas, the *parum litterati* may indeed interpret with a rigid fidelity to the letter or with a blindness to the function of internally cited hypotexts.

This tension between monitory intent and the possible realities of reception is already inherent in William's Anecdote of the Ass. Although not absolutely essential to understanding that the young man is an ass only because he is an idiot, the *Pseudo-Clementine Recognitions* and the *De civitate Dei* greatly help, since they alert the recipient of the tale to the dominant diegetic and performative theme of transformation. Therefore, to explicate a hermeneutic effect that William does not directly countenance, the real reader or listener may become a different type of figurative ass simply for failing to note these subtle signals for interpretative caution. Since these signals are provided by the real author rather than his delegated narrator, William could potentially be charged with precisely the mockery he attempts to abjure. To object to this last point by saying that William endeavors to distance himself from the monk merely compounds the problem, since he uses the *Recognitions* to do so and thereby reveals his ploy only to those familiar with a relatively abstruse text. Consequently, by introducing the theme of asinine stupidity, even as a receptive effect that should never be imposed by the accomplished, William implicitly provides an unflattering characterization of those who would not understand his own narrative shifts, his own transformation of hearsay into fact, his own fiction of oral performance.

Similar problems of hermeneutic perspective are found in Geoffrey's drama of credulous reception. In this instance the hypotextual presence of the *Pseudo-Clementine Recognitions*—here complemented by Plautus's *Amphitryon*—is absolutely crucial to the function of the metamorphosis at issue, and a relatively advanced *litteratura* is therefore required to explicate the figurative significance of the episode. Yet Geoffrey nevertheless effects a definitive shift away from his predecessor's concerns. Showing none of William's monitory abhorrence, he is the first author of the Insular tradition to embrace magic as the sign of his own power and to manifest no hesitation in promulgating potentially beguiling fictions and figuratively creating asses as a result.

Assessed in this regard, it is Geoffrey and not William who went on to exert a decisive influence on subsequent Latin and vernacular writing: by refabricating the obscure British past, he precipitated the confusion between *historia* and *fabula* that was to preoccupy authors for the rest of the century, and he thereby helped create the context in which, above all others, the interpretative acumen of the contemporary public was to be challenged. These initiatives unquestionably inspire the writing of Gerald, that self-styled *daemon* of Latin letters. Less obviously, but no less definitively, Geoffrey's precedent also informs Benoît's *Troie*. Diegetically fabricated by three authorial personae who excel in architecture, divination, language, and necromancy, *Troie* is a product of the same power of magical creativity that is configured by Merlin's—and, through him, Geoffrey's—prophetic insight into a future-now-past ("ingenium in futuris dicendis") and talents in structural contrivance ("ingenium in operationibus machinandis"). To be sure, Benoît follows William rather than Geoffrey in his efforts to write against elitism and to define the responsibilities that accompany erudition. But, these efforts notwithstanding, the possibility of misprision I mentioned earlier still obtains. As the thirteenth-century scribes responsible for the alternative prologue to *Troie* imply, Benoît's internal gestures to the literate are so densely allusive that they do indeed surpass the ken of "cil qui n'entendent la letre." *Troie* is enlightening only if explicated as such by the literate mediator, and it accordingly remains a plea that could fail to convey its message. In its emphasis on potentially inscrutable performance, it warns the unlettered that their own receptive dispositions are being dramatized. Yet it invites them only to question and leaves to *litterati* the right to choose between clarification and invisibility, between the power to enlighten and the prerogative to occlude.

Benoît diverges from both William and Geoffrey, however, in his sustained concern with the material rewards that should fall to the literate. In this he was unquestionably the product of his times. While William rejected lucre as a debasing *cupiditas* and Geoffrey wrote in an effort to end a period of incipient austerity that plausibly explains the silence he cast over his own financial ambitions,[1] Benoît was active during the reign of Henry II, in which the fiscal mechanisms of the realm and its Continental territories were restored and refined and *litterati* were led in ever increasing numbers to pursue careers in secular administration. His shrewd assessments of the value he has accrued through his commercial enterprise and his efforts to leave the resultant written gold indelibly imprinted with his own signature—and, perhaps, his personal seal of authorial propriety—bespeak the mercantile ethos of the new Troy that was vaunted by FitzStephen in his *Vita Sancti Thomae* and by FitzNigel in his meditations on the cabalistic sacraments obeyed and perpetuated at the Exchequer.

Indulging in precisely the mockery that William denounced some sixty years earlier, Gerald is to be differentiated from all the other authors I consider: book 2 of his *Topographia* is offered to a regal ass with the expectation that it will be not be accepted as a faithful account of Irish society, and it is designed primarily to victimize the incredulous rather than the credulous recipient. Written to be rejected in its pretense to fact, it nonetheless serves to articulate political concerns, divorcing the Anglo-Normans from the truth of Ireland, clarifying the global dichotomy established in book 1, and preparing the musical communion celebrated in book 3. When Gerald finally comes to advance music as a medium for significance that transcends the contingencies of the letter, he is not, strictly speaking, glorifying a form of literacy. He does, however, manipulate the tensions of restriction and prerogative that his Insular predecessors had associated with the literate and the graphemic art they control, thereby pushing the figurative necromancy elaborated earlier in the century to its final conclusion: not only is sense hidden through the intricacies of arcane discourse; even those who are privy to Gerald's verbal manipulations are led to understand that another, superior vehicle for meaning exists beyond language, and that they, the privileged exegetes of the written word, are as isolated from its harmonies as the unlettered themselves. The exclusive circle of initiates that results is ethnic in its constitution and territorial in its claims: the great musical communion with the natural world is reserved for the Cambro-Normans, who arrogate suzerainty over Ireland, and it is aggressively denied to the rival Anglo-Norman polity. Thus Gerald appropriates and alters the power of hermeneutic privilege adumbrated by William of Malmesbury, whose Anecdote of the Ass lies at the foundation of the rhetorical maneuvers enacted throughout book 2 of the *Topographia*. What William foresaw as the elitism of a particular social sphere Gerald transforms into a device of political affirmation, delineating a new form of communicative privilege that serves to differentiate and glorify one populace over all others.

INSULAR MAGIC, FRENCH ROMANCE: THE EXAMPLE OF CHRÉTIEN'S *CLIGÉS*

That the conflation of magic and literacy should so pervade the writing of twelfth-century England inevitably raises the question of contemporary France. Throughout the period under consideration, but most particularly in the latter half of the century, the political boundaries between the two kingdoms were extremely fluid. As either duke or count of a number of Continental domains, the king of England was vassal—in name at least—to the king of France.[2] Yet, this relationship notwithstanding, Henry II made considerable encroachments into French domains, gaining effective dominion over such territories as Armagnac and the Auvergne, to which his claims of suzerainty were strongly disputed.[3] Just as the frontiers of the lands owing varied degrees of fealty to the two monarchs frequently shifted, so too did the political allegiances of the barony, in both France and England itself. Henry overcame the most forceful threat to his power in 1174 by defeating a coalition formed of not only Continental magnates such as Louis of France and Philip of Flanders, but also a number of his own subjects, including his sons (among them Henry the Younger, heir to the throne, and Richard, later the Lionheart) and the earls of Chester and Leicester.[4] With political frontiers and loyalties in constant flux, the cultural distinctions between the nobles of the two realms remained negligible. While Insular authors strove, as early as the 1120s, to encourage the new overlords of England to identify with the land they now ruled,[5] English nobles continued to speak French throughout the period (even though many displayed a sound command of English and some were bilingual),[6] and, following their Norman ancestors, they observed aristocratic social rituals that were predominantly Continental in origin.[7] An analogous commonality of culture applied to *litterati:* Wace, for example, states that he received a rudimentary instruction in letters in Normandy before spending several years in France to perfect his skills and further his studies,[8] and Gerald was by his own account a student in Paris, and he returned there later in his career briefly to teach.[9] Similarly, the literate were mobile in their secular employment or religious duties: although perhaps born and raised in a territory owing direct fealty to the French Crown,[10] Benoît was associated with the English court and participated, however ambiguously, in writing the vernacular history of the Angevin line.[11] Conversely, John of Salisbury eventually left his native England to become archbishop of the French see of Chartres.[12]

Even without corroborating evidence, this constant political and cultural interaction would make it highly unlikely that magic was used as a trope for literacy only by authors who were either Insular in origin or active under the patronage of Insular magnates. Indeed, the testimony of contemporary texts eloquently speaks otherwise. For instance, Alain de Lille, who was staunchly French in his political allegiances, conflates magic and literacy as part of an admonition against the snares of poetic reference and does so as a warning that is of general application and not directed solely at literate French contemporaries. This one example is sufficient in itself to demonstrate that the figurative resonance of magic was a cultural phenomenon that existed on both sides of the Channel, and no doubt for similar reasons: in both kingdoms, the literate were restricted in number, and in both their talents could have attracted the same distrust or fear.[13]

Nevertheless, while writers throughout the francophone domains demonstrably used magic as a trope for literate power, the specific contexts in which they did so varied according to precise economic and social conditions that did not obtain elsewhere. Among the authors I consider, only William of Malmesbury is an analogue to Alain. His appeals to the responsibilities of the literate entail no ethnic inflection, and they could conceivably have been read by contemporaries to apply to *litterati* not only in England, but also in France and, indeed, anywhere in western Europe. Benoît, Gerald, and most particularly Geoffrey, on the other hand, confront problems that were contextually unique to the British Isles. Although he endeavors to deconstruct his vernacular fiction for an unlettered audience that could have included both English and French magnates, Benoît responds to the quintessentially Insular concern with the Trojan prehistory of Britain.[14] In a similar manner, while Gerald's mockery of Henry could plausibly have appealed to the subjects of Philip Augustus, his celebration of the natural plenitude of Ireland exclusively serves the political cause of his Cambro-Norman brethren, and it is ultimately as disobliging to the French as to their Anglo-Norman rivals. Finally, though obviously writing in a language comprehensible to the *litterati* of France, Geoffrey employs magic as a trope for his refabrication of a past that is politically and geographically alien to the French and offered as a proleptic type for the *imperium* the contemporary English should ideally rule.[15]

A comprehensive study of French permutations on the interrelated themes of magic and literacy would necessarily have to engage works produced on the Continent that were of both general implication (such as Alain's *De planctu*) and specific Continental resonance. Such a project is still to be undertaken. Nevertheless, as a series of final remarks, I would like to consider one Continental author's romance response to the *Historia regum,* since it represents something of a definitive shift in the significance that was accorded to the Arthurian past and, through it, a "magical" literacy developed in and for England. The author in question is Chrétien de Troyes and the romance is *Cligés.*

Chrétien was associated with the courts of Champagne and Flanders between the late 1160s and early 1190s,[16] and he was the first author of the Arthurian tradition to redirect specifically Insular conflations of magic and literacy to the service of contemporary France. Because he was active in Continental domains that owed no fealty to England, he is, technically speaking, beyond the purview of this study. Nevertheless, the canonical position he occupies in the discipline of medieval studies invites analysis—however brief—of the role he played in modifying Arthurian initiatives.

Chrétien's most significant predecessor in transposing the British past into the vernacular was Wace, author of the *Roman de Brut,* the most widely known and successful of several Old French translations of the *Historia regum.*[17] Wace's work constitutes a challenge to the contemporary public that involves, to a particularly acute degree, the receptive difficulties William of Newburgh went on to broach in stating, "Anyone who is not apprised of the truth of historical events incautiously admits the vanity of fables" ("qui rerum gestarum veritatem non didicit, fabularum vanitatem indiscrete admittit" [*Historia rerum Anglicarum,* proem]). Following the "First Variant" of the *Historia regum,* which he for the most part uses as his paradigm, Wace avoids any mention of Geoffrey[18] and never openly nuances the historicity of his material. Rather, he presents himself as a vernacular medium through which the anterior written truth of an unnamed source will be communicated,[19] at one point intervening contrastively to sanction his own enterprise:

> En cele grant pais ke jo di,
> Ne sai si vus l'avez oï,
> Furent les merveilles pruvees
> E les aventures truvees
> Ki d'Artur sunt tant recuntees
> Ke a fable sunt aturnees.
> Ne tut mençunge, ne tut veir,
> Tut folie ne tut saveir.
> Tant unt li cunteür cunté
> E li fableür tant flablé
> Pur lur cuntes enbeleter,
> Que tut unt fait fable sembler.
> (9787–98)

[I do not know if you have already heard this, but it was during the long period of peace I have just mentioned that the marvels were experienced and the adventures undergone that are being so often told about Arthur that they are in the process of becoming fable. They are not entirely false, nor entirely true; neither complete folly, nor complete sense. Storytellers have told so many stories and confabulators woven so many fables in an effort to give their tales a finer form that they have made everything appear to be fable.]

According to Wace, the circulating oral tales of Arthurian marvel and adventure are unreliable testimonies to history because they have been repeatedly retold and literally embellished to the point of distorting the events they were originally intended to commemorate.[20] By antiphrasis, these remarks serve to validate the historical accuracy of *Brut* itself, which Wace in his prologue identifies as a translation of a book and therefore as a vernacular version of a truth that has achieved the authoritative fixity he considers compromised by the oral tradition. Now it must be stressed that this contrast is strategic. Wace knew his material to be apocryphal, and he permits himself the freedom of disguising the fact for political reasons: he maintains the illusion of truth in order to create through Arthur a truthfully historical antecedent and monarchic type upon which subtly to celebrate the advent of Henry II.[21] But, however historically justified the cause, the effect vitiates the faithful transcription of history itself: by never openly avowing his material to be largely fiction, Wace permits the confusion of *fabula* and *historia* that William of Newburgh, almost fifty years later, imputed to any reader who would admire the *Historia regum*.

To what extent this confusion perplexed the contemporary public can only remain the object of speculation. Nevertheless, by the mid-1170s two vernacular authors had dismantled the historical truth of Arthurian Britain, thereby working to dispel whatever problems of perspective *Brut* may have left unresolved. The first is Wace himself, who in his complementary history of Normandy, the *Roman de Rou*, anecdotally identifies his prior Brythonic undertaking as precisely the *folie* he considers storytellers to promote to the detriment of historical fact.[22] The second is Chrétien.

In his five romances, Chrétien demonstrates that he had read Wace's two dynastic works with great attention to detail,[23] and in the prologue to *Cligés* he makes clear intertextual reference to *Brut*. Anticipating the journey undertaken by the eponymous hero's father to the famed Arthurian court, Chrétien observes:

Tant fu preuz et de fier corage,
Que por pris et por los conquerre
Ala de Grece an Angleterre,
Qui lors estoit Bretaingne dite.[24]
(14–17)

[He was of such valor, of such daring courage, that, to gain renown and recognition, he went from Greece to England, which at that time was called Britain.]

This allusion to toponymic change echoes one of the dominant motifs of *Brut,* in which Wace repeatedly uses place-names to reflect the discontinuity of Insular *imperium* and several times over comments on the repercussions of the shift from "Bretaingne" to "Angleterre." The following, for example, outlines the definitive moment of Anglo-Saxon expansionism and the occlusion of the Britain that Arthur had ruled only a few generations before:

Pur un lignage dunt cil furent
Ki la terre primes reçurent
Se firent Engleis apeler
Pur lur orine remenbrer,
E Englelande unt apelee
La terre ki lur ert dunee.
Tant dit Engleterre en français
Cum dit Englelande en engleis;
Terre a Engleis, ço dit li nuns,
Ço en est l'espositiuns.
Des que Brutus de Troie vint
Tut tens Bretaine sun nun tint
Jesqu'al terme que jo vus di
Que par Gurmund sun nun perdi.[25]
(13643–56)

[In memory of the lineage from which they sprang, those who first took over the land called themselves "English," thus commemorating their origin. They also called the land given over to them "England." "Angleterre" means the same in French as "England" in English, that is, duly expounded, "Land of the English." Britain retained its name from the time Brutus arrived from Troy to the moment I have mentioned when this name was lost through the actions of Gormond.]

By returning to the preoccupations of his predecessor, Chrétien relates his own material to Wace's vernacular initiative. However, while he may devote his romance to the "Bretaingne" that preceded the arrival of the Anglo-Saxons and is glorified in Insular letters, he does so merely to emphasize the superiority of another realm:

Par les livres que nos avons
Les feiz des anciiens savons
Et del siecle qui fu jadis.
Ce nos ont nostre livre apris,
Que Grece ot de chevalerie
Le premier los et de clergie.
Puis vint chevalerie a Rome
Et de la clergie la some,
Qui or est an France venue.
Deus doint qu'ele i soit retenue,
Et que li leus li abelisse
Tant que ja meis de France n'isse
L'enors qui s'i est arestee.
(27–39)

[Through the books we have, we know of the deeds of ancient peoples and gain a familiarity with the world as it once was. And our books have taught us the following: that it was in Greece that chivalry and learning first gained renown, and that it was then Rome that inherited chivalry and the sum of learning, which has now come to France. May God grant that it be retained there, that this land so nurture it that the honor now gracing France may never leave.]

Not only does Chrétien celebrate the intellectual preeminence of late-twelfth-century France as a historical reality and by zeugma vaunt its chivalric glories;[26] he also undermines the historical truth of the very period of the past that he, the preeminent cleric of the cultured French domains, will use in the text proper to demonstrate the cultural supremacy he glorifies. Significantly, he omits from his narrative of military dominance any allusion to the third of the powers said to have dominated the West, the British kingdom ruled by Arthur, which Wace, following Geoffrey, describes expanding its *imperium* to cover France and all of northern Europe and depicts overcoming precisely the sovereign might of Rome to which Chrétien alludes.[27] This omission becomes all the more eloquent in the light of the sources Chrétien adduces to authenticate his brief history of empire and culture: it is because of books that "we know of the deeds of ancient peoples and gain a familiarity with the world as it once was" ("les feiz des anciiens savons / et del siecle qui fu jadis" [28–29]), and it is because of them ("ce nos ont nostre livre apris" [30]) that we know the two great hegemonies of the past to have been Greece and Rome. For the same reason, logic decrees that it is also because of these books that we know nothing of the Arthurian Britain that supposedly achieved a comparable position of political dominance. This has the effect of denying historiographic integrity to the Insular tradition of British glory that Wace disseminated into the French vernacular: in translating the *Historia regum* to create *Brut,* Wace certainly wrote a book of his own; but what his book has to say finds no place in the European history Chrétien has read elsewhere and himself reproduces in his prologue.

Once disclosed, the fiction of the Arthurian past necessitates a reappraisal of the book from which Chrétien has already claimed to have derived the story he himself will tell:

> Ceste estoire trovons escrite,
> Que conter vos vuel et retreire,
> An un des livres de l'aumeire
> Mon Seignor saint Pere a Biauveiz.
> De la fu li contes estreiz,
> Don cest romanz fist Crestiiens.
> Li livres est mout anciiens,
> Qui tesmoingne l'estoire a voire;
> Por ce feit ele miauz a croire.
>
> (18–26)

[The account of the past that I wish to relate to you can be found in writing in one of the books of the library of my Lord Saint Peter's in Beauvais. It is from there that the tale from which Chrétien made this romance was extracted. The book is extremely ancient and bears truthful witness to the narrative, and, for this reason, the narrative itself gains an even greater claim to our credence.]

This written paradigm is introduced immediately before the comments on military and cultural history, and, by juxtaposition, its witness to the past is utterly compromised. Since books tell us of Greece and Rome and omit the magnificent conquests of Arthurian Britain, then the story of Cligés is itself denied any relationship with the bibliographic tradition Chrétien goes on to paraphrase. For this tale is itself set in the reign of Arthur, and it depicts an era of magnificence during which the fame of Britain had extended even as far as Greece, inspiring Cligés's father to travel to the Insular shores "to gain renown and recognition" ("por pris et por los conquerre" [15]). Thus Chrétien subverts the very truth he claims to respect: by proscribing the military suzerainty of Arthurian Britain from his prefatory remarks on the military history of the West, he undermines the historical pretensions not only of the Insular tradition, but also of his own romance.

The alleged source of the tale consequently lends itself to two possible interpretations. First, the book may indeed have existed, but, if this is so, then Chrétien takes pains to isolate the information it conveys from the consensus of historical writing by disclosing the extent to which it is absent from other sources. Second, the book may be a fiction in its own right, as historically inauthentic as the tale Chrétien himself will tell. In either case, Chrétien has availed himself of precisely the topos of *inventio* that inaugurated the Insular tradition he goes on to channel to a new cause. His *livres mout anciiens* far too closely recalls Geoffrey's paradigm to be the result of mere coincidence. Not only is it introduced as the source of a tale formed of the British material Geoffrey conjured into being; it is also the precise vernacular equivalent of the *liber vetustissimus* that Geoffrey claims to have translated to produce the *Historia regum* itself.[28] Since Wace never so much as mentions an extremely ancient book, it is legitimate to state that Chrétien shows he has gained his knowledge of the apocryphal British past not only from *Brut*, but also from its Latin source. He demonstrates this knowledge, moreover, further to dismantle the work of his Insular antecedents. Using the bibliographic topos to confer authority on his material ("[li livres] tesmoingne l'estoire a voire" [25]), yet proceeding to subvert the authoritative truth he thereby creates and as a result undermining either the historical accuracy or indeed the existence of the book he professes to translate, Chrétien inevitably evokes and subverts the *liber vetustissimus* itself, that alleged origin and source of the Insular tradition he arrogates for romance.

It is further to dispel any illusion over the historicity of his work that, as Michelle Freeman has demonstrated, Chrétien presents his own artifice as a form of creative necromancy.[29] Complementing Freeman's analysis of the content of the philter through which Chrétien configures the romance, I would like to comment briefly on its function and effects. It is administered to the emperor Alis on his first night of marriage to the German princess Fenice, who, having already fallen in love with Cligés and found her affection reciprocated, refuses to give herself to another man; and it is designed to make its unwitting recipient believe he is having carnal relations with his new wife when in fact he is never even touching her body (lines 3196–372). In fine, the draught and the text it metonymically evokes are contrivances through which fiction is made to appear fact. There is, however, a distinction in the way they are received: while Alis is diegetically deceived and accepts the fiction, the listener or reader of the romance has already by this stage heard or read the prologue, in which the author takes pains to distinguish between the historiographic canon and his own enterprise and in which he implicitly differentiates between history and fable.

Chrétien's recourse to this internal drama of alluring fiction also finds its analogue in the *Historia regum*. Once again:

> Uther took the drugs given by Merlin and assumed Gorlois's appearance. So the king spent that night with Ingerna and enjoyed the pleasures he had longed for. He had fooled her with the false appearance he had assumed. He had also fooled her with lying words he ornately composed.[30] (137)

The two scenes of nuptial displacement do not cohere in every detail: the gendered roles are reversed, with Chrétien's Emperor Alis placed into a position occupied by Geoffrey's Ingerna, and the fiction differs in nature, Alis spending the night with an insubstantial chimera he believes to be his wife and Ingerna spending the night with a man of flesh and blood she believes to be her husband. In view of these differences, it is unwarranted to argue a direct filiation between the episodes. It is also unnecessary. At hand is a particular topos through which the two authors countenance the same issues. In both cases a necromantic preparation is administered to ensure that an unwitting dignitary makes love to a spousal surrogate and the victim is fully deceived, and in both cases prospective problems of reception are confronted, although to differing effect. The *medicamen* Geoffrey proffers in his writing may either cure or stupefy, clarify or mislead, according to the insight brought to bear by those to whom it is administered. Chrétien's vernacular audience, in contrast, receives in the very prologue the antidote to the *poisons* of romance that is later configured through Tessala's philter.[31] Like Geoffrey, therefore, Chrétien is a sorcerer of words. But he endeavors to make those who form his audience into discerning initiates who appreciate the virtuosity of his performance and do so with no risk of confusing its result with the reality it is purported to be.

In dismantling an apocryphal past for a vernacular public, Chrétien responds to the same desire to educate that impels Benoît. But his approach is far more direct. Whereas Benoît relies on the cooperation of a *litteratus* who will mediate the hypotextual significance of the *De excidio Troiae historia,* the *Ephemeris belli Troiani,* and the *Gesta regum Anglorum,* Chrétien presupposes in his public no more than an acquaintance with the Insular tradition of Arthurian majesty. While there were no doubt some Continental magnates who lacked such knowledge, there were equally undoubtedly a large number who were perfectly qualified to negotiate for themselves the implications of *Cligés,* and this simply because the *Historia regum* had given rise to several translations — most notably that of Wace — that celebrate in unambiguous and linguistically accessible terms the British hegemony Chrétien subverts.

Indeed, the very fact that the *Historia regum* and its translations were so successful can be adduced to clarify Chrétien's decision to proscribe the Arthurian *imperium* from history. The glories of the Insular past were created by Geoffrey as a hypothetical model for the expansionist future that he considered his Insular contemporaries should strive to achieve; and, some twenty years later, the Arthur who ruled this British hegemony was subtly transformed by Wace to reflect the new king of England, ruler of Western France and primary political rival to the French Crown, Henry Plantagenet. In short, the apocryphal history of Britain that was so widely known on the Continent was aggressively Insular at its origins, and it became obliquely anti-French in its later vernacular guise. This expansionist tenor is entirely erased by Chrétien, who as a

Frenchman writing for the French in effect discloses the imperial fiction of Britain in order to undermine the pretensions of the contemporary Angevin realm. Rejecting the claim to preeminence disseminated by his Insular predecessors, he posits France as the true locus of military and cultural supremacy, as the third of the great hegemonies of the West, and as the heir to Greece and Rome in its flourishing devotion to letters. And he himself brings this new center of intellectual vitality an unmatched sophistication by turning the written magic of England against the propagandistic cause it was originally intended to serve.

Notes

Introduction

1. "In the twelfth century everyone was convinced that the goods appropriated by the secular lords from the fruits of peasant toil should not be employed solely to conduct war for the defense of the realm. These fiscal levies seemed justified only if they were partly applied to the advancement of knowledge and the cultivation of religious art. The patronage of high culture became one of the missions of the nobility" (Georges Duby, "The Culture of the Knightly Class: Audience and Patronage," in *Renaissance and Renewal in The Twelfth Century*, ed. Robert L. Benson and Giles Constable, with Carol D. Lanham [Cambridge, Mass.: Harvard University Press, 1982], 248–62; here 254).

2. "The cultural monopolies until then retained by the Church were now clearly challenged: the chivalric society too intended to participate in high culture. Its dream was to appropriate 'clerisy'—meaning the knowledge of the schools" (ibid., 250).

3. "From the end of the eleventh century on, there is mounting evidence of young men who neither belonged to the ranking nobility nor were destined for the Church, and yet were taught at home by private tutors or duly sent off to schools" (ibid., 255).

4. "If the number of students continued to increase during the twelfth century, it was because more and more careers were opening up for those who had finished their studies. The most accessible and most attractive careers were not ecclesiastical. Lay society clamored for the services of men who possessed such training, and it was ready to pay them handsomely.... Demand was so pressing, and the response so enthusiastic, that during the last decades of the century the leaders of the Church began to reconsider the purpose of the cathedral schools and thought of taking measures to stem the flight of their graduates into more or less secular professions. Hired in ever growing numbers by the courts, where their function—increasingly judged essential—received ever greater rewards, these intellectuals were the artisans who brought the lay and learned cultures together, and the most effective propagators of a 'renaissance' for which the school was the great studio" (ibid., 257).

5. One of Duby's examples is the *Historia comitum Ghisnensium* (The history of the counts of Guines), which was "written in a small principality—a satellite of the county of Flanders—at the very beginning of the thirteenth century. Its author, Lambert of Ardres, is precisely one of those household clerics who were the most effective agents of acculturation" (ibid., 261). Another is a regional history of the lords of Amboise, Duby's response to which I shall quote in due course.

6. "Younger sons were either placed in collegiate churches or entrusted to private tutors. First-born sons were expected only to become skilled in physical exercises and faith-

ful to the warrior's code. Educating the mind through study carried the risk, or so it was thought, of spoiling the body" (ibid., 260).

7. M. T. Clanchy, *From Memory to Written Record: England 1066–1307,* 2nd ed. (Oxford: Blackwell, 1993); Franz H. Bäuml, "Varieties and Consequences of Medieval Literacy and Illiteracy," *Speculum* 55 (1980): 237–65.

8. "[A] fundamental difference between medieval and modern approaches to literacy is that medieval assessments concentrate on cases of maximum ability, the skills of the most learned scholars *(litterati)* and the most elegant scribes, whereas modern assessors measure the diffusion of minimal skills among the masses. Consequently modern assessments of literacy have been primarily concerned with the minimal ability of persons to sign their own names and the development of elementary schools in which this ability is taught as the basic educational skill" (Clanchy, *From Memory to Written Record,* 88).

9. "The automatic coupling of reading with writing and the close association of literacy with the language one speaks are not universal norms, but products of modern European culture. . . . [R]eading and writing were not automatically coupled at the end of the twelfth century, nor was a minimal ability to perform these actions described as literacy. Writing was a skill distinct from reading because the use of parchment and quills made it difficult" (Clanchy, *From Memory to Written Record,* 232). See also Bäuml, "Varieties and Consequences," 240, drawing upon the earlier findings of V. H. Galbraith, "The Literacy of the Medieval English Kings," *Proceedings of the British Academy* 21 (1935): 201–38.

10. Bäuml, "Varieties and Consequences," 241.

11. See, for example, James Westfall Thompson, *The Literacy of the Laity in the Middle Ages,* University of California Publications in Education 9 (Berkeley and Los Angeles: University of California Press, 1939): "Literacy during the Middle Ages may be measured almost wholly by the extent of the knowledge and use of the Latin language" (v); Herbert Grundmann, "Litteratus—illiteratus: Der Wandel einer Bildungsnorm vom Altertum zum Mittelalter," *Archiv für Kulturgeschichte* 40 (1958): 1–65: "*Illitterati* und *idiotae,* die also des Lateins, des Lesens und Schreibens unkundig waren" (8).

12. Bäuml, "Varieties and Consequences," 240. See also D. H. Green, "Orality and Reading: The State of Research in Medieval Studies," *Speculum* 65 (1990): 267–80, passim, but especially 274: "When Grundmann claims for his definition of medieval literacy that it comprises an ability not only to read but also to write, we may ask whether, in formulating his definition in this way, he is not anachronistically applying standards of literacy to the Middle Ages derived from the modern period or, to a less extent, from the Roman antiquity which was his starting point."

13. Bäuml "Varieties and Consequences," 240.

14. "Sed haec vulgariter ficta crediderit aliquis, quod soleat populus litteratorum famam laedere, dicens illum loqui cum daemone quem in aliquo viderint excellentem opere" (William of Malmesbury, *Gesta regum Anglorum,* ed. William Stubbs as *De gestis regum Anglorum,* 2 vols. [London: Her Majesty's Stationery Office, Rolls Series, 1887 and 1889; reprint, New York: Kraus, 1964], 2.167 [vol. 1, p. 193]). From now on the work will usually be referred to as the *Gesta regum,* with reference to book and section number only. Here, as in all other cases throughout this study, the translation is my own.

15. Studies on magic as a perceived reality in the Middle Ages are legion. The most informative are Lynn Thorndike's *The Place of Magic in the Intellectual History of Europe* (New York: Columbia University Press, 1905) and his comprehensive *The History of Magic and Experiential Science*, 8 vols. (New York: Macmillan and Columbia University Press, 1923–58). For more focused studies of magic in England in the period preceding the High Middle Ages, see the essays in *Anglo-Saxon Magic*, ed. Godfrid Storms (The Hague: Nijhoff, 1948), and Jane Crawford, "Evidences for Witchcraft in Anglo-Saxon England," *Medium Aevum* 32 (1963): 99–116. Although not exclusively devoted to the twelfth century, Jeffrey Burton Russell's *Witchcraft in the Middle Ages* (Ithaca, N.Y.: Cornell University Press, 1972) and *Lucifer: The Devil in the Middle Ages* (Ithaca, N.Y.: Cornell University Press, 1984) provide pertinent background information. A useful introduction to the phenomenon is Richard Kieckhefer's *Magic in the Middle Ages* (Cambridge: Cambridge University Press, 1989). For a study of magic as a theme in the medieval romance, see DeLaWarr Benjamin Easter, *A Study of the Magic Elements in the Romans d'Aventure and the Romans Bretons* (Baltimore, Md.: Furst, 1906). At no point, however, does Easter approach magic as a trope, and his methodology is purely descriptive.

16. Brian Stock, *The Implications of Literacy: Written Language and Models of Interpretation in the Eleventh and Twelfth Centuries* (Princeton, N.J.: Princeton University Press, 1983).

17. "The effects [of literacy] on higher culture were particularly noticeable. As methods of interpretation were increasingly subjected to systematic scrutiny, the models employed to give meaning to otherwise unrelated disciplines more and more clustered around the concept of written language" (ibid., 3); "For literacy, as it actually penetrated medieval life and thought, brought about a transformation of the basic skills of reading and writing into instruments of analysis and interpretation. It was, so to speak, the ontological cement binding the apparently isolated activities" (11).

18. His discrete studies have been brought together in Hans Robert Jauss, *Toward an Aesthetic of Reception*, trans. Timothy Bahti, Theory and History of Literature 2 (Minneapolis: University of Minnesota Press, 1982). Jauss's seven theses of response are laid forth in chapter 1.

19. "The relationship of literature and reader has aesthetic as well as historical implications. The aesthetic implication lies in the fact that the first reception of a work by the reader includes a test of its aesthetic value in comparison with works already read" (ibid., 20); "The new text evokes for the reader (listener) the horizon of expectations and rules familiar from earlier texts, which are then varied, corrected, altered, or even just reproduced" (23); "The specific disposition toward a particular work that the author anticipates from the audience can also be arrived at, even if explicit signals are lacking, through three generally presupposed factors: first, through familiar norms or the immanent poetics of the genre; second, through the implicit relationships to familiar works of the literary-historical surroundings; and third, through the opposition between fiction and reality, between the poetic and the practical function of language, which is always available to the reflective reader during the reading as a possibility of comparison" (24); "This horizon of the expectable is constituted for the reader from out of a tradition or series of previously known works, and from a specific attitude, mediated by one (or more) genre and dissolved through new works" (79).

20. In ibid., chapter 3, "Theory of Genres and Medieval Literature."

21. Most notably Flaubert's *Madame Bovary* (ibid., 42–45), Goethe's *Faust* and poems by Valéry (110–38), and Baudelaire's *Spleen II* (139–85).

22. For a wider discussion of literary competence and reader response, consult Jonathan Culler, *Structuralist Poetics: Structuralism, Linguistics, and the Study of Literature* (Ithaca, N.Y.: Cornell University Press, 1975), 113–30. As Culler points out, the recipient is adequate to the task of interpretation only if he or she recognizes the presence and function of a specific literary semiotics in the work he or she reads or hears. To be sure, such an argument is implicit in Jauss's methodology. But it is finally somewhat lost in Jauss's primary concern with the fact, rather than the process, of changing horizons. It can also be noted that Culler's cautionary remarks apply even more forcefully to the medieval context that I shall consider, since the conventions of signification that must be recognized were at this time the almost exclusive domain of the Latin language, itself a relatively exclusive domain of a clerical minority.

23. Especially Ovid's *Metamorphoses;* see, for example, Jean Dornbush, "Ovid's *Pyramus and Thisbe* and Chrétien's *Le Chevalier de la Charrete,*" *Romance Philology* 36 (1982): 34–43.

24. For instance, Stephen G. Nichols has argued that a knowledge of Augustine's *Confessions* is crucial to the understanding of the affective interiority portrayed in the vernacular *Enéas;* see Nichols, "Amorous Imitation: Bakhtin, Augustine, and *Le Roman d'Enéas,*" in *Romance: Generic Transformation from Chrétien de Troyes to Cervantes,* ed. Kevin Brownlee and Marina Scordilis Brownlee (Hanover, N.H.: University Press of New England, 1985), 47–73.

25. The relationship between Macrobius's *Commentarium in Somnium Scipionis* and Chrétien de Troyes's *Erec et Enide* (for example) has been analyzed by Stefan Hofer, "Beiträge zu Kristian, II: Kristian und Macrobius," *Zeitschrift für Romanische Philologie* 48 (1928): 130–31; and Thomas Elwood Hart, "Chrestien, Macrobius, and Chartrean Science: The Allegorical Robe as Symbol of Textual Design in the Old French *Erec,*" *Medieval Studies* 43 (1981): 250–96, and "The *Quadrivium* and Chrétien's Theory of Composition: Some Conjunctures and Conjectures," *Symposium* 35 (1981): 57–86. On Martianus Capella's *De nuptiis Mercurii et Philologiae* as a palimpsest to the same work, see Karl D. Uitti, "A propos de philologie," trans. Eric Hicks, *Littérature* 41 (1981): 30–46; Uitti, "Vernacularization and Old French Romance Mythopoesis with Emphasis on Chrétien's *Erec et Enide,*" in *The Sower and His Seed: Essays on Chrétien de Troyes,* ed. Rupert T. Pickens (Lexington, Ky.: French Forum, 1983), 81–115; Sally Musseter, "The Education of Chrétien's Enide," *Romanic Review* 73 (1982): 147–66; and my own "From Apuleius's Psyche to Chrétien's Erec and Enide," in *The Search for the Ancient Novel,* ed. James Tatum (Baltimore, Md.: Johns Hopkins University Press, 1994), 347–69, especially 350.

26. The term *litteraturae peritus* is derived from William of Malmesbury's *Gesta regum Anglorum.* I shall return to this in chapter 2.

27. The term *parum litteratus* is derived from Gerald of Wales's *Expugnatio Hibernica.* I shall return to this in chapter 5.

28. The *auditor* or *audiens,* evoked by Alain de Lille in the *De planctu Naturae.* I shall return to this in chapter 2.

29. Paul Zumthor, *La lettre et la voix* (Paris: Éditions du Seuil, 1987). Many of the arguments found in this work are anticipated in Zumthor's slightly earlier studies: *Introduction à la poésie orale* (Paris: Éditions du Seuil, 1983); "The Text and the Voice," *New Literary History* 16 (1984): 67–92; and "Spoken Language and Oral Poetry in the Middle Ages," *Style* 19 (1985): 191–98.

30. "Le texte auditivement reçu engendre la conscience commune, à la manière dont le langage engendre la société qui le parle: effet d'autant plus fort que ce texte est moins appropriable, moins marqué par un individu concret qui en revendiquerait, comme nous disons, les 'droits'" (ibid., 173); "Le signifiant du signifié textuel est un être vivant. Hors jargon, je traduirais que le sens du texte se lit dans la présence et le jeu d'un corps humain. Le texte devient *chaud*...: la performance n'est divertissement que de façon seconde; elle n'est en rien commodité; elle est communication de vie, sans réserve" (ibid., 292).

31. "Que, de tel texte du XIIe siècle, on pût prouver (supposons-le) que son mode d'existence avait été principalement oral, cela nuisait gravement, vers 1960–1965 encore, en France du moins, à son prestige. De tel texte admiré, tenu pour 'chef-d'oeuvre,' un préjugé très fort intersdisait à la plupart des lecteurs érudits d'admettre qu'il eût pu ne point être écrit et, dans l'intention de l'auteur, offert à la seule lecture" (ibid., 8). It will be noted that Zumthor situates this problem in the early 1960s. Yet the very fact that *La lettre et la voix* appeared some twenty-five years later reveals that Zumthor perceived an ongoing need to counter its effects. Such concerns are certainly not confined to medieval studies. In a less polemical context than Zumthor's, Walter J. Ong has repeatedly sought to erase distorting modern assumptions (such as the insubstantial oxymoron of "oral literature") in a variety of anthropological works. Of these, the most pertinent to the present discussion is *Orality and Literacy: The Technologizing of the Word* (London: Routledge, 1988), particularly chapter 1, "The Orality of Language."

32. "Au début de notre siècle, la 'littérature' embrassait ainsi, à l'échelle mondiale, de manière exclusive les faits et les textes homologues à ceux qu'engendrait la pratique dominante de l'Europe occidentale: eux seuls concernaient la conscience critique, crédités qu'on les avait de caractères relevant, selon l'opinion unanime, de sa compétence. L'ensemble de présupposés régissant cette attitude d'esprit tenait en quelque façon au centralisme politique depuis longtemps instauré par la majorité des États européens. Il s'accordait aux tendances mythificatrices, voire allégorisantes, qui y présidaient à l'élaboration des 'histoires nationales': exaltation de héros personnifiant le surmoi collectif; confection d'un Livre d'Images où fonder un sens qui justifiât le fait présent; les voix de Jeanne d'Arc, la croisade de Barberousse ou le bûcher de Jean Hus" (Zumthor, *La lettre et la voix*, 8).

33. "Que [le texte] soit reçu par lecture individuelle directe, ou par audition et spectacle, modifie profonément son effet sur le récepteur, donc sa signifiance" (ibid., 24).

34. "Mieux valait nier l'évidence, et cette menace dont on avait lieu de redouter qu'à court terme elle ne ruine la stabilité d'une philologie assise sur des siècles de certitudes" (ibid., 7).

35. "D'où, pour le médiéviste, une aporie critique, puisqu'il ne peut saisir *in situ* la performance. Pourtant, cette impossibilité ne justifie en rien la négligence avec laquelle on tend à mettre entre parenthèses, sinon, avec superbe, à ignorer, le problème" (ibid., 294).

36. Especially in Zumthor, *Parler du Moyen Age* (Paris: Éditions de Minuit, 1980), 35–36.

37. "Il n'est pas, tant s'en faut, inconcevable de reconstituer (dans plusieurs cas particuliers que l'on tiendra pour exemplaires, et fût-ce en s'aidant avec prudence de travaux ethnologiques) les facteurs de l'opération performancielle (temps, lieu, circonstances, contexte historique, acteurs) et de percevoir, au moins globalement, la nature des valeurs investies—dont celles que véhicule ou produit le texte" (Zumthor, *La lettre et la voix*, 294).

38. And this according to Zumthor himself, who acknowledges the phenomenon as "la surenchère à laquelle nous avons assisté, au cours des années 70 et 80, en France plus qu'ailleurs, dans les études sur le *roman*" (ibid., 307), and defines its primary effect as "une grave distorsion *moderno-centriste* de l'idée que nous nous faisons du 'moyen âge'" (307).

39. "Dans le nombre, très minoritaire, des hommes capables de déchiffrer leurs lettres, seule une poignée appartenait au groupe clos des professionnels de l'écriture. Celle-ci, jusqu'au XIIIe siècle, fait ainsi presque figure de privilège de classe et ne peut entrer dans le réseau général des communications sociales qu'en maintenant des liens avec la voix" (ibid., 116). Stock concurs: "Medieval and early modern society hovered between... extremes: there was a tiny minority who were truly literate and a much larger majority for whom communication could take place only by word of mouth. Down to the age of print and in many regions long afterwards, literacy remained the exception rather than the rule. Despite primary schools, cheap paper, spectacles, and the growing body of legal and administrative material, the masses of both town and countryside as late as the Reformation remained relatively indifferent to writing. For this vast group, marginal to literacy, the graphic world represented only a complex set of signs, frequently tied to relations of authority" (Stock, *The Implications of Literacy*, 13–14).

40. "Reste que toujours le facteur décisif immédiat de la mise par écrit fut l'intention soit d'enregistrer un discours préalablement prononcé, soit de préparer un texte destiné à la lecture publique ou au chant dans telle ou telle circonstance. L'écriture n'était qu'un relais provisoire de la voix" (Zumthor, *La lettre et la voix*, 135).

41. This is not to say that the romance necessarily relied on a literate cleric for its performance. Although most probably composed through the technology of writing (at least in the early, extremely complex and protracted form represented by the *romans antiques*) and although usually delivered through reading aloud, romances were on occasion recited from memory. On this, along with contemporary evidence, see Joseph J. Duggan, "Performance and Transmission, Aural and Ocular Reception in the Twelfth- and Thirteenth-Century Vernacular Literature of France," *Romance Philology* 43 (1989): 49–58, and Evelyn Birge Vitz, "Rethinking Old French Literature: The Orality of the Octosyllabic Couplet," *Romanic Review* 77 (1986): 307–21, which anticipates her wide-ranging study, *Orality and Performance in Early French Romance* (Cambridge: D. S. Brewer, 1999), especially 86–163.

42. *Le Roman de Thèbes*, ed. Léopold Constans, 2 vols., Société des Anciens Textes Français (Paris: Firmin Didot, 1890), lines 1–4.

43. This cultural function has been well analyzed by Robert W. Hanning in "The Social Significance of Twelfth-Century Chivalric Romance," *Medievalia et Humanistica*, n.s., 3 (1972): 3–29, and "The Audience as Co-Creator of the First Chivalric Romances," *Yearbook*

of English Studies 2 (1981): 1–28 (in which Hanning considers precisely the passages from *Thèbes* I have just quoted). The one minor objection I have with the latter article is Hanning's concern with "the audience," a monolithic concept that creates a specious sense of uniform reception. It is not so much that the romance is cocreated by author-performer and audience at each session. Rather, *a number of romances* are cocreated, in precise proportion to the number of listeners, and this plurality of "cocreations" would inevitably display distinctions in insight arising from divergences in literate competence.

44. *Le Conte de Floire et Blancheflor,* ed. Jean-Luc Leclanche, Classiques Français du Moyen Age 105 (Paris: Champion, 1983), lines 823–26. On the figure of Barbarin as an interpolation, see p. 6 of the editor's introduction.

45. Michelle A. Freeman, *The Poetics of "Translatio Studii" and "Conjointure": Chrétien de Troyes's "Cligés"* (Lexington, Ky.: French Forum, 1979).

46. See ibid., 91–139.

47. Benoît de Sainte-Maure, *Roman de Troie;* the edition used will be that of Léopold Constans, 6 vols., Société des Anciens Textes Français (Paris: Firmin Didot, 1904–12), with reference to line number only.

48. See n. 3 above. Duby's prior work on the "iuvenes" who followed the chivalric ethos is found in "Les 'jeunes' dans la société aristocratique dans la France du Nord-Ouest au XIIe siècle," in *Hommes et structures du Moyen Age* (Paris: Mouton, 1973), 213–25.

49. See Ralph V. Turner, *Men Raised from the Dust: Administrative Service and Upward Mobility in Angevin England* (Philadelphia: University of Pennsylvania Press, 1988), in which Turner considers the careers of William de Sainte-Mère-Eglise, bishop of London; Geoffrey fitz Peter, earl of Essex; William of Briwerre; Henry of London, archbishop of Dublin; Thomas of Moulton; and Stephen of Segrave.

50. As Turner points out, learning became a highly remunerative qualification during the reigns of the first four Angevins: "Perhaps the question of new men *versus* magnates in Henry II's last years can be answered by looking at the role of education and literacy in late twelfth-century government. The magnates were more likely to offer their monarch the older feudal virtues of loyalty to sworn lord, good counsel, and military prowess than they were proficiency with letters and numbers. More and more, the king required intimates who were numerate and literate, masters of skills needed for administration. The best known illustration of how high mastery of these new disciplines could carry one is Thomas Becket, who had been a 'clerk and accountant' before entering Henry II's service" (ibid., 9). I shall further pursue the course Turner proposes in order to demonstrate that education and literacy became *flaunted* prerogatives, objectified by writers of the era and—however fantastically—celebrated as devices of control.

1. WILLIAM OF MALMESBURY

1. Among representative judgments of William's stature are the following: "His ability to see the wood for the trees is, in that age, extraordinary; but for expressing it he is nearly unique" (V. H. Galbraith, *Historical Research in Medieval England* [London: Athlone Press, 1951], 15); "William of Malmesbury was perhaps the greatest, and is certainly the most admired, of the Anglo-Norman historians" (James Campbell, "Some Twelfth-Century Views of the Anglo-Saxon Past," *Peritia* 3 [1984]: 131–50; here 136); "William of Malmesbury [was] the greatest English historian after Bede" (D. R. Howlett, "The Literary Context of Geoffrey of Monmouth: An Essay on the Fabrication of Sources," *Arthuriana* 5 [1995]: 25–69; here 26). For a notable recent example of a study that widely draws on William's writings, consider the notes to Marjorie Chibnall's *Anglo-Norman England, 1066–1166* (Oxford: Blackwell, 1986), in particular 85–100.

2. Respectively *Gesta regum Anglorum* 2.171; 2.205; 2.169 and 171; 2.206; 2.207. One of these anecdotes has had an undeniable longevity: William's tale of the statue and the ring reappears, at a distance of some seven hundred years, as Mérimée's *La Vénus d'Ile.*

3. For a response of this type, see Rodney Thomson in the extraordinarily erudite and perspicacious monograph devoted to William's education and reading, *William of Malmesbury* (Woodbridge, England: Boydell, 1987). Although with no elaboration, Thomson shows a sensitivity to the potential significance of William's anecdotes, which he characterizes as "notorious and baffling fables and folk-tales, apparently (but only apparently?) introduced as light relief" (139). The most penetrating analysis to date of William's anecdote of the Campus Martius, however, is found in chapter 3 of Monika Otter's *Inventiones: Fiction and Referentiality in Twelfth-Century English Historical Writing* (Chapel Hill: University of North Carolina Press, 1996). I shall return to Otter's arguments (and to my differing interpretation) in due course.

4. In the front matter to his edition of the *Gesta regum,* Stubbs observes that they "belong to a common treasury of entertainments meant for the diversion of uncritical listeners" (vol. 2, lxxii). Similarly, Antonia Gransden in *Historical Writing in England, c. 550 to c. 1307* (London: Routledge & Kegan Paul, 1974) attributes "the secular, in places gay, almost frivolous, tone of the *Gesta regum*" to William's "desire to entertain" (171).

5. See Arturo Graf, *Miti, leggende e superstitizioni del Medioevo,* 2 vols. (Florence: Forni, 1980), who characterizes William as "[un] gran raccoglitore, gran narratore, caloroso, efficace e credulo, di storie incredibili" (vol. 2, 16–17).

6. Alain de Lille, *De planctu Naturae,* ed. Nikolaus M. Häring, *Studi Medievali* 19 (1978): 797–879; both examples at 837. I reconsider the sale of naked *falsitas* in due course.

7. "An ignoras quomodo . . . in superficiali littere cortice falsum resonat lira poetica, interius uero auditoribus secretum intelligentie altioris eloquitur, ut exteriori falsitatis abiecto putamine dulciorem nucleum ueritatis secrete intus lector inueniat?"

8. "Poete tamen aliquando hystoriales euentus ioculationibus fabulosis quadam eleganti sutura confederant, ut ex diuersorum conpetenti iunctura ipsius narrationis elegantior pictura resultet."

9. At this early stage, it must be emphatically stated that William's Gerbert does not remotely correspond to the historical figure. On this, see Massimo Oldoni's two extremely detailed and well-reasoned articles: "Gerberto e la sua storia," *Studi Medievali,* 3rd series, 18 (1977): 629–704, and "A fantasia dicitur fantasma," *Studi Medievali,* 3rd series, 21 (1980): 493–622. As will become clear, I agree with the general tenor of Oldoni's arguments. I disagree, however, with his reading of William of Malmesbury.

10. "Erat juxta Romam in campo Martio statua, aerea an ferrea incertum mihi, dexterae manus indicem digitum extentum habens, scriptum quoque in capite 'Hic percute.'"

11. "Quod superioris aevi homines ita intelligendum rati quasi ibi thesaurum invenirent, multis securium ictibus innocentem statuam laniaverant" (2.169).

12. "Sed illorum Gerbertus redarguit errorem, longe aliter ambiguitate absoluta: namque meridie, sole in centro existente, notans quo protenderetur umbra digiti, ibi palum figit; mox superveniente nocte, solo cubiculario laternam portante comitatus, eo contendit. Ibi, terra solitis artibus dehiscens, latum ingredientibus patefecit introitum: conspicantur ingentem regiam, aureos parietes, aurea lacunaria, aurea omnia" (2.169).

13. "Mox superveniente nocte, solo cubiculario laternam portante comitatus, eo contendit. Ibi, terra solitis artibus dehiscens, latum ingredentibus patefecit introitum."

14. "Illis qui haec quae scribimus non intelligunt, hoc dico: me ita non esse reprehendendum, quia haec non intelligunt: tanquam si lunam veterem uel novam sidusve aliquod minine clarum vellent videre, quod ego intento digito demonstrarem; illis autem nec ad ipsum digitum meum videndum sufficiens esset acies oculorum, non propterea mihi succensere deberent. Illi vero qui etiam istis praeceptis cognitis atque perceptis, ea quae in divinis Scripturis obscura sunt intueri nequiverint, arbitrentur se digitum quidem meum videre posse, sidera vero quibus demonstrandis intenditur, videre non posse." Augustine's text is from J. P. Migne, *Patrologiae cursus completus: Series latina*, vol. 34 (Paris: Éditions Migne, 1887), cols. 15–122. From now on this work will be designated as the *De doctrina;* reference will be to book and section.

15. Neither Graf nor Oldoni identify the statue as an index for Augustine, and neither reads the anecdote as a commentary on interpreting the written sign. Nonetheless, Oldoni's study in particular is complementary to my own in its constant emphasis on the forces of ignorance that Gerbert encountered (and at times vigorously attacked). See above all "Gerberto e la sua storia," 676–81, for illuminating remarks on efforts by Gerbert's contemporaries to argue (with predictable biblical citation) that the City of God—and, for that matter, the city of Rome—is to be inherited by the intellectually innocent—"Unde eius [Christ's] vicarii et eius discipuli apostolicis et euangelicis sunt instituti doctrinis, et non ornatu sermonum, sed ratione et sensu verborum; quia scriptum est 'Stulta mundi elegit Deus, ut confundat fortia.' Et ab initio mundi non elegit Deus oratores et philosophos, sed illiteratos et rusticos" (excerpt from letter by Leo, abbot of San Bonifacio in Rome, to Hugh Capet and his son Robert; quoted by Oldoni, "Gerberto e la sua storia," 679). From these remarks it becomes clear that Gerbert was himself accused during his own lifetime of the perceived crime of ornate language and an apparent disregard for the literal that are central to William's anecdote.

16. Donatus (mid–fourth century) subsumed figures of diction into the discipline of grammar in book 3 (the "Barbarismus") of his *Ars grammatica* (or *Ars maior*). James J. Murphy describes the historical circumstances of this shift in his *Rhetoric in The Middle Ages: A History of Rhetorical Theory from St. Augustine to the Renaissance* (Berkeley and Los Angeles: University of California Press, 1974), 32–37. For a probing analysis of the exegetical and literary ramifications of rhetorical and grammatical figuration, see Rita Copeland, *Rhetoric, Hermeneutics, and Translation in the Middle Ages: Academic Traditions and Vernacular Texts* (Cambridge: Cambridge University Press, 1991).

17. The commentary on Augustine that I provide makes no claim to being particularly interpretative, and it is little more than a paraphrase of those aspects of the *De doc-*

trina that I consider apposite to William's *Gesta regum*. For genuinely searching studies, I refer the reader to the following: on oratory, homiletics, and conversion, Narciso Jubany, "San Agustín y la formación oratoria Cristiana," *Analecta Sacra Tarraconensia: Revista de Ciencias Histórico-Eclesiásticas* 15 (1943): 9–22; on semiotics, Raffaele Simone, "Semiologia agostiniana," *La cultura* 7 (1969): 88–117; R. A. Markus, "St. Augustine on Signs," *Phronesis* 2 (1957): 68–83; B. Darrell Jackson, "The Theory of Signs in St. Augustine's *De doctrina christiana*," *Revue des études augustiniennes* 15 (1969): 9–49; Marcia L. Colish, *The Mirror of Language: A Study of the Medieval Theory of Knowledge*, rev. ed. (Lincoln: University of Nebraska Press, 1983), 7–54 (particularly 41–46).

18. These terms are defined by Donatus in 3.6 of the *Ars grammatica* as follows: "allegoria est tropus, quo aliud significatur quam dicitur, ut 'et iam tempus equum fumantia solvere colla,' hoc est 'carmen finire'"; "aenigma est obscura sententia per occultam similitudinem rerum, ut 'mater me genuit, eadem mox gignitur ex me,' cum significet aquam in glaciem concrescere et ex eadem rursus effluere"; "parabole est rerum genere dissimilium conparatio, ut 'qualis mugitus fugit cum saucius aram taurus' et cetera" (this, alongside *icon* and *paradigma,* is a subdivision of *homoeosis*); "metaphora est rerum verborumque translatio. haec fit modis quattuor, ab animali ad animale, ab inanimali ad inanimale, ab animali ad inanimale, ab inanimali ad animale"; "catachresis est usurpatio nominis alieni, ut parricidam dicimus qui occiderit fratrem, et piscinam quae pisces non habet. haec enim nisi extrinsecus sumerent, suum vocabulum non haberent"; "ironia est tropus per contrarium quod conatur ostendens, ut 'egregiam vero laudem et spolia ampla refertis tuque puerque tuus' et cetera. hanc nisi gravitas pronuntiationis adiuverit, confiteri videbitur quod negare contendit"; "antiphrasis est unius verbi ironia ut [bellum lucus et Parcae] bellum, hoc est minime bellum, et lucus eo quod non luceat, et Parcae eo quod nulli parcant"; text in H. Keil, *Grammatici latini,* 8 vols. (Leipzig: Teubner, 1864), vol. 4.

19. "Quorum cognitio propterea Scripturarum ambiguitatibus dissolvendis est necessaria, quia cum sensus, ad proprietatem verborum si accipiatur, absurdus est, quaerendum est utique ne forte illo vel illo tropo dictum sit quod non intelligimus; et sic pleraque inventa sunt quae latebant."

20. "Cum enim figurate dictum sic accipitur, tanquam proprie dictum sit, carnaliter sapitur. Neque ulla mors animae congruentius appellatur, quam cum id etiam quod in ea bestiis antecellit, hoc est, intelligentia carni subjicitur sequendo litteram. Qui enim sequitur litteram, translata verba sicut propria tenet, neque illud quod proprio verbo significatur, refert ad aliam significationem. . . . Ea demum est miserabilis animae servitus, signa pro rebus accipere; et supra creaturam corpoream oculum mentis ad hauriendum aeternum lumen levare non posse."

21. "[D]octrinae omnes Gentilium non solum simulata et superstitiosa figmenta gravesque sarcinas supervacanei laboris habent, quae unusquisque nostrum duce Christo, de societate Gentilium exiens, debet abominari atque devitare; sed etiam liberales disciplinas usui veritatis aptiores, et quaedam morum praecepta utilissima continent, deque ipso uno Deo colendo nonnulla vera inveniuntur apud eos; quod eorum tanquam aurum et argentum, quod non ipsi instituerunt, sed de quibusdam quasi metallis divinae providentiae, quae ubique infusa est, eruerunt, et quo perverse atque injuriose ad obsequia daemonum abutuntur, cum ab eorum misera societate sese animo separat, debet ab eis auferre christianus ad usum justum praedicandi Evangelii."

22. "Talia illum adversis praestigiis machinatum fuisse constans vulgi opinio est. Veruntamen, si quis verum diligenter exsculpat, videbit nec Salomonem, cui Deus ipse dederit sapientiam, hujusce inscium commenti fuisse."

23. For a differing reading, see Otter, *Inventiones,* chapter 3. While I am in complete agreement with Otter in viewing William's subterranean world as a trope, I consider it to signify a repository of knowledge to be excavated by the scholar and not a world of fiction potentially created by a negative pendant of the author.

24. See, for example, both Graf and Oldoni, who, by failing to identify the statue with Augustine, in effect halt at precisely the verbal surface William himself invites the reader figuratively to excavate.

25. "Sed haec vulgariter ficta crediderit aliquis, quod soleat populus litteratorum famam laedere, dicens illum loqui cum daemone quem in aliquo viderint excellentem opere."

26. "Unde Boetius, in libro de Consolatione Philosophiae, queritur se propter studium sapientiae de talibus notatum, quasi conscientiam suam sacrilegio polluisset ob ambitum dignitatis" (2.167).

27. "Haec Boetius. Mihi vero fidem facit de istius sacrilegio inaudita mortis excogitatio. Cur enim se moriens, ut postea dicemus, excarnificaret ipse sui corporis horrendus lanista, nisi novi sceleris conscius esset? Unde in vetusto volumine quod in manus meas incidit, ubi omnium apostolicorum nomina continebantur et anni, ita scriptum vidi: 'Johannes, qui et Gerbertus, annos quatuor, mensem unum, dies decem; hic turpiter vitam suam finivit.'"

28. Stubbs considers this confusion "a fatal mistake," "the most unfortunate blunder in the whole of the works of William of Malmesbury" (*Gesta regum,* vol. 1, li); he elaborates further in vol. 2, lxxiii–iv.

29. Two copies of this text still exist: Cambridge University Library Kk. 4. 6 and British Library Harl. 633. The first dates from the 1130s and the second from the end of the century. Wilhelm Levison, the first to notice affinities between this compendium and William's treatment of the papacy, concluded that it must have been employed simply as his paradigm; see Levison, "Aus Englischen Bibliotheken II," *Neues Archiv für ältere deutsche Geschichtskunde* 35 (1910): 333–431. Elaborating on Levison's findings, Thomson shows that it was in fact William himself who oversaw its production, sometime between the appearances of the first and later recensions of the *Gesta regum*; see Thomson, *William of Malmesbury,* chapter 6.

30. Thomson, *William of Malmesbury,* 73–74: "By 1125, on the completion of the first edition of the *Gesta Regum,* he had been to Oxford, where he investigated the archives of Saint Frideswide's. But the evidence of the *Gesta Pontificum* shows that by the same date he had made a grand tour of England, visiting Thorney, Rochester, Sherborne, Crowland, Hereford, York, Carlisle, Shaftesbury, Bath, Durham, Wareham, Corfe, Gloucester, Bangor, Coventry and Winchester and perhaps Tavistock. The *Antiquity of Glastonbury,* written between 1129 and 1135, enables us to add Glastonbury and Bury, where he found historical works which interested him, and by the second edition of the *Gesta Regum,* c. 1135, he had seen records at Milton Abbas."

31. On the dates of William's works in general, see ibid., chapter 1; for the composition of the *Gesta regum* in particular, see 3–4.

32. Cf. Oldoni's discussion in "A fantasia dicitur fantasma," 537–44, summed up in the following: "Il fatto che sia presente in Guglielmo di Malmesbury un binomio del tipo Gerberto/Giovanni vale soprattutto a significare che nelle fonti del Maresberiense già circola, e siamo dunque fra XI secolo e primissimo XII, la volontaria confusione riguardante la morte di due papi spesso sovrapposti" (543–44). There is indeed a "volontaria confusione" at hand here. But it does not predate William.

33. "Urgebat ipse fortunas suas, fautore diabolo, ut nihil quod semel excogitasset imperfectum relinqueret. Denique thesauros olim a gentilibus defossos, arte nigromantiae molibus eruderatis inventos, cupiditatibus suis implicuit. Adeo improborum vilis in Deum affectus; et ejus abutuntur patientia, quos ipse mallet redire quam perire."

34. Compare William's "thesauros olim a gentilibus defossos . . . cupiditatibus suis implicuit" with Augustine's "[gentiles] de quibusdam quasi metallis divinae providentiae, quae ubique infusa est, eruerunt."

35. With the result of contravening one of Augustine's most urgently stated distinctions and fully revealing the *cupiditas* that impels him: "Charitatem voco motum animi ad fruendum Deo propter ipsum, at se atque proximo propter Deum: cupiditatem autem, motum animi ad fruendum se et proximo et quolibet corpore non propter Deum" (3.10).

36. "Sed reperit tandem ubi magister suus haereret, et, ut dici solet, quasi cornix cornici oculos effoderet, dum pari arte temptamentis ejus occurreret."

37. "Et illi ergo, et isti me reprehendere desinant, et lumen oculorum divinitus sibi praeberi deprecentur. Non enim si possum membrum meum ad aliquid demonstrandum movere, possum etiam oculos ascendere, quibus vel ipsa demonstratio mea vel etiam illud quod volo demonstrare, cernatur" (proem).

38. "Illi vero qui etiam istis praeceptis cognitis atque perceptis, ea quae in divinis Scripturis obscura sunt intueri nequiverint, arbitrentur se digitum quidem meum videre posse, sidera vero quibus demonstrandis intenditur, videre non posse" (proem).

39. "Conspicantur ingentem regiam, aureos parietes, aurea lacunaria, aurea omnia; milites aureos aureis tesseris quasi animum oblectantes; regem metallicum cum regina discumbentem, apposita obsonia, astantes ministros, pateras multi ponderis et pretii, ubi naturam vincebat opus. In interiori parte domus carbunculus, lapis inprimis nobilis et parvus inventu, tenebras noctis fugabat. In contrario angulo stabat puer, arcum tenens extento nervo et arundine intenta. Ita in omnibus, cum oculos spectantium ars pretiosa raptaret, nihil erat quod posset tangi etsi posset videri."

40. "Continuo enim ut quis manum ad contingendum aptaret, videbantur omnes illae imagines prosilire, et impetum in praesumptorem facere. Quo timore pressus Gerbertus, ambitum suum fregit."

41. "Sed non abstinuit cubicularius, quin mirabilis artificii cultellum, quem mensae impositum videret, abriperet; arbitratus scilicet, in tanta praeda, parvum latrocinium posse latere. Verum mox omnibus imaginibus cum fremitu exsurgentibus, puer quoque, emissa arundine in carbunculum, tenebras induxit; et, nisi ille monitu domini cultellum rejicere accelerasset, graves ambo poenas dedissent. Sic insatiata cupiditatis voragine, laterna gressus ducente, discessum."

42. "Talia illum adversis praestigiis machinatum fuisse constans vulgi opinio est. Veruntamen, si quis verum diligenter exsculpat, videbit nec Salomonem, cui Deus ipse dederit sapientiam, hujusce inscium commenti fuisse.... credo quod qui dederit Salomoni virtutem super daemones, ut idem historiographus testatur, adeo ut dicat etiam suo tempore fuisse viros qui illos ab obsessis corporibus expellerent, apposito naribus patientis anulo habente sigillum a Salomone monstratum, credo, inquam, quod et isti hanc scientiam dare potuerit, nec tamen affirmo quod dederit."

43. Again, eliding the reputed magic of Gerbert with the wisdom of Solomon, and inviting the accomplished reader to exhibit both: "Talia illum adversis *praestigiis* machinatum fuisse constans vulgi opinio est. Veruntamen, si quis verum diligenter exsculpat, videbit nec Salomonem, cui Deus ipse dederit sapientiam, hujusce inscium commenti fuisse" (2.169; emphasis added).

44. "Sed haec vulgariter ficta crediderit aliquis, quod soleat *populus* litteratorum famam laedere, dicens illum loqui cum daemone quem in aliquo viderint excellentem opere" (2.167; emphasis added); "Talia illum adversis praestigiis machinatum fuisse constans *vulgi* opinio est" (2.169; emphasis added).

45. See Stubbs, *Gesta regum*, vol. 1, xliii–lxii. The dedication appears only in the second and third recensions of the work, both of which Stubbs dates after 1135.

46. Lay illiteracy has already been considered. But clerics also displayed disparate degrees of competence, arising from divergences in intelligence, training, and application. For the problems of clerical illiteracy in the Anglo-Norman domains during the High Middle Ages, see Thompson, *The Literacy of the Laity*, 166, and Clanchy, *From Memory to Written Record*, 241–42.

47. The still canonical study of oral performance and auditory reception in the Middle Ages is Ruth Crosby's "Oral Delivery in the Middle Ages," *Speculum* 11 (1936): 88–110; its influence on Zumthor's *La lettre et la voix* is clear, especially between 83–106. For a divergent approach that at times excessively privileges sight over sound in a vernacular context, see Manfred Günter Scholz, *Hören und Lesen: Studien zur primären Rezeption der Literatur im 12. und 13. Jahrhundert* (Wiesbaden: Franz Steiner, 1980), particularly 189–91. On the difficulties of accepting some of Scholz's conclusions, see the critical reviews his work has received from Dieter Kartschoke in *Internationales Archiv für Sozialgeschichte der Literatur* 8 (1983): 253–66 and D. H. Green in "On the Primary Reception of Narrative Literature in Medieval Germany," *Forum for Modern Language Studies* 10 (1984): 289–308.

48. On the reiterative modes of reception and revision that reading affords and listening inhibits, see Jack Goody and Ian Watt, "The Consequences of Literacy," in *Comparative Studies in Society and History* 5 (1962–63): 304–45, at 339–40.

49. The distinction I am making of course concerns reading and listening as *primary* modes of receiving data. Since the ability to scan the written text silently was an extremely rare accomplishment throughout the Middle Ages, solitary reading itself usually entailed *sotto voce* utterance, creating conditions in which medieval writing almost always partly depended on the voice for its intelligibility. Yet, because involving the oralization of the visual, such cases still initially rely on sight. For further information on the voice as a supplement to the eye, see Walter J. Ong, "Orality, Literacy, and Medieval Textualization," *New Literary History* 16 (1984): 1–12; Manfred Günter Scholz, "On Presentation and Reception:

Guidelines in the German Strophic Epic of the Late Middle Ages," trans. Rebecca Williams Duplantier and Crozet Deplantier Jr., *New Literary History* 16 (1984): 137–51; and Zumthor, *La lettre et la voix*, 117.

50. "Praestigium vero Mercurius dicitur invenisse quod ex eo sic dicitur quod aciem praestringat oculorum, fuitque magorum peritissimus, ut quascunque res vellet invisibiles faceret aut ut videbatur in alias species transformaret" (1.9). The text is from J. P. Migne, *Patrologiae cursus completus: Series latina*, vol. 199 (Paris: Garnier, 1900), cols. 379–822; here 407. I shall refer to the *Policraticus* by both book and chapter and by column number. When necessary, I will replace the editor's punctuation with my own.

51. The function of the narrator is formulated with useful concision by Tzvetan Todorov, *Introduction to Poetics*, trans. Richard Howard, Theory and History of Literature 1 (Minneapolis: University of Minnesota Press, 1981), 27–40, especially 38–40. For more detailed critical studies, see Gérard Genette, *Figures II* (Paris: Éditions du Seuil, 1969), 195–222, and *Figures III* (Paris: Éditions du Seuil, 1972), 225–67. The most penetrating analyses of the narrator in medieval literature are Scholz, *Hören und Lesen*, 1–113, particularly 1–34, and Evelyn Birge Vitz, *Medieval Narrative and Modern Narratology: Subjects and Objects of Desire* (New York: New York University Press, 1989).

52. The English is given earlier in this chapter.

53. "[D]icam quod a quodam loci nostri monacho, genere Aquitanico, aetate provecto, arte medico, in pueritia audisse me memini" (2.170). The monk's first-person voice then intervenes, with William providing the appropriate "aiebat" to create the illusion of direct quotation ("'Ego,' *aiebat*, 'septennis . . . in Italiam veni'").

54. "Nam et nos cum essemus in Italia audiebamus talia de quadam regione illarum partium, ubi stabularias mulieres inbutas his malis artibus in caseo dare solere dicebant quibus uellent seu possent uiatoribus, unde in iumenta ilico uerterentur et necessaria quaeque portarent postque perfuncta opera iterum ad se redirent; nec tamen in eis mentem fieri bestialem, sed rationalem humanamque seruari, sicut Apuleius in libris quos asini aurei titulo inscripsit, sibi ipsi accidisse, ut accepto ueneno humano animo permanente asinus fieret, aut indicauit aut finxit." The text is from the edition of *De civitate Dei* by B. Dombart and A. Kalb in *Corpus Christianorum, Series Latina, XLVIII: Aurelii Augustini Opera Pars XIV, 2* (Turnholt: Brepols, 1955); here 18.18. In view of this transposition, it is extremely incautious to follow Oldoni ("A fantasia dicitur fantasma," 567–68) and read William literally in his assertion that he heard the tale of the crones from an Aquitanian traveler.

55. "Refert ille se asinum fuisse, modo hominem, omnemque casum exponit. Miratus famulus ad dominum detulit; dominus ad apostolicum Leonem, dico, nostro seculo sanctissimum; convictae anus idem fatentur. Dubitantem papam confirmat Petrus Damianus, litteraturae peritus, non mirum si haec fieri possint; productoque exemplo de Simone Mago, qui Faustinianum in Simonis figura videri, et a filiis horreri fecit, instructiorem de cetero in talibus reddidit" (2.171).

56. See *Recognitions* 10.52 (in which "Clement" is speaking in the first person): "cumque haec diceret, supervenit pater et invenit Petrum nobis de se loquentem. cumque salutasset, satisfacere coepit et causam exponere, ob quam foris mansisset. nos autem respicientes ad eum expavimus, vultum in eo Simonis videntes, vocem tamen patris nostri audiebamus.

cumque refugeremus eum et execraremur, stupebat pater quod tam austere cum eo ageremus et barbare. solus tamen Petrus erat qui vultum eius naturalem videbat." Simon himself is described planning this stratagem in 10.58. The text is from the edition of Bernhard Rehm, *Die Pseudoklementinen: II, Rekognitionen in Rufins Übersetzung* (Berlin: Akademie-Verlag, 1965).

57. "[M]agnum suis commodis emolumentum habentes asinum qui transeuntium detineret oculos miraculo gestuum, quocunque enim modo praecepisset anus, movebatur asinus. Nec enim amiserat intelligentiam, etsi amiserat loquelam."

58. Cicero, for example, quite happily uses the term in the vocative when addressing the utterly loathed Piso: "quid nunc te, asine, litteras docem? Non opus est verbis, sed fustibus" (*In L. Calpurnium Pisonem*, ed. N. H. Watts, in *Cicero: The Speeches*, Loeb Classical Library [London: Heinemann and Putnam's, 1931], section 30). Cicero is also prepared to use this abusive word in mockery of himself. For example, addressing Atticus: "Scio te voluisse et me asinum germanum fuisse" (*Letters to Atticus*, ed. E. O. Winstedt, Loeb Classical Library, 3 vols. [London: Heinemann and Putnam's, 1928], vol. 1, section 4.5). Terence quite frequently uses the term; see, for instance, *Heauton Timorumenos*, line 877: "Sunt dicta in stulto, caudex, stipes, asinus, plumbeus"; also, *Eunuchus*, lines 597–98: "Tum equidem istuc os tuom inpudens uidere nimium uellem, qui esset status, flabellulum tenere te asinum tantum" (*The Comedies of Terence*, ed. Sidney G. Ashmore [New York: Oxford University Press, 1908]). There is no evidence that William knew either of the two Ciceronian texts; however, he did know both *Heauton Timorumenos* and *Eunuchus*. On William's quotation of these plays, see Thomson, *William of Malmesbury*, 49.

59. Even this erases certain other ambiguities. The use of "modo" in the last period ("refert ille se asinum fuisse, modo hominem, omnemque casum exponit") is rather elusive. Stubbs's punctuation implies a distinction justified by a straightforward reading: the entertainer has been an ass, but is now once more a man. However, to give "modo" the meaning of "now" (as I have) is questionable. The word can have a temporal sense, but is usually accompanied by another adverb in a contrastive construction rendering something like the English "now" in "now he does one thing, now another": for example, "modo negat, modo ait" (the second "modo" could also be replaced by practically any other adverb of time, including "nunc," "interdum," "aliquando," "tum"). Nevertheless, used alone, it cannot be denied its far more usual restrictive sense of "only," giving the reading "He stated that he himself had been an ass, only a human one, and explained the whole situation."

60. The following is the definition of *medicamentum* from P. G. W. Glare's *Oxford Latin Dictionary* (Oxford: Clarendon, 1982): "1. A substance administered to produce spec. effects upon the body, medicament, drug. b (with gen.) a medicament intended to produce (a specified effect). 2. A curative medicament, remedy. b (transf.) 3. malum ~um, A harmful drug, poison; (also occ. ~um alone). 4. A cosmetic. 5. A substance used to treat plants, land, wine and other things, a preparation. 6. A dye." Glare defines the synonym *medicamen* in the same terms, except for entry 3, which he curiously omits. However, Charlton T. Lewis and Charles Short, *A Latin Dictionary* (Oxford: Clarendon, 1969) do—correctly—attest the negative implications of both words, defining *medicamen* as "[a] drug, medicament, in a good and a bad sense, meaning both a healing substance, remedy, medicine, and, as also *medicamentum* and the Gr. *pharmakon*, a poisonous drug, poison."

61. This displacement is permitted by the extraordinarily wide semantic field of *medicamentum* itself, which alongside its medicinal senses can also mean "rhetorical embellishment" (see Lewis and Short, who cite Cicero's usage), thereby already collapsing the monk's twin fields of expertise.

62. Simon catalogs his powers in *Pseudo-Clementine Recognitions* 2.9. Since many of these are reproduced by the magicians to be considered in later chapters, it is apposite to introduce them here. By his own testimony, Simon can make himself invisible to anyone who should try to seize him, and then reappear when he wishes ("possum enim facere ut volentibus me conprehendere non appaream et rursus volens videri palam sim"). If ever he needs to find a means of escape, he can burrow through mountains, passing through the rock as if it were clay ("si fugere velim montes perforem et saxa quasi lutum pertranseam"). When he leaps from a great height, he is borne unharmed to the ground ("si me de monte excelso praecipitem, tamquam subvectus ad terras inlaesus deferar"). When bound in chains, he frees himself unaided and leaves his aggressors bound in his stead ("vinctus memetipsum solvam, eos vero qui vincula iniecerint vinctos reddam"). He makes the doors of prisons open of their own accord if he is inside ("in carcere conligatus claustra sponte patefieri faciam"). He animates statues and passes them off for real people ("statuas animatas reddam, ita ut putentur ab his qui vident homines esse"). He makes new trees suddenly sprout up and immediately grow shoots ("novas arbores subito oriri faciam et repentina virgulta producam"). He throws himself into fire and does not burn ("in ignem me ipsum iniciens non ardeam"). He can change his appearance yet reveal to chosen observers that he still retains his own face ("vultum meum commuto, ut non agnoscar, sed et duas facies habere me possum hominibus ostendere"). He can create sheep and goats, make young boys grow beards, and fly through the air ("ovis aut capra efficiar, pueris parvis barbam producam, in aerem volando invehar"). He can reveal the location of fabulous quantities of gold ("aurum plurimum ostendam"). And he can make and unmake kings ("reges faciam eosdemque deiciam").

63. "Simon vehementissimus est orator, in arte dialectica et syllogismorum tendiculis enutritus, quod autem est omnibus gravius, et in arte magica valde exercitatus; et ideo metuo, ne forte tam valide ex omni parte munitus, apud eos qui ignorant eum, falsa allegans putetur vera defendere."

64. Here, as elsewhere, I use the word "travesty" in its literal sense of "dressing up" or "disguise," and I do not intend that it convey any moralizing judgment on my part (cf. "a travesty of justice").

65. Recall the example used by Peter Damian: "productoque exemplo de Simone Mago, qui Faustinianum in Simonis figura videri, et *a filiis horreri fecit*."

2. Geoffrey of Monmouth and John of Salisbury

1. The list could continue, but for the present purposes it is already long enough. For fuller discussions of *litteratura*, see Stock, *The Implications of Literacy*, 12–87, and Zumthor, *La lettre et la voix*, 299–322.

2. "An ignoras quomodo poete sine omni palliationis remedio auditoribus nudam falsitatem prostituunt, ut quadam mellite delectationis dulcedine uelut incantatas audientium aures inebrient?"

3. We note that Alain's twelfth-century lexicon already binds together the three senses that subtend the modern English and Romance derivations of the Latin verb: "to enchant," "enchanter," "incantare," and "encantar" all distantly derive from the act of singing, and all, depending on context, mean either "to delight" or "to bewitch."

4. For Alain's Latin in full, see the notes to chapter 1.

5. A case in point is William of Jumièges, who dedicated his *Gesta Normannorum ducum* to the unlettered William the Conqueror and therein pointedly cites the presence of literate advisers who will presumably help their king comprehend the work: "Vestraeque quidem majestatis latera ambiunt praeclari viri, litterarum peritia admodum eruditi, qui strictis galdiis civitatem circumeuntes, eliminatais pravorum insidiis, tectum Salomonis divinae legis pervigili munimine satagunt tueri." Text ed. J.-P. Migne as the *Historia Northmannorum,* in *Patrologiae cursus completus: Series latina,* vol. 149 (Paris: Éditions Migne, 1853), cols. 779–914; here col. 779. For further comments on the Conqueror's analphabetism, see Thompson, *The Literacy of the Laity,* 167.

6. "Henricus, junior filius Willelmi magni, natus est in Anglia anno tertio postquam pater eam adierat; infans jam tum omnium votis conspirantibus educatus egregie, quod solus omnium filiorum Willelmi natus esset regie, et ei regnum videretur competere. Itaque tirocinium rudimentorum in scholis egit litteralibus, et litterarum mella adeo avidis medullis indidit, ut nulli postea bellorum tumultus, nulli curarum motus, eas excutere illustri animo possent. Quamvis ipse nec multum palam legeret, nec nisi summisse cantitaret; fuerunt tamen, ut vere confirmo, litterae, quamvis tumultuarie libatae, magna supellex ad regnandum scientiae, juxta illiam Platonis sententiam, qua dicit 'Beatam esse rempublicam si vel philosophi regnarent, vel reges philosopharentur.'... Itaque pueritiam ad spem regni litteris muniebat; subinde, patre quoque audiente, jactitare proverbium solitus, 'Rex illiteratus, asinus coronatus.'" I have emended Stubbs's reading of the second period. He accepts the "librorum mella" of his paradigm as the direct object of "indidit." But this forces the later "eas" to refer back to "avidis medullis," the only feminine plural that antecedes. This is neither particularly satisfying nor particularly comprehensible: "no tumults in war and no upheavals in administration could banish them ['the thirsting fibers'?] from his illustrious mind." My reading, "litterarum mella" (attested by Stubbs's MSS *Aa, Aah*), provides a grammatically correct antecedent in "litterae" and makes more sense.

7. It can be noted in passing that the implicit butt of the jibe William scripts for Henry is none other than William the Conqueror, to whom, figuratively asinine attributes notwithstanding, William of Jumièges dedicated his Latin account of the Norman dukes.

8. Ovid, *Metamorphoses,* ed. Frank Justus Miller, rev. G. P. Gould, 2 vols., Loeb Classical Library (Cambridge, Mass.: Harvard University Press; London: Heinemann, 1984), vol. 2. The story of Midas is told between 11.85 and 11.193. References will be to book and line number.

9. "[I]lle male usurus donis ait 'effice, quicquid / corpore contigero, fulvum vertatur in aurum.'"

10. "'[D]a veniam, Lenaee pater! peccavimus' inquit."

11. "[V]iderat hoc famulus, qui cum nec prodere visum
dedecus auderet, cupiens efferre sub auras,
nec posset reticere tamen, secedit humumque
effodit et, domini quales adspexerit aures,
voce refert parva terraeque inmurmurat haustae
indiciumque suae vocis tellure regesta
obruit et scrobibus tacitus discedit opertis."

12. It can also be noted that, although directly derived from Augustine, William's use of the underground vault to configure a text in the anecdote of Gerbert corresponds with the Ovidian trench dug as a repository for written words. There is also perhaps an Ovidian reminiscence in William's colorful assertion that the two hags who make the young man seem an ass ingest the money they earn from their victims ("nummos inde acceptos ingurgitantes"): the metaphor reads as a variation on Midas literally discovering that the food he attempts to eat has been turned into gold.

13. For factual comments on the patronage of vernacular works in England during this era, see Jean Blacker, *The Faces of Time: Portrayal of the Past in Old French and Latin Historical Narrative of the Anglo-Norman Regnum* (Austin: University of Texas Press, 1994), 167–90.

14. "[C]reber harundinibus tremulis ibi surgere lucus
coepit et, ut primum pleno maturuit anno,
prodidit agricolam; leni nam motus ab austro
obruta verba refert dominique coarguit aures."

15. I shall return to John later in this chapter and to Gerald in chapter 5.

16. See "Literate Readings of the Romance" in the introduction.

17. Li rois mande un encanteor;
ne savoit on a icel jour
nul millor trover ne son per.
Tres bien faisoit home tranler,
de la piere faisoit fromages,
encanteres estoit molt sages.
Les bués faisoit en l'air voler
et les asnes faisoit harper. (805–12).

18. "Or escoutez, seignor marchis!
Espine, a vos, non a vasal:
Marc a orelles de cheval."
Bien ont oï le nain parler.
. . . .
Au roi dïent priveement:
"Rois, nos savon ton celement."
Li rois s'en rist et dist: "Ce mal
Que j'ai orelles de cheval,
M'est avenu par cest devin:
Certes, ja ert fait de lui fin."

(Béroul, *Le Roman de Tristan*, ed. Ernest Muret, rev. L. M. Defourques, Classiques Français du Moyen Age 12 [Paris: Champion, 1982], lines 1332–35, 1341–46.) This is evidently a transposition of Ovid's tale of Midas, and it would seem bound up with Mark's inability to "read" his wife. Sadly, the fragmented state of Béroul's text prohibits any more than this tentative suggestion.

19. For an analysis of the sociocultural criteria behind the development of such terms as these, see Zumthor, *La lettre et la voix*, 107–27.

20. See my *Historical Fabrication, Ethnic Fable, and French Romance in Twelfth-Century England* (Lexington, Ky.: French Forum, 1998), chapter 3 (on Geoffrey's use of Stonehenge as a circular symbol demarcating certain of his own contrivances) and, with relevance to later, vernacular developments, chapters 6–8 (on Benoît de Sainte-Maure's written refabrication of Troy).

21. William of Newburgh, *Historia rerum Anglicarum*, proem: "Gaufridus hic dictus est, agnomen habens Arturi, pro eo quod fabulas de Arturo, ex priscis Britonum figmentis sumptas et ex proprio auctas, per superductum Latini sermonis colorem honesto historiae nomine palliavit." The text is from the edition of Richard Howlett in *Chronicles of the Reigns of Stephen, Henry II, and Richard I*, 4 vols. (London: Her Majesty's Stationery Office, Rolls Series, 1884–89; reprint, New York: Kraus, 1964), vol. 1, 3–408, and vol. 2, 415–500.

22. I myself deal with William's ethnic bias in *Historical Fabrication*, chapter 12.

23. The bibliography on Geoffrey's fabrications is ample, but consult in particular J. S. P. Tatlock, *The Legendary History of Britain: Geoffrey of Monmouth's "Historia Regum Britanniae" and Its Early Vernacular Versions* (Berkeley and Los Angeles: University of California Press, 1950); Walter F. Schirmer, *Die frühen Darstellungen des Arthurstoffes*, Arbeitsgemeinschaft für Forschung des Landes Nordrhein-Westfalen 73 (Cologne: Westdeutscher Verlag, 1957); Robert W. Hanning, *The Vision of History in Early Britain from Gildas to Geoffrey of Monmouth* (New York: Columbia University Press, 1966), 121–76; Gransden, *Historical Writing in England, c. 550 to c. 1307*, 203; Christopher N. L. Brooke, "Geoffrey of Monmouth as a Historian," in *Church and Government in the Middle Ages: Essays Presented to C. R. Cheney on His Seventieth Birthday*, ed. Christopher N. L. Brooke, D. E. Luscombe, G. H. Martin, and Dorothy Owen (New York: Cambridge University Press, 1976), 77–91; Valerie I. J. Flint, "The *Historia regum Britanniae* of Geoffrey of Monmouth: Parody and Its Purpose. A Suggestion," *Speculum* 54 (1979): 447–68; R. William Leckie Jr., *The Passage of Dominion: Geoffrey of Monmouth and the Periodization of Insular History in the Twelfth Century* (Toronto: University of Toronto Press, 1981); and D. R. Howlett, "The Literary Context of Geoffrey of Monmouth: An Essay on the Fabrication of Sources," *Arthuriana* 5 (1995): 25–69. Also relevant are Neil Wright's comments in the front matter to his definitive edition, *The "Historia Regum Britannie" of Geoffrey of Monmouth I: Bern, Burgerbibliothek, MS. 568* (Cambridge: D. S. Brewer, 1984).

24. See in particular the studies by Brooke, Flint, and Howlett cited above.

25. "Praeterea in libro suo, quem Britonum historiam vocat, quam petulanter et quam impudenter fere per omnia mentiatur, nemo nisi veterum historiarum ignarus, cum in librum illum inciderit, ambigere sinitur. Nam qui rerum gestarum veritatem non didicit, fabularum vanitatem indiscrete admittit."

26. "Cum ergo nec tenuem de his veteres historici fecerint mentionem, liquet a mendacibus esse conficta quaecunque de Arturo atque Merlino, ad pascendam minus prudentium curiositatem, homo ille scribendo vulgavit."

27. That Geoffrey used both Henry's *Historia Anglorum* and William's *Gesta regum* as structural and thematic paradigms has been well argued by Flint, "The *Historia regum Britanniae* of Geoffrey of Monmouth: Parody and Its Purpose," passim.

28. Bäuml uses this term to designate the romance illusion of fact in "Varieties and Consequences," 255–59, particularly 256; his precedent is followed to lucid effect by Gabrielle M. Spiegel in the context of works by Wace and Benoît in *Romancing the Past: The Rise of Vernacular Prose Historiography in Thirteenth-Century France* (Berkeley and Los Angeles: University of California Press, 1993), 62. Both are ultimately inspired by Peter Haidu's "Repetition: Modern Reflections on Medieval Aesthetics," *Modern Language Notes* 92 (1977): 875–87, in which fiction is analyzed as both an affront to the more conservative tenets of medieval linguistic philosophy and a liberating movement toward new formulations of truth.

29. "Uocatus confestim Merlinus, cum in presentia regis astitisset, iussus est consilium dare quo rex desiderium suum in Ingerna expleret. Qui comperta anxietate quam rex patiebatur pro ea commotus est super tanto amore et ait: 'Ut uoto tuo potiaris utendum est tibi nouis artibus et tempore tuo inauditis. Scio medicaminibus meis dare figuram Gorlois ita ut per omnia ipse videaris. Si itaque parueris, faciam te prorsus similare eum, Ulfin uero Iordanum de Tintagol, familiarem suum. Alia autem specie sumpta adero tertius poterisque tuto adire oppidum ad Ingernam atque aditum habere.' Paruit itaque rex diligentemque animum adhibuit." The text is from Wright, *The "Historia Regum Britannie" of Geoffrey of Monmouth I: Bern, Burgerbibliothek, MS. 568,* here paragraph 137. All subsequent references will be to this edition, followed by the relevant paragraph number.

30. "[Uther] commisit se medicaminibus Merlini et in speciem Gorlois transmutatus est.... Commansit itaque rex ea nocte cum Ingerna et sese desiderata uenere refecit. Deceperat namque eam falsa specie quam assumpserat. Deceperat etiam ficticiis sermonibus quos ornate conponebat" (137).

31. Tatlock, *The Legendary History of Britain,* 47, 361.

32. The result is an early and sophisticated version of the procedure that a number of modern French critics have called *la mise en abyme,* the refraction of the text within the text that serves to clarify the primary mechanisms of composition and/or theme. On this, consult in particular Lucien Dällenbach, *Le récit spéculaire: Essai sur la mise en abyme* (Paris: Éditions du Seuil, 1977). Geoffrey's internal drama fulfills Dällenbach's functional criteria at every turn. First, the correspondence between internal and external interpretants is only partial: if the diegetic clarification were perfectly to reflect its wider object, then the text would be internally reproduced in its totality up to the point of its reproduction, at which point it would be reproduced once again, and so on indefinitely. Second, aspects of both theme (corresponding with Dällenbach's *énoncé*) and performance (Dällenbach's *énonciation*) are dramatized, sequentially in the orchestration of false appearances and in the delivery of lying yet ornate words.

33. Tatlock was the first definitively to demonstrate that Geoffrey redeployed the classical myth of Amphitryon and Alcmene in orchestrating the circumstances of Arthur's conception (see *The Legendary History of Britain,* 317). In passing, it can also be noted that by so doing Geoffrey has left the modern critic with an exemplary enigma of medieval intertextuality: although the most obvious precedent he could have employed is Plautus's *Amphitryon,* tradition would have it that this work could not have been available to him at the time. For a discussion of such problems of clear yet apparently untenable filiation (and a proposed means for their solution), see my "From Apuleius's Psyche to Chrétien's Erec and Enide," passim.

34. "[C]um a poetis deorum pluralitas sompniatur uel ipsi dii uenereis ferulis manus subduxisse dicuntur, in hiis falsitatis umbra lucescit. Nec in hoc poeta a sue proprietatis genere degener inuenitur.... Quia ergo, ut poete testati sunt, plerique homines predicamentalibus Veneris terminis ad litteram sunt abusi, narratio uero illa, que uel deos esse uel ipsos in Veneris gignasiis lasciuisse mentitur, in nimie falsitatis uesperascit occasum" (Natura to the narrator/protagonist; 837–38).

35. "Haec cum juxta historicam veritatem a venerabili Beda expositam constet esse rata, cunta quae homo ille de Arturo et ejus vel successoribus vel, post Vortigirnum, praedecessoribus scribere curavit, partim ab ipso, partim et ab aliis, constat esse conficta.... Denique Vortigirno facit succedere Aurelium Ambrosium.... illique dat successorem Utherpendragon fratrem ejus... plura de Merlino suo profusa mentiendi libertate interserens. Defuncto quoque Utherpendragon facit succedere Arturum filium in regno Britanniae, a Vortigirno quartum; sicut noster Beda ponit Ethelbertum, Augustini susceptorem, in regno Anglorum ab Hengisto quartum. Itaque regnum Arturi et ingressus in Britanniam Augustini concurrere debuerunt. Sed quantum mera historiae veritas hoc loco compositae praejudicet falsitati, vel lippienti mentis acie clare videri potest."

36. To cite William of Newburgh: "Quomodo enim historiographi veteres, quibus ingenti curae fuit nihil memorabile scribendo omittere, qui etiam mediocria memoriae mandasse noscuntur, virum incomparabilem, ejusque acta supra modum insignia, silentio praeterire potuerunt? Quomodo, inquam, vel nobiliorem Alexandro Magno Britonum monarcham Arturum, ejusque acta, vel parem nostro Esaiae Britonum prophetam Merlinum, ejusque dicta, silentio suppresserunt?" (*Historia rerum Anglicarum,* proem).

37. Cf. Jauss: "The new text evokes for the reader (listener) the horizon of expectations and rules familiar from earlier texts, which are then varied, corrected, altered, or even just reproduced" (23).

38. For all of these meanings of *medicamen/medicamentum,* see the notes to chapter 1.

39. See, again, William of Newburgh: "Et hunc quidem Merlinum patre incubo daemone ex femina natum fabulatur, cui propterea tanquam patrissanti excellentissimam atque latissimam tribuit praescientiam futurorum; cum profecto et veris rationibus et sacris literis doceamur daemones, a luce Dei seclusos, futura nequaquam contemplando praescire: sed quosdam futuros eventus ex signis sibi quam nobis notioribus, conjiciendo magis quam cognoscendo colligere.... Quid enim minus in praescientia duntaxat futurorum tribuit suo Merlino quam nos nostro Esaiae: nisi quod ejus vaticiniis non audet inserere 'Haec dicit Dominus,' et erubuit inserere 'Haec dicit diabolus,' quippe hoc debuit congruere vati incubi daemonis filio" (*Historia rerum Anglicarum,* proem).

40. "Nam et artes perierant, evanuerant jura, fidei et totius religionis officia quaeque corruerant, ipseque recti defecerat usus eloquii, nisi in remedium infirmitatibus humanae litterarum usum mortalibus divina miseratio procurasset"; "Exempla majorum, quae sunt incitamenta et fomenta virtutis, nullum omnino corrigerent aut servarent nisi pia sollicitudo scriptorum et triumphatrix inertiae diligentia eadem ad posteros transmisisset"; "Quis enim Alexandros sciret aut Caesares, quis Stoicos aut Peripateticos miraretur, nisi eos insignirent monumenta scriptorum? Quis apostolorum et prophetarum amplexanda imitaretur vestigia nisi eos posteritati divinae litterae consecrassent?"; "Nihil ergo consiliosius est captatoribus gloriae quam litteratorum et scribentium maxime gratiam promereri. Inutiliter enim eis geruntur egregia, perpetuis tenebris obducenda, nisi litterarum luce clarescant"; "Nam a vitiis redimitur animus et suavi et mira quadam etiam in adversis jucunditate reficitur, cum ad legendum vel scribendum utilia mentis intendit acumen. Nullam in rebus humanis jucundiorem aut utiliorem occupationem invenies, nisi forte divinitus compuncta devotio" (prologue to book 1; 385–86).

41. For biographical details, see the front matter of Cary J. Nederman's *"Policraticus": Of the Frivolities of Courtiers and the Footprints of Philosophers* (Cambridge: Cambridge University Press, 1990), which is a translation of chapters 1–3 of book 1 and most of books 3–8. On John's political thought, see Richard H. Rouse and Mary H. Rouse, "John of Salisbury and the Doctrine of Tyrannicide," *Speculum* 42 (1967): 693–709; Hans Leibeschütz, *Medieval Humanism in the Life and Writings of John of Salisbury* (Nendeln: Kraus, 1968); Cary J. Nederman and J. Brückmann, "Aristotelianism in John of Salisbury's *Policraticus*," *Journal of the History of Philosophy* 21 (1983): 203–29; and two articles by Nederman, "The Aristotelian Doctrine of the Mean and John of Salisbury's Concept of Liberty," *Vivarium* 24 (1986): 128–42, and "A Duty to Kill: John of Salisbury's Theory of Tyrannicide," *Review of Politics* 50 (1988): 365–89. Also relevant is R. W. Southern's discussion of English twelfth-century philosophical and political theorists in *Medieval Humanism and Other Studies* (Oxford: Blackwell, 1970), 151–80.

42. "Postquam autem sederit in solio regni sui describet sibi Deuteronomium legis hujus in volumine, accipiens exemplar a sacerdotibus Leviticae tribus, et habebit secum legetque illud omnibus diebus vitae suae, ut discat timere Dominum Deum suum et custodire verba et caeremonias ejus, quae in lege praecepta sunt." John is here quoting Deuteronomy 17.

43. "Ex quibus liquido constat quam necessaria sit principibus peritia litterarum qui legem Domini quotidie revolvere lectione jubentur. . . . Hoc utique sine difficultate illitteratus non faciet. Unde et in litteris, quas regem Romanorum ad Francorum regem transmisisse recolo, quibus hortabatur ut liberos suos liberalibus disciplinis institui procuraret, hoc inter caetera eleganter adjecit, quia rex illitteratus est quasi asinus coronatus."

44. "Si tamen, ex dispensatione ob egregiae virtutis meritum, principem contingat esse illitteratum [an extraordinarily generous excuse], eumdem agi litteratorum consiliis, ut ei res recte procedat, necesse est. Assistant ergo ei Nathan propheta et Sadoc sacerdos et fideles filii prophetarum qui cum a lege Domini divertere non patiantur, et, quam ipsa oculis et animo non ostendit linguis suis introducant quasi quodam aurium ostio litterati."

45. I shall return to these points (and nuance them) in chapters 3 and 5.

46. "Nunc vero nobilium in eo sapientia declaratur si venaticam noverint, si in alea damnabilius fuerint instituti, si naturae robur effeminatae vocis articulis fregerint, et modis et musicis instrumentis, virtutis immemores obliviscantur quod nati sunt. Verum a parentibus haec pernicies manat ad liberos. Quid enim faciet filius nisi quod patrem viderit facientem?"

47. John's misogyny is, of course, classic of the era, as indeed is his other favored topos of opprobrium, the homophobic charge of homoeroticism that for him, as for many other authors, follows on from his own perverse accusations of the feminine male. On medieval misogyny in general, see R. Howard Bloch, *Medieval Misogyny and the Invention of Western Romantic Love* (Chicago: University of Chicago Press, 1991); for a full discussion of John's use of effeminacy as a device of censure, see Cary J. Nederman and N. E. Lawson, "The Frivolities of Courtiers Follow the Footprints of Women: Historical Women and the Crisis of Virility in John of Salisbury," in *Ambiguous Realities: Medieval and Renaissance Women*, ed. J. Watson and C. Levin (Detroit: Wayne State University Press, 1987), 82–96.

48. "Philosophi gentium justitiam quae politica dicitur praeceptis et moribus informantes, cujus merito respublica hominum subsistit et viget, unumquemque suis rebus et studiis voluerunt esse contentum, urbanis et suburbanis, colonis quoque vel rusticis, sua singulis loca et studia praescribentes. Sollicitudo singulorum et omnium utilitati publicae serviebat" (1.3; 390).

49. "Quae vero naturae sunt peraeque sunt omnium; quae officii sua sunt singulorum. Aliud itaque ex officio, aliud ex natura, licet naturae vis ex officio debeatur" (1.2; 389).

50. "Parricidii siquidem species est impugnare jura naturae, et sacrilegii instar parentis leges evacuare et matri omnium honorem debitum non referre" (1.2; 389–90).

51. "Et primi quidem Thebani, si fidem sequamur historiae, eam communicandam omnibus statuerunt. Ex quo suspecta sit omnibus gens foeda parricidiis, incestibus detestanda, insignis fraude, nota perjuriis, hujus artificii, vel potius malificii, in primis praecepta congessit" (1.4; 390).

52. "Quae postmodum ad gentem mollem imbellemque, levem et impudicam—Phrygios loquor—tansmitteret" (1.4; 390).

53. "In auras itaque raptum tradunt [Graeci] ab aquila Dardanium venatorem ad pocula, a quibus a[d] illicitos et innaturales transiret amplexus. Eleganter utique cum et levitas ferri possit ab alite et voluptas sobrietatis ignara cujuscunque libidine prostitui non erubescit." I have here emended the printed text, the second clause of which reads "a quibus *ab* illicitos et innaturales transiret amplexus," which makes no sense and seems to be a typesetting error.

54. "Non illam dico quam parit pax, patientia, benignitas, longanimitas, gaudium in Spiritu sancto, sed quae amica epulis, potationibus, conviviis, modulationibus et ludis, cultibus operosius exquisitis, stupris et variis immunditiis, animos etiam graviores effeminat et quodam naturae ludibrio molliores et corruptiores facit esse viros quam feminas."

55. "Naturae robur effeminatae vocis articulis freg[unt]" (1.5; 400); "Nascuntur ergo majoribus haeredes quidem degeneres et qui virilem sexum muliebri mollitie dehonestant" (ibid.); "Ante conspectum Domini, in ipsis penetralibus sanctuarii, lascivientis vocis luxu quadam ostentatione sui muliebribus modis notularum articulorumque caesuris stupentes animulas emollire nituntur" (1.6; 402).

56. *Specularii:* "Specularios vocant qui in corporibus levigatis et tersis, ut sunt lucidi enses, pelves, cyathi, speculorumque diversa genera divinantes, curiosis consultationibus satisfaciunt" (1.12; 408); *mathematici, genethliaci,* and *horoscopi:* "Mathematici sunt, licet appellatio generaliter omnia complectatur, qui a positione stellarum, situque firmamenti, et planetarum motu, quae sint ventura conjiciunt. . . . Quorum et genethliaci, qui geneses, id est natalitias horas attendunt, imitantur errorem. . . . Iidem vero horoscopi nominantur" (ibid.); *chiromantici:* "Chiromantici sunt qui a manuum inspectione rerum vaticinantur abscondita" (ibid.); *conjectores:* "Conjectores sunt qui artificio quodam sibi vindicant somniorum interpretationem" (ibid.); *augures:* "Augurium vero quod est in avium observatione" (1.12; 409); *aruspices,* who also make predictions based on the hours: "Aruspices sunt inspectores horarum, praescribentes quid qua hora fieri expediat. . . . Aruspicium quoque in extorum inspectione viget" (1.12; 407); *salissatores:* "Salissatores qui ex saltu membrorum aut inopinato corporis motu prosperum aliquid futurum autumant, vel adversum" (1.12; 409).

57. "Vultivoli sunt qui ad affectus hominum immutandos in molliori materia—cera forte vel limo—eorum quos pervertere nituntur effigies exprimunt" (1.12; 408); "Imaginarii sunt qui imagines quas faciunt quasi in possessionem praesidentium spirituum mittunt ut ab eis de rebus dubiis doceantur" (ibid.); "Arioli [sunt] qui circa aras nefandas preces aut exsecrata sacrificia faciunt" (1.12; 407); "sortilegi sunt qui, sub nomine fictae religionis superstitiosa quadam observatione, rerum pollicentur eventus" (1.12; 409); "Pythii sunt quos spiritus Pythonicus replet, et frequentius in virginibus exercetur ut magis ludificet; ac, si immundissimo spiritui placeat, integritas mentis ac corporis" (1.12; 408); "necromanti[a] inde dicitur, quod tota in mortuorum inquisitione versatur. Cujusvis ea esse videatur, ut, ad interpretationem veri, mortuos valeat suscitare" (ibid.).

58. *Somnia:* "Somnium vero cujus appellatio communis est, licet in specie propria censeatur, per quaedam involucra rerum gerit imagines, in quibus conjectorum praecipue disciplina versatur" (2.15; 429); *visiones:* "Porro visionum alia manifestior est ut quae clara rei occurrit imagine, alia profundiorem desiderat intellectum, ut cum rem admista species figurarum obnubilat" (2.15; 430); *oracula:* "Cum vero res per quietem alio nuntiante clarescit, si tamen enuntiantis honesta cuique persona sit et venerabilis, in oraculorum speciem cadit. Est enim oraculum, ut ait quidam, divina voluntas ore hominis enuntiata" (2.15; 431).

59. "Multifarie siquidem multisque modis suam Deus instruit creaturam, et nunc elementorum vocibus, nunc sensibilium aut insensibilium rerum indiciis, prout electis noverit expedire, quae ventura sunt manifestat" (2.2; 416–17).

60. "Utraque autem, modo ex elementis dispositione Creatoris, modo ex natura rerum, modo ex malitia daemonum homines Domino permittente ludificantium, provenire dicuntur. Sed quae, et quomodo, quave de causa, judicium quidem difficile est, et frequenter incertum et saepe altius quam ut ab homine valeat expediri" (2.3; 418).

61. "Et licet quandoque, quae honesta vel recta sunt, ut se in loco mundo velle servari, vel solum Deum, quando aliquid quaeritur precibus et muneribus invocandum praecipiat, maligni tamen spiritus hanc esse fallaciam certissimum est, qui, ut minus caveatur, innocentiae vel justitiae praecepta plerumque videtur afferre" (2.19; 442–43; here in the context of astrology).

62. "Caeterum quod simpliciorum animos movet, scilicet per hujusmodi consultationem abscondita futurorum manifestari, non posse nisi per manum ejus in cujus potestate sunt tempora et momenta, nodum non ingerit quaestionis. Licet enim futurorum sit unus arbiter, qui et Deus et Dominus omnium est, tamen ex signis interdum hominibus innotescunt" (2.28; 473).

63. "Manet itaque usquequaque immobilis integritas scientiae Dei, et si quid varietatis alicui inest, non tam scientis quam scitorum mutabilitas est. Licet enim quae scientia Dei complectitur mutabilitati subjaceant, ipsa tamen alterationis vices ignorat et, uno singulari aspectu et individuo, omnium quae dici aut quocunque sensu excogitari possunt universitatem claudit et continet" (2.21; 445).

64. "Multifarie siquidem multisque modis suam Deus instruit creaturam, et nunc elementorum vocibus, nunc sensibilium aut insensibilium rerum indiciis, prout electis noverit expedire, quae ventura sunt manifestat" (2.2; 416–17). John further elaborates at a later stage: "Hic vero intelliguntur signa quaecunque quovis indicio divinam homini innuunt voluntatem. Signum siquidem est quod se ipsum sensui et praeter se aliquid animo ostendit" (2.14; 428).

65. "Futuras itaque tempestates aut serenitates signa quaedam antecedentia praeloquuntur, ut homo qui ad laborem natus est ex his possit sua exercitia temperare. Hinc agricolae, hinc nautae familiaribus quibusdam experimentis quid quo tempore geri oporteat colligunt, qualitatem temporis futuri ex eo quod praeteriit medientes" (2.2; 417).

66. "Futuram etiam sanitatem, aut aegritudinem, aut statum quem dicunt neutralitatem, fatalitatem quoque ipsam, ex praecedentibus signis agnoscunt, et interdum, si causas noverint, efficacissime curant" (2.2; 417).

67. "Omnis etenim regula alicui generi rerum accommodata est. Si vero traducatur ad aliud, statim in veritatem impingit obnoxiam falsitati. Si ergo mathematici probabilis matheseos, id est doctrinalis essent fine contenti, et veram possent assequi positionem stellarum et ex signis suis sobria eruditione secundum quod naturaliter proveniunt qualitatem praescire temporum et speculationis suae jucundissimum carpere fructum. Cum vero dilatant phylacteria sua et magnificant fimbrias, dum constellationibus et planetis nimium virtutis ascribunt, eis nescio quam auctoritatem operum ascribentes, in Creatoris prorumpunt injuriam; et dum coelestia quae tractant ad sobrietatem non sapiunt, juxta Apostolum stulti sunt. Vide in quantum erroris abyssum, ab ipsis coelestibus cadant. Constellationibus suis ascribunt omnia. Tu videris an fiat ei injuria, qui fecit coelum et terram et omnia quae in eis sunt. Deinde eam constellatio rebus necessitatem indicit, ut arbitrii perimat libertatem" (2.19; 442). So also John's definition of *mathematici:* "Ac si stellarum choreas applicationesque unius ad alteram constet rebus quae ex arbitri libertate proveniunt quamdam necessitatis praestare originem, quorum et genethliaci, qui geneses, id est natalitias horas attendunt, imitantur errorem" (1.12; 408). For John's complex reconciliation of free will and Providence, see 2.21 (444), the preoccupations of which are summarized in its chapter heading, "An possint a Deo sciri quae non sciuntur; et quod rerum mutabilitas ei nequaquam est infligenda; et quod idem est scientia, praescientia, dispositio, providentia et praedestinatio; et quod vera infinita sunt, ut numerus eorum non queat augeri vel minui; et quod providentia nullam necessitatem rebus inducit."

68. "[M]endacii pater... cum his notis resperserit creaturam ipsum creaturae sic infam[at] auctorem. Postremo animulas miserorum fraude deceptas inevitabilium vaticinio futurorum in elationis tumorem suspendere, vel desperationis abyssum praecipitare dementia est."

69. "Quod vel ex eo patet quod mulierculis et viris simplicioribus et infirmioribus in fide ista proveniunt."

70. "Et nunc quidem res ut sunt, nunc aliter intuetur, nunc simpliciter, nunc composite, nunc distincta conjungit, nunc conjuncta distrahit, et disjungit" (2.18; 437).

71. "Disjuncta conjungit ut si 'humano capiti cervicem jungat equinam . . . varias inducens undique plumas,' ut juxta poetam 'turpiter atrum desinat in piscem mulier formosa superne'" (2.18; 437).

72. Today's canonical reading somewhat differs from the version John reproduces. Compare lines 1–4 in the edition of H. Rushton Fairclough in *Horace: Satires, Epistles, and Ars Poetica* (Cambridge, Mass.: Harvard University Press; London, Heinemann, 1978).

73. "Hunc vero ad auditores suos verbo trajiciunt poetae, cum hircocervum, centaurum describunt, et chimaeram."

74. "Porro cum res aliter quam sint, componendo inspicit, eo quod cassus est, et a rerum veritate deficiens."

75. For the Latin, see the notes to chapter 1.

76. "Sed licit aliter quam sint, dum tamen simpliciter conjuncta disjungat, non inanis erit conceptio, quae totius investigationis sapientiae expeditissimam parit viam. Hic est enim totius philosophiae instrumentum, quod et mentem mira subtilitate exacuit, et res singulas a se invicem naturae suae proprietate distinguit. Si abstrahentem tuleris intellectum, liberalium artium officina peribit, cum citra ipsius operam nulla earum rite haberi valeat aut doceri. Hic itaque sicut formam sine materia, sic et materiam aggreditur sine forma; et quod propriae virtutis potentia tenere non sufficit, suo quodam defectu interdum comprehendit, ut si videantur tenebrae non videndo et non audiendo silentium audiatur."

77. "At nostra aetas prolapsa ad fabulas, et quaevis inania, non modo aures et cor prostituit vanitati, sed oculorum et aurium voluptate, suam mulcet desidiam, luxuriam ascendit, conquirens undique fomenta vitiroum. Nonne piger desidiam instruit, et somnos provocat instrumentorum suavitate, aut vocum modulis, hilaritate canentium, aut fabulantium gratia, sive quod turpius est ebrietate vel crapula?"

78. There is in fact some possibility that the *histriones* and *mimi* John lambastes include storytellers themselves in their number and that they are therefore the equivalent of the vernacular *jongleur.* As Duggan argues in "Performance and Transmission," 50, the art of the *jongleur* accommodated gestural mime and freedoms of bodily movement, and, I would add, these could certainly have scandalized morally conservative thinkers such as John. On the general opprobrium attached to such vocal/gestural performers in the period leading to the twelfth century, consult J. D. A. Ogilvy, "*Mimi, Scurrae, Histriones:* Entertainers of the Early Middle Ages," *Speculum* 38 (1963): 608–19.

3. Benoît de Sainte-Maure

1. I shall consider the more hyperbolic of these accounts in chapter 5.

2. On such representatives of the nobility, including even minor knights, Clanchy remarks: "By 1200, and certainly by 1300, they had usually learned enough Latin to cope with the documents which came their way. But this restricted knowledge of literacy was a pragmatic, rather than a positive contribution to their intellectual education. A little Latin, learned from a relatively ignorant priest, did not educate a man in the culture of imperial or Christian Rome, and hence it did not make him a *litteratus* in the traditional sense" (*From Memory to Written Record,* 250–51).

3. Salemon nos enseigne e dit,
E sil list om en son escrit,
Que nus ne deit son sen celer,
Ainz le deit om si demostrer
Que l'om i ait pro e honor,
Qu'ensi firent li ancessor.
Se cil qui troverent les parz
E les granz livres des set arz,
Des philosophes les traitiez,
Dont toz li monz est enseigniez,
Se fussent teü, veirement
Vesquist li siegles folement:
Come bestes eüssons vie. (1–13)

4. MSS *M2* (late 12th cent.) and *N* (early 13th cent.). Here, as in all subsequent cases, I follow Constans, *Le Roman de Troie* (vol. 1, 1–66), for sigla and dating.

5. This version appears in the reproduction of MS *K* (mid–13th cent.) that Aristide Joly published some thirty years before Constans's edition in *Benoît de Sainte-More et le "Roman de Troie" ou Les métamorphoses d'Homère et de l'épopée gréco-latine en France au Moyen Age* (Paris: Franck, 1870). MS *B* (late 13th cent.) also has the reading "cil qui entendent la letre"; *C* has "antendra."

6. For a general description of the progressive increase of literacy during this period, see Harvey J. Graff, *The Legacies of Literacy* (Bloomington: Indiana University Press, 1987), 62–74.

7. As Clanchy observes: "Elementary instruction in reading and writing started from Latin because that was the traditional language of literacy and sacred Scripture. Those who wrote in the vernaculars, whether in Middle English or French, were building novel and complex structures on a foundation of Latin. Neither Middle English nor French was sufficiently standardized, or well enough established as a literary language, to become the basis of elementary instruction in reading and writing until well after 1300. If a person in Edward I's reign or earlier had learned to read in English or French but not in Latin, he could never have become *litteratus,* nor could he have understood the majority of writings circulating in his own lifetime because they were in Latin. English and French had to have become common business and literary languages before it was practical and desirable to initiate literate skills with them" (*From Memory to Written Record,* 233–34). On the primacy of Latin as a graphemic code see also Grundmann, "Litteratus—illitteratus," 1–15; Bäuml, "Varieties and Consequences," 240–41; Stock, *The Implications of Literacy,* 6, 26–27; and Zumthor, *La lettre et la voix,* 132–34.

8. The following studies broach *Troie* in terms of translation, but they lay only a cursory emphasis on Benoît's Latin paradigms, and, as studies of adaptation rather than intelligibility, they address neither the contrivance of history nor the magical prerogatives

that will be central to my concerns: Aimé Petit, *Naissances du roman. Les techniques littéraires dans les romans antiques du XIIe siècle*, 2 vols. (Paris: Champion; Geneva: Slatkine, 1985–86); Penny Sullivan, "Translation and Adaptation in the *Roman de Troie*," in *The Spirit of the Court: Selected Proceedings from the Fourth Congress of the International Courtly Literature Society* (Toronto 1983), ed. Glyn S. Burgess, Robert A. Taylor, Alan Deyermond, Dennis Green, and Beryl Rowland (Cambridge: D. S. Brewer, 1985), 350–59; Emmanuèle Baumgartner, "Vocabulaire de la technique littéraire dans le *Roman de Troie* de Benoît de Sainte-Maure," *Cahiers de lexicologie* 51 (1987): 39–48; Barbara Nolan, *Chaucer and the Tradition of the "Roman Antique"* (Cambridge: Cambridge University Press, 1992), 14–47.

9. "Ephemeridem belli Troiani Dictys Cretensis, qui in ea militia cum Idomeneo meruit, primo conscripsit litteris Punicis, quae tum Cadmo et Agenore auctoribus per Graeciam frequentabantur" (*Ephemeridos belli Troiani libri a Lucio Septimio ex Graeco in Latinum sermonem translati*, ed. Werner Eisenhut [Leipzig: Teubner, 1973]; prefatory epistle of Lucius Septimius to Q. Aradius Rufinus).

10. "[D]einde post multa saecula collapso per vetustatem apud Gnosum, olim Cretensis regis sedem, sepulchro eius, pastores cum eo devenissent, forte inter ceteram ruinam loculum stagno affabre clausum offendere ac thesaurum rati mox dissolvunt. [N]on aurum neque aliud quicquam praedae, sed libros ex philyra in lucem prodierunt. [A]t ubi spes frustrata est, ad Praxim dominum loci eos deferunt, qui, commutatos litteris Atticis, nam oratio Graeca fuerat, Neroni Romano Caesari obtulit, pro quo plurimis ab eo donatus est."

11. "[Gyges], cum terra discessisset magnis quibusdam imbribus, descendit in illum hiatum aëneumque equum, ut ferunt fabulae, animadvertit, cuius in lateribus fores essent; quibus apertis corpus hominis mortui vidit magnitudine invisitata anulumque aureum in digito; quem ut detraxit, ipse induit (erat autem regius pastor), tum in concilium se pastorum recepit. Ibi cum palam eius anuli ad palmam converterat, a nullo videbatur, ipse autem omnia videbat; idem rursus videbatur, cum in locum anulum inverterat. Itaque hac opportunitate anuli usus reginae stuprum intulit eaque adiutrice regem dominum interemit, sustulit, quos obstare arbitrabatur, nec in his eum facinoribus quisquam potuit videre. Sic repente anuli beneficio rex exortus est Lydiae." The text is from the edition of Cicero's *De officiis* by Walter Miller, Loeb Classical Library (Cambridge, Mass.: Harvard University Press; London: Heinemann, 1975); here 3.9.

12. The significance of Gyges in the works of Herodotus, Plato, and, to a lesser extent, Cicero has already been examined by Marc Shell in *The Economy of Literature* (Baltimore, Md.: Johns Hopkins University Press, 1978). Shell provides further analyses of this topic in his later *Money, Language, and Thought: Literary and Philosophic Economies from the Medieval to the Modern Era* (Berkeley and Los Angeles: University of California Press, 1982), but without an emphasis on Gyges. For discussions of verbal semiology and financial transaction in a medieval context, see R. A. Shoaf, *Dante, Chaucer, and the Currency of the Word: Money, Images, and Reference in Late Medieval Poetry* (Norman, Okla.: Pilgrim, 1983), and, in more general terms, R. Howard Bloch, *Etymologies and Genealogies: A Literary Anthropology of the French Middle Ages* (Chicago: University of Chicago Press, 1983), particularly chapter 5, "The Economics of Romance." A thoroughly convincing study of the myth of Gyges in its relationship to a specific medieval text is Eugene Vance's "Chrétien's *Yvain* and the Ideologies of Change and Exchange," which appears as chapter 5 of *Mervelous*

Signals: Poetics and Sign Theory in the Middle Ages (Lincoln: University of Nebraska Press, 1986). I differ from Vance by approaching invisibility as a trope first and foremost for the manipulation of knowledge and understanding, and by making finance a secondary, dependent issue.

13. "[S]i nemo sciturus, nemo ne suspicaturus quidem sit, cum aliquid divitiarum, potentiae, dominationis, libidinis causa feceris, si id dis hominibusque futurum sit semper ignotum, sisne facturus?"

14. "[Q]uoniam iuris natura fons sit, hoc secundum naturam esse, neminem id agere ut ex alterius praedetur inscitia."

15. "Omnes enim trahimur et ducimur ad cognitionis et scientiae cupiditatem, in qua excellere pulchrum putamus, labi autem, errare, nescire, decipi et malum et turpe ducimus. In hoc genere et naturali et honesto duo vitia vitanda sunt, unum, ne incognita pro cognitis habeamus iisque temere assentiamur; quod vitium effugere qui volet (omnes autem velle debent), adhibebit ad considerandas res et tempus et diligentiam."

16. "Ubi enim iudicium emptoris est, ibi fraus venditoris quae potest esse?"

17. Edward Champlin has recently argued that the Latin translator Septimius is to be identified as Serenus Sammonicus, who flourished during the reign of Septimius Severus and was the renowned (if eccentric) author of a treatise on the sturgeon with scales that grow backward. If Champlin is right, then the translation dates not from the fourth century A.D. (as, for example, Eisenhut maintains in his edition of the *Ephemeris* [viii]), but from the late second or the early third century. See "Serenus Sammonicus," *Harvard Studies in Classical Philology* 85 (1981): 189–212.

18. For information on the two manuscript filiations, see Eisenhut's introduction to his edition of the *Ephemeris*, xi–xlvii.

19. "[C]ontinuoque ad suum dominum, Eupraxidem quendam nomine, pertulerunt. [Q]ui agnitas, quaenam essent, litteras Rutilio Rufo, illius insulae tunc consulari, obtulit. [I]lle cum ipso Eupraxide ad Neronem oblata sibi transmisit existimans quaedam in his secretiora contineri. [H]aec igitur cum Nero accepisset, advertissetque Punicas esse litteras, harum peritos ad se evocavit. [Q]ui cum venissent, interpretati sunt omnia. [C]umque Nero cognosset antiqui viri, qui apud Ilium fuerat, haec esse monumenta, iussit in Graecum sermonem ista transferri, e quibus Troiani belli verior textus cunctis innotuit. [T]unc Eupraxidem muneribus et Romana civitate donatum ad propria remisit. annales vero nomine Dictys inscriptos in Graecam bibliothecam recepit."

20. On Henry's expansionsist policies, see W. L. Warren, *Henry II* (Berkeley and Los Angeles: University of California Press, 1973), particularly 53–237.

21. Illic praecipiti Nero fulmine concutit orbem,
Indulgens sceleri, cogit plus velle furorem
Quam furor ipse velit; quicquid distillat ab illo
Nequitiae, totum sese partitur in orbem.

(Alain de Lille, *Anticlaudianus* 1.5; ed. Thomas Wright in vol. 2 of *Anglo-Latin Satirical Poets and Epigrammatists of the Twelfth Century* [London: Her Majesty's Stationery Office, Rolls Series, 1872; reprint, New York: Kraus, 1964], 279.)

22. Illic pannoso plebescit carmine noster
Ennius, et Priami fortunas intonat; illic

Maevius in coelos audens os ponere mutum,
Gesta ducis Macedum tenebrosi carminis umbra
Pingere dum temptat, in primo limine fessus
Haeret, et ignavam queritur torpescere musam. (1.5)

For the identification of Nero with Henry II consult M. Hutchings, "L'*Anticlaudianus* d'Alain de Lille: Étude de chronologie," *Romania* 50 (1924): 1–13. James J. Sheridan suggests probable candidates for Alain's incompetent scriveners in *Alain de Lille: "Anticlaudianus"; or, The Good and Perfect Man* (Toronto: Pontifical Institute of Mediaeval Studies, 1973), 51, nn. 32, 34.

23. For factual arguments demonstrating Henry's patronage of letters, see Diana B. Tyson, "Patronage of French Vernacular History Writers in the Twelfth and Thirteenth Centuries," *Romania* 100 (1979): 180–222; Jean-Guy Gouttebroze, "Henry II Plantagenêt, patron des historiographes anglo-normands de langue d'oïl," in *La littérature angevine médiévale: Actes du Colloque du semedi 22 mars*, ed. Georges Cesbron (Maulévrier: Hérault, 1981), 91–105. The canonical work, however, is Ulrich Broich's "Heinrich II. als Patron der Literatur seiner Zeit," in *Studien zum literarischen Patronat im England des 12. Jahrhunderts* (Cologne: Westdeutscher Verlag, 1962), 27–203; it is preceded by a short essay by Walter F. Schirmer, "Die kulturelle Rolle des englischen Hofes im 12. Jahrhundert" (9–23), which also considers the Norman kings and Henry's Angevin successors. These last two studies are extremely informative in historical matters. Neither is interpretative.

24. Rollo, *Historical Fabrication*, chapters 6–8.

25. They are, once again "trei sage engeigneor" (16650), "trei sage devin" (16729), and "trei poëte, sages dotors, / qui mout sorent de nigromance" (14668–69).

26. The numerology of Mercury under his various guises was passed on to the Middle Ages primarily through Martianus Capella's *De nuptiis Mercurii et Philologiae*, particularly 2:102–5, ed. Adolf Dick, rev. Jean Préaux (Stuttgart: Teubner, 1969). For an analysis of the traditions in which Martianus was working, see William Harris Stahl, Richard Johnson, and E. L. Burge, *Martianus Capella and the Seven Liberal Arts*, 2 vols. (New York: Columbia University Press, 1971 and 1977), vol. 1, 35–37.

27. The following is the relevant part of "Cornelius's" epistolary preface to the *De excidio*: "Cum multa ago Athenis curiose, inveni historiam Daretis Phrygii ipsius manu scriptam, ut titulus indicat, quam de Graecis et Troianis memoriae mandavit. [Q]uam ego summo amore conplexus continuo transtuli. [C]ui nihil adiciendum vel diminuendum rei reformandae causa putavi, alioquin mea posset videri. [O]ptimum ergo duxi ita ut fuit vere et simpliciter perscripta, sic eam ad verbum in latinitatem transvertere, ut legentes cognoscere possent, quomodo res gestae essent: utrum verum magis esse existiment, quod Dares Phrygius memoriae commendavit, qui per id ipsum tempus vixit et militavit, cum Graeci Troianos obpugnarent, anne Homero credendum, qui post multos annos natus est, quam bellum hoc gestum est. [D]e qua re Athenis iudicium fuit, cum pro insano haberetur, quod deos cum hominibus belligerasse scripserit." The text is from the edition of Ferdinand Meister, *Daretis Phrygii de excidio Troiae historia* (Leipzig: Teubner, 1873). It will be noted that no mention is made of a quest for grammar books in a small library.

28. Chrétien de Troyes, *Erec et Enide*, ed. Mario Roques, Classiques Français du Moyen Age 80 (Paris: Champion, 1981), lines 13–14.

29. We could push these ambiguities still further. For what it is worth, *aumaire*, that place of the written word, anaphonically echoes and thematically glosses the already forcefully determined presence of *Omers* (oblique case *Omer*), whom Benoît has already by this stage of the prologue identified as the primary historian of the distant past (lines 45–55). In this case, Benoît may be implying that Cornelius actually composed the book of Dares after careful perusal of Homer's work. Whether this argument stands depends on three debatable points: first, to adduce paronomasia in a language that has since vocalically altered is a rickety enterprise; second, and dismissing the previous point in order to posit an accurate reconstruction of the twelfth-century phoneme, *aumaire* and *omer* are only approximate homophones, the first distinguished by its initial diphthong ("au" ≠ "o"), its vocalized final vowel ("e"), and, perhaps also, by the vocalic length of its second syllable ("-mai-" > "-mer"); third, the pun requires a certain amount of grammatical scrambling to be comprehensible. It is quite possible in twelfth-century French to speak of the author in place of his text: alongside the logical "trover el livre" (10556, for example) and "trover en l'estoire" (2860), Benoît's usage also accommodates "trover en l'autor" (914) and even "trover lisant en Daire" (26246). This construction, however, does not directly correspond to "querre [and subsequently 'trover'] en un aumaire," which includes an indefinite article. If the pun is accepted, nonetheless, this only approximate grammar would not necessarily vitiate the phonic reminiscence it conveys. The onomastic function of *aumaire* has after all been meticulously prepared. Homer's name has already been made textually present in the immediately preceding passage and, under the circumstances of oral performance or vocalized individual reading, its resonance would still be perceptible at a distance of only seventeen lines. But, however all this may be, phonic allusion to Homer is not a prerequisite to unraveling the other equivocations of the passage: whatever *aumaire* is intended to convey, Benoît still suggests that Cornelius is extracting writing from writing.

30. The *De officiis* was certainly known in England during the twelfth century. A copy still survives that was transcribed under the personal supervision of William of Malmesbury and bears corrections and annotations in William's own hand. It is found in Bodleian Library MS Rawlinson G. 139, which also contains Cicero's *Partitiones oratoriae*, the *Declamationes maiores XIX* of the pseudo-Quintilian, and a florilegium of the *Noctes Atticae* of Aulus Gellius. It is written in the hands of seven different scribes; William's own marginal and interlinear notes and corrections run as far as f. 137v. For further information on the manuscript, see Thomson, *William of Malmesbury*, 53, 86–87. William also demonstrates his knowledge of Cicero's treatise by quoting it several times over in the *Gesta regum:* "ut nunquam minus solus esset quam cum solus esset" (1:60; on Bede), corresponding to *De officiis* 3.1, "nec minus solum quam cum solus esset" (on Cato); "quid vero est stultius quam quod libenter facias curare ne diutius facere possis?" (4:313; on William Rufus's unwise prodigality), cf. *De officiis* 2.15, "quid autem est stultius quam quod libenter facias curare ut id diutius facere non possis?"; "Si violandum est jus, gratia civium violandum est; aliis rebus pietatem colas" (4:389; proffered as Caesar's words), cf. *De officiis* 3.21, "Nam si violandum est ius, regnandi gratia / Violandum est; aliis rebus pietatem colas" (in verse, also attributed to Caesar). None of this, of course, proves that Benoît had firsthand acquaintance with Cicero's treatise. But it does demonstrate that Insular *litterati* of the era had access to the work.

31. On these problems, see Hanning, "The Audience as Co-Creator," 1.

32. Other examples are usefully paraphrased by Zumthor, *La lettre et la voix*, 60–82, 249–63.

33. As Hanning argues in "The Audience as Co-Creator," passim, those constituting the twelfth-century audiences of chivalric romances clearly displayed an immense sophistication in negotiating the sense of the oralized artifact. The romances of Chrétien, which Hanning uses as his main paradigms, constantly impose a simultaneous identification with and distance from their protagonists, creating a response that is fundamentally an act of criticism (and, ultimately, self-evaluation). Although Hanning does not directly broach questions of Latin intertextuality, he does suggest a level of engagement that would actively seek out the meaning of any arcane reference. Penny Eley gives a lucid analysis of Benoît's mediating role in "Author and Audience in the *Roman de Troie*," in *Courtly Literature: Culture and Context*, ed. Keith Busby and Erik Kooper (Amsterdam: Benjamins, 1990), 179–90, especially 185: "[T]he implied relationship between author and audience is that of master and pupil, the one teaching, the other lending substance to the narrative. The author speaks with authority: the authority of the source to which he has access, and his authority as learned mediator between Latin and vernacular cultures"; and 187: "The author's attempt to control the audience's response shows that more than one response is thought to be possible. In other words, such interventions suggest that the audience is being invited to participate in the process of literature in a different way [from that characteristic of the *chanson de geste*]: their activity now seems to involve assessment and interpretation on an individual level, as well as celebrations of what is held in common." I fully concur and shall demonstrate that the trope of magic is integrally bound up with these mediating designs.

34. This assessment is based Zumthor's oralized reading of Gautier d'Arras's *Heracle*; see *La lettre et la voix*, 212.

35. To use an author I myself shall consider as an example, Gerald of Wales performed his *Topographia Hibernica* at Oxford in three sittings protracted over three days. See chapter 5.

36. On romances in general being delivered in discrete sections, see Crosby, "Oral Delivery in the Middle Ages," 101, and Duggan, "Performance and Transmission," 51–52.

37. For the Latin, see chapter 1.

38. See Rollo, *Historical Fabrication*, chapter 8.

39. Qui onques en la Chambre esteit,
Si se veeit veraiement,
Senz deceveir, apertement.
Li mireors n'ert mie faus. (14686–89)

40. Bataille d'ors ne de sengler,
De grip, de tigre, de lion,
Ne vol d'ostor ne de faucon
Ne d'espervier ne d'autre oisel,
Gieu de dame e de dameisel,
Ne parlemenz ne repostauz,
Batailles, traïsons n'assauz,
Ne nef siglant par haute mer,

Ne nus divers peissons de mer,
Ne batailles de champions,
N'omes cornuz ne marmions,
Ne serpenteaus volanz, hisdos,
Nuitons ne mostres perillos. (14724–36)

41. Quant cil de la Chambre conseillent,
A l'endormir e quant il veillent,
Sone e note tant doucement,
Ne trait dolor ne mal ne sent
Quil puet oïr ne escouter.
Fol corage ne mal ne penser.
N'i prent as genz, ne fous talanz. (14791–97)

42. Li dameiseaus, qui tant est genz,
Après le son des estrumenz,
Prent flors de mout divers semblanz,
Beles e fresches, bien olanz;
Adonc les giete a tel plenté
Desus le pavement listé
Que toz en est en fin coverz:
C'est en estez e en iverz. (14805–12)

43. Quar ceus de la Chambre esguardot
E par signes lor demostrot
Que c'ert que il deveient faire
E que plur lor ert necessaire:
A conoistre le lor faiseit
Si qu'autre ne l'aperceveit.
S'en la Chambre fussent set cent,
Si seüst chascuns veirement
Que l'image li demostrast
Iço que plus li besoignast.
Ço qu'il mostrot ert bien segrei:
Nel coneüst ja rien fors sei,
Ne jo ne nus, fors il toz sous. (14865–77)

44. For the Latin, see the notes to chapter 1.

45. Premierement l'ont desarmé
E de vin blanc set feiz lavé
En chieres especes boilli.
Anceis qu'il fust enseveli,
L'ont mout bien aromatizié,
E le ventre del cors sachié.
Ostee en ont bien la coraille,
Feie e poumon e l'autre entraille.
Le cors dedenz ont embasmé,
Sin i mistrent a grant plenté. (16507–16)

46. See Rollo, *Historical Fabrication,* chapter 8. Other studies that consider the furnishings of the tomb, but with no reference to the tensions of literacy and disclosure they imply, are Emmanuèle Baumgartner, "Tombeaux pour guerriers et Amazones: Sur un motif descriptif de l'*Enéas* et du *Roman de Troie,*" in *Contemporary Readings of Medieval Literature,* Michigan Romance Studies 8, ed. Guy Mermier (Ann Arbor: Michigan Romance Studies, 1989), 37–50; R. Buchtal, "Hector's Tomb," in *Essays in Honor of E. Panofsky,* ed. M. Meiss (New York: New York University Press, 1961), 29–36; and Marc-René Jung, "Hector Assis," in *Romania Ingeniosa* (New York: Peter Lang, 1987), 153–69.

47. Complementing this emphasis on the responsibilities of the *clergiez,* Benoît describes how the Trojans dedicate an entire religious foundation to preserving the memory committed to the tomb:

Li temples fu si establiz
Que de sainz homes e d'esliz
I a li reis mis un covent,
E s'i avront mout richement
Lor vivre a trestoz sofisant.
Ne sai qu'alasse porloignant:
Mais onques cors de chevalier,
Dès le derrain jusqu'al premier,
Ne jut en terre a tel honor
Ne ne fera ja mais nul jor. (16849–58)

[The temple was designed, according to the king's wishes, to include a monastery of holy, elect men. There they will always receive their sustenance in perfect sufficiency. I shall say no more on this matter, save to point out that never has the corpse of a knight, whatever his status, been interred with such honor, nor ever will be.] Although Benoît nowhere states that these resident *litterati* are actually present when the entombed signifiers are made accessible to the community, he forcefully suggests as much by lending them the sole function of perpetuating and glorifying the memory the tomb itself encloses.

48. Wace, *Le Roman de Rou,* ed. Anthony Holden, 3 vols., Société des Anciens Textes Français (Paris: Picard, 1970–73): "Troisième partie," lines 1–10.

49. See the notes to chapter 1.

50. With *aveir:* lines 159–60, 841–42, 1329–30, 3905–6, 5319–20, 6355–56, 13447–48, 13653–54, 18303–4, 25159–60, 26809–10, 26921–22, 29027–28; with *valeir:* lines 10495–96, 25431–32; with *poëir:* lines 769–70, 1121–22, 1287–88, 1731–32, 2247–48, 18703–4, 24777–78, 25055–56.

4. William FitzStephen, Richard FitzNigel, Benoît de Sainte-Maure

1. For detailed discussions of the administrative policies that characterized the early years of Henry's reign, see Emilie Amt, *The Accession of Henry II in England: Royal Government Restored, 1149–1159* (Woodbridge, England: Boydell, 1993), passim, with 113–32 devoted to the Exchequer; and Chibnall, *Anglo-Norman England, 1066–1166,* 105–57. For later developments, see Warren, *Henry II*, 241–396; and, for an account of the procedures Henry refined, consult C. Warren Hollister and John W. Baldwin, "The Rise of Administrative Kingship: Henry I and Philip Augustus," *American Historical Review* 83 (1978): 867–905, especially 867–91.

2. To quote Ralph Turner from the introduction to his biographical studies: "Traditionally, high birth was considered necessary for candidates for high ecclesiastical office, but Henry II and his sons found nothing wrong with elevating royal clerks from lower levels of the knightly class or from prosperous bourgeois families, such as Henry of London, to episcopal thrones" (*Men Raised from the Dust*, 8).

3. "In the traditionalists' view, only those courtiers who demonstrated 'courtly' or chivalric conduct deserved knightly rank. Instead, the *familiares regis* too often presented qualities that might be more appropriate for bureaucrats or for the bourgeoisie" (ibid., 2).

4. One such figure is Gerald of Wales, whose opinions of certain administrators (and, indeed, their regal masters) will be considered in chapter 5.

5. "Inter nobiles orbis urbes, quos fama celebrat, civitas Londoniae, regni Anglorum sedes, una est quae famam sui latius diffundit, opes et merces longius transmittit, caput altius extollit. . . . Ab occidente duo castella munitissima; muro urbis alto et magno duplatis heptapylae portis intercontinuante. . . . Item sursum ab occidente palatium regium eminet super fluvium . . . duobus millibus ab urbe, suburbio frequenti continuante. . . . Urbe Roma, secundum chronicorum fidem, satis antiquior est. Ab eisdem quippe patribus Trojanis haec prius a Bruto condita est, quam illa a Remo et Romulo. . . . Civitas Londonia peperit aliquot qui regna plurima et Romanum sibi subdiderunt imperium; et plurimos alios, quos mundi dominos virtus evexit ad deos, ut fuerat in Apollinis oraculo Bruto promissum:

'Brute, sub occasu solis, trans Gallica regna,
Insula in oceano est undique clausa mari.
Hanc pete; namque tibi sedes erit illa perennis:
Hic fiet natis altera Troja tuis.
Hic de stirpe tua reges nascentur; et ipsis
Totius terrae subditus orbis erit.'"

(William FitzStephen, *Vita Sancti Thomae, Cantuariensis archiepiscopi et martyris*, ed. James Craigie Robertson in *Materials for the History of Thomas Becket, Archbishop of Canterbury*, vol. 3 [London: Her Majesty's Stationery Office, Rolls Series, 1877; reprint, New York: Kraus, 1963], Prologue, paragraphs 2, 5, 12, 19.) The quoted verse is from Geoffrey's *Historia regum*, and it corresponds more closely to the First Variant than to the Vulgate version. Compare the two readings of paragraph 16 in Neil Wright's editions of the respective texts, *The "Historia Regum Britannie" of Geoffrey of Monmouth I: Bern, Burgerbibliothek, MS. 568* and *The "Historia Regum Britannie" of Geoffrey of Monmouth II: The First Variant Version: A Critical Edition* (Cambridge: D. S. Brewer, 1988).

6. "Praeterea est in Londonia supra ripam fluminis, inter vina in navibus et cellis vinariis venalia, publica coquina. Ibi quotidie pro tempore est invenire cibaria, fercula, assa, pista, frixa, elixa, pisces, pisciculos, carnes grossiores pauperibus, delicatiores divitibus, venationum, avium, avicularum. . . . Haec equidem publica coquina est, et civitati plurimum expediens, et ad civilitatem pertinens."

7. "Londonia et modernis temporibus reges illustres magnificosque peperit, imperatricem Mathildem, Henricum regem tertium, et beatum Thomam archiepiscopum, martyrem Christi gloriosum."

8. On this issue, see, for example, William of Newburgh, *Historia rerum* 1.3: "Factoque concilio, eidem filiae suae et susceptis vel suscipiendis ex ea nepotibus, ab episcopis, comitibus, baronibus, et omnibus qui alicujus videbantur esse momenti, regnum Angliae cum ducatu Normanniae fecit jurari."

9. Modern scholarship on Becket is extensive. Among the recent biographies see Richard Winston, *Thomas Becket* (New York: Knopf, 1967); David Knowles, *Thomas Becket* (Stanford: Stanford University Press, 1971); and Frank Barlow, *Thomas Becket* (Berkeley and Los Angeles: University of California Press, 1986). The following are also useful, though less detailed: Egbert Türk, *Nugae Curialium: Le Règne d'Henri Plantegenêt (1154–1189) et l'éthique politique* (Geneva: Droz, 1977), 8–25, and Warren, *Henry II*, chapter 13. On the effects of Becket's career, see Beryl Smalley, *The Becket Conflict and the Schools: A Study of Intellectuals in Politics* (Oxford: Blackwell, 1973), and, for a fascinating narrative of later efforts to locate his relics, see John Butler, *The Quest for Becket's Bones: The Mystery of the Relics of St Thomas Becket of Canterbury* (New Haven, Conn.: Yale University Press, 1995).

10. It is for this reason that medieval accounts of Becket's life and death are comparable in volume to those produced during the twentieth century—Robertson's *Materials for the History* runs to seven copious volumes.

11. "In ingressu Gallicanarum villarum et castrorum, primi veniebant garciones pedites, 'fruges consumere nati,' quasi ducenti quinquaginta, gregatim euntes sex vel deni, vel plures simul, aliquid lingua sua pro more patriae suae cantantes"; "Sequebantur aliquo intervallo canes copulati et leporarii in loris et laxis suis, seu quo alio dignentur nomine, cum concuratoribus et sequacibus suis"; "Quaeque etiam biga habebat canem alligatum vel supra vel subtus, magnum, fortem et terribilem, qui ursum vel leonem domiturus videretur"; "Duae bigae solam cervisiam trahebant, factam in aquae decoctione ex adipe frumenti, in cadis ferratis, donandam Francis, id genus liquidi plasmatis mirantibus, potum sane salubrem, defaecatum, colore vineo, sapore meliori"; "Habuit duodecim summarios. [S]upra quemque summarium erat vel simia caudata, vel 'humani simulator simius oris'"; "[O]cto scrinia . . . cancellarii continebant supellectilem, auream scilicet et argenteam. . . . Aliae coffrae et clitellae cancellarii continebant monetam, aes plurimum quotidianis ejus impensis et donis sufficiens"; "Habuit etiam viginti quatuor mutatoria vestimentorum. [Aliae coffrae continebant] vestes ejus"; "Unus summarius capellae sacra vasa et altaris ornamenta et libros portabat, caeterorum praeambulus"; "Circiter ducentos in equis secum habuit de familia sua, milites, clericos, dapiferos, servientes, armigeros, nobilium filios militantes ei pro armis, omnes instructos. Omnes isti et omnis eorum sequela novo festivo fulgebant ornatu vestium, quisque pro modo suo"; "Postremo, cancellarius et aliqui familiares ejus circa eum."

12. "Mirabilis est ipse rex Anglorum, cujus cancellarius talis et tantus incedit."

13. *Historia rerum Anglicarum* 2.1: "Mox castella nova, quae in diebus avi sui nequaquam exstiterant, complanari praecepit, praeter pauca in locis opportunis sita, quae vel ipse retinere vel a pacificis ab regni munimen retineri voluit. . . . Talia novi principis initia fuere [et] fugiebant lupi rapaces, vel mutabantur in oves; aut si non vere mutabantur, metu tamen

legum innoxii cum ovibus morabantur. Conflabantur gladii in vomeres, et lanceae in falces, nullusque jam exercebatur ad proelium, sed omnes olim optatae et nunc Deo propitio indultae pacis, vel fovebantur otiis, vel intendebant negotiis."

14. "Miseratione Dei, consilio cancellarii, et cleri et baronum regni . . . castella omnia per Angliam corruunt, praeter antiquas pacis conservandae turres et oppida; corona Angliae, revocatis defectionibus, redintegratur; exhaeredatis jura paterna restituntur; de sylvarum latibulis ad villas prodeunt latrones, et communi gaudentes pace teneri, conflant gladios in vomeres, lanceas in falces. . . . Hujus cancellarii industria et consilio, annitentibus ordinatis Dei, et comitibus et baronibus, nobile illud regnum Angliae, tanquam ver novum, renovatur, ecclesia sancta honoratur."

15. "Cancellarius Thomas regni sedem, palatium Londoniae, prius fere ruinam, reparari facit."

16. "Cancellarii Angliae dignitas est, ut secundus a rege in regno habeatur; ut altera parte sigilli regii, quod et ad ejus pertinet custodiam, propria signet mandata; ut capella regis in ipsius sit dispositione et cura; ut vacantes archiepiscopatus, episcopatus, abbatias et baronias, cadentes in manu regis, ipse suscipiat et conservet; ut omnibus regis assit conciliis, et etiam non vocatus se ingerat; ut omnia sigilliferi regii, clerici sui, manu signentur, omnia cancellarii consilio disponantur."

17. FitzNigel was also, later in his life, bishop of London. For biographical details and dating, consult the edition of the *Dialogus de Scaccario* by Charles Johnson, revised F. E. L. Carter and D. E. Greenway (Oxford: Clarendon, 1983), xv–xx. This is the paradigm for all subsequent quotations. Since some of the sections of this edition are extremely lengthy, I shall refer first to book and section and then to page number. Following the editors, I shall call the author FitzNigel, rather than the equally common alternative FitzNeal.

18. In this connection, it can be noted that Chrétien de Troyes perhaps makes an oblique reference to the Exchequer in *Le Conte du Graal* when he describes Gauvain using a chessboard as a shield to defend himself against an aggressive troop of *borjois;* see lines 5891–6023 in the edition of William Roach, Textes Littéraires Français 71 (Geneva: Droz, 1959). If so, this may be a burlesque recognition of efforts made on the part of the aristocracy to defend its interests by employing a technology associated with the new masters of money, and therefore with the disposers of an increasingly hegemonic and threatening power.

19. "Magnus est hic cuius fidei totius regni cura immo et cor regis committitur. Scriptum quippe est: 'ubi est thesaurus tuus ibi est et cor tuum.'"

20. "Licet autem tabula talis scaccarium dicatur, transumitur tamen hoc nomen ut ipsa quoque curia, que consedente scaccario est. . . . [C]ertum est quod magnorum auctoritate roboratur adeo ut nulli liceat statuta scaccarii infringere uel eius quauis temeritate resistere. Habet enim hoc commune cum ipsa domini regis curia in qua ipse in propria persona iura discernit quod nec recordationi nec sententie in eo late licet alicui contradicere" (Magister).

21. "Huic autem curie tam insignis auctoritas est cum propter regie ymaginis excellentiam que in sigillo eius in thesauro indiuidua lege seruatur tum propter eos qui assident ut dictum est quorum sollertia totus regni status indempnis seruatur" (Magister).

22. "Videre mihi uideor fieri posse ratione calculandi ut idem denarius pro calculo missus nunc unum solidum nunc libram nunc centum nunc mille significet" (Discipulus).

23. "Sic est quibusdam tamen appositis. Itemque fieri potest eisdem demptis, si calculatori placeat, ut qui mille significat gradatim descendens unum significet" (Magister).

24. "Sic fit ut quiuis de plebe, cum homo sit et aliud esse non possit, temporalibus appositis uoluntate presidentis ab imo conscendat in summum ac deinceps fortune lege seruata retrudatur in imum, manens quod fuerat, licet uideatur ratione dignitatis et status a se sibi mutatus" (Discipulus).

25. This emphasis on the advancement granted to men of lowly origins amply corroborates the upward mobility that Ralph Turner biographically studies in *Men Raised from the Dust:* "This revolution in government demanded a new kind of royal servant, someone beginning to resemble the modern bureaucrat. Evidence of these new officials in England is the spread of practical manuals for the instruction of civil servants. Two of the best examples come from the end of Henry II's reign: Richard fitz Neal's *Dialogus de Scaccario* and the *Tractatus de legibus et consuetudinibus regni Anglie* attributed to Glanvill. The Angevin monarchs relied less on men with military resources to staff their councils and offices and more on graduates of the schools or men with practical administrative experience, men with financial, legal, and record-keeping skills" (11).

26. "Nescis quod sermo tuus non capit in omnibus" (Magister).

27. "[Q]uicquid aliis uideatur, mihi satis placet quod ex hiis alia conicis. In mundanorum enim tribulis mistici intellectus flores querere laudabile est. Nec in hiis tantum que commemoras set in tota scaccarii descriptione sacramentorum quedam latibula sunt" (Magister).

28. See 1.4 (14); 1.5 (26); 2.1 (69).

29. "[F]ieri potest per falsarios et nummorum decurtatores uel detonsores. Noueris autem monetam Anglie in tribus falsam deprehendi, in falso scilicet pondere, in falsa lege, in falsa imagine" (Magister).

30. "He takes the chosen coins, which he personally counts and places in a charcoal vessel positioned in the furnace. Then, in accordance with the procedures of metallurgy, he reduces them to a single mass, and rids the now fused silver of its impurities" ("Quos [fusor] suscipiens manu propria numerat et sic disponit eos in uasculum ignitorum cinerum quod in fornace est. Tunc igitur, artis fusorie lege seruata, redigit eos in massam, conflans et emundans argentum" [Magister, 1.6; 37]). The discrepancy between the weight of the ingot and the pound represents the quantity of base material that has been purged in the crucible or the amount of silver already clipped from the coins, and more silver is then added by the Sheriff responsible in order to supplement the difference.

31. "[D]um rotuli corriguntur, facta omnium trium collatione, facile erit errata corrigere" (Magister).

32. "Quod si forte per negligentiam, uel alium quemlibet casum, contigerit eum errare in scriptura rotuli uel in nomine uel in numero uel in causa in quibus uis maior scripture consistit, non presumat abradere, set linea subtili subducta cancellet et scribat in serie quod oportet" (Magister).

33. "Non facile nisi manifesto uitio rasure cedunt" (Magister).

34. "[Vicecomes] posset enim, quod vellet, impune delere, mutare uel minuere, cum non exstet aliquod penes barones eius rescriptum" (Discipulus); "Posset fortasse si uellet, set foret hoc insani capitis argumentum, si tantis se sponte periculis opponeret, praesertim cum non auferre sic regis debita posset set uix differre: omnia namque debita de quibus summonitiones fiunt, alias diligenter annotata seruantur, unde non posset quis a debito suo, etiam procurante uicecomite, hac arte liberari" (Magister).

35. "Si quis ergo, sicut jam susurrari audio, post me scribendi de talibus munus attemptaverit, mihi debeat collectionis gratiam, sibi habeat electionis materiam."

36. It is also with some irony that we compare *Rou* with Benoît's *Chronique des ducs* and observe just how accurate Wace's predictions in some cases proved to be. On the relationship between these two vernacular histories of the Normans, see H. Andresen, "Ueber die von Benoît in seiner normannischen Chronik benutzten Quellen, insbesondere über sein Verhältnis zu Dudo, Wilhelm von Jumièges und Wace," *Romanische Forschungen* 2 (1886): 477–538, in which, alongside Wace's *Rou,* the works of William of Jumièges and William of Poitiers are also considered as paradigms for the information Benoît gives on the ducal tenures of Richard II through the Conqueror and his sons.

37. Benoît de Sainte-Maure, *Chronique des ducs de Normandie,* ed. Carin Fahlin, 2 vols. (Uppsala: Almqvist and Wiksells, 1951–67), lines 41370–74. For the identification of Benoît as the author of both *Troie* and the *Chronique,* see Falin, *Étude sur le manuscrit de Tours de la "Chronique des ducs de Normandie" par Benoît* (Uppsala: Almqvist and Wiksells, 1937), 141–72.

5. Gerald of Wales

1. Neo-Platonism: a *Cosmographia* written in imitation of Bernardus Silvestris; ethnography: the *Topographia Hibernica,* the *Itinerarium Kambriae,* and the *Descriptio Kambriae;* political ethics: the *De principis instructione;* secular history: the *Expugnatio Hibernica* (also called the *Historia vaticinalis* by its author); ecclesiastical reform: the *Gemma ecclesiastica.* The editions that will be used are those published in the Rolls Series: the *Cosmographia* in *Giraldi Cambrensis De rebus a se gestis Libri III, Invectionum libellus, Symbolum electorum,* ed. J. S. Brewer (London: Her Majesty's Stationery Office, 1861; reprint, New York: Kraus, 1966), 341–49; the *Topographia* and *Expugnatio* in *Giraldi Cambrensis Opera. Vol. V,* ed. James F. Dimock (London: Her Majesty's Stationery Office, 1867; reprint, New York: Kraus, 1964), 1–204, 207–411; the *Itinerarium* and *Descriptio* in *Giraldi Cambrensis Itinerarium Kambriae et Descriptio Kambriae,* ed. Dimock (London: Her Majesty's Stationery Office, 1868; reprint, New York: Kraus, 1964), 3–152, 155–227; the *De principis* in *Giraldi Cambrensis Opera. Vol. VIII,* ed. George Warner (London: Her Majesty's Stationery Office, 1891); and the *Gemma ecclesiastica* in *Giraldi Cambrensis Gemma ecclesiastica,* ed. J. S. Brewer (London: Her Majesty's Stationery Office, 1862; reprint, New York: Kraus, 1964). I shall continue to refer to the works in the abbreviated forms used above. The longer works will be referred to by book and chapter, and the shorter by page number.

2. To consider two examples taken from the *Topographia:* 1.31, on experiments he observed that were conducted to gauge the effects of a thong made of Irish leather on an English toad, and 2.19, on the written advice he sent an Irish synod with respect to a prophetic werewolf and his dying werewolf spouse. I shall return to both of these.

3. Autobiography: the *De rebus a se gestis,* ed. J. S. Brewer in *Giraldi Cambrensis De rebus a se gestis Libri III, Invectionum libellus, Symbolum electorum* (London: Her Majesty's

Stationery Office, 1861; reprint, New York: Kraus, 1966), 1–122; florilegium: the *Symbolum electorum* (of which the *Cosmographia* forms part); ed. Brewer in the same volume of the Rolls Series as the *De rebus a se gestis,* 199–395; literary self-promotion: the *Catalogus brevior librorum suorum* and the epistolary "Ad capitulum Herefordense de libris a se scriptis" ("To the Chapter of Hereford, on Books written by the Self"), both ed. Brewer in the same volume of the Rolls Series as the *De rebus a se gestis,* 421–23 and 409–19.

4. In his own opinion, Gerald restored to letters a dignity unsurpassed since the days of ancient Rome. The incident that prompted this extravagant claim was the first public recitation of the *Topographia,* which took place in Oxford in the early 1190s. This was protracted over a period of three days, and the final performance was apparently attended by practically the entire population of the town. Gerald describes this literary prodigy in *De rebus a se gestis* 2.16: "Sumptuosa quidem res et nobilis, quia renovata sunt quodammodo authentica et antiqua in hoc facto poetarum tempora; nec rem similem in Anglia factam vel praesens aetas vel ulla recolit antiquitas." Assessed in context, this is really quite predictable. The prologue to *De rebus* begins with the most spectacular set piece of self-celebration to be found in twelfth-century letters (if not, indeed, all medieval writing). Gerald advances himself as a worthy object of documentation and imitation and aligns his own (auto-)biographical practice with the Greats of ancient Greece: "Inclitorum gesta virorum quondam Graï veteres primo per imagines deinde per scripta tenacius et expressius memoriae commendabant; quatinus exacti temporis virtutum extantium aemula posteritas posset imitatione laudibili ad similia provocari. Fabulosis enim seu relationibus seu lectionibus, quibus hyperbolica promuntur et impossibilia, ad imitationem nullus accenditur. Sed ubi vera viri virtus emicat, ibi ad imitandum et virilia complexandum mens virtuosa consurgit. Unde viri cujusdam nostri temporis inclite gesta, quae vel oculis conspexi vel ipso referente notavi, scolastico stilo, simplici tamen et non exquisito, perpetuae memoriae commendare curavi.... Pars igitur operis hujus prima de ortu Giraldi continet, pueritiae gestis atque adolescentiae; secunda vero de gestis virilis aetatis ejusdem et robustae; tertia vero de gestis provectioris aetatis et maturae, laboribus immensis atque periculis et persecutionibus plena."

5. The *Retractationes,* ed. Brewer in the same volume of the Rolls Series as the *De rebus a se gestis,* 425–27.

6. Concerning two of the poems he inserted into his personal florilegium and thereby promulgated as particularly egregious examples of his own talents: "Item: in *Symbolo electorum,* inter versus nostros metricos, duos appositos de duelli descriptione, et duos de dolenti missa consolatione, et quatuor de renuentis solatia responsione, alienos noverit esse lector et non nostros" (426). The purloined lines in question constitute brief poems in their own right, respectively *Symbolum electorum* 2.16, 17, 20 (pp. 363–64). We note that, while willing to admit the authorship of another, Gerald in a somewhat characteristic move fails to specify to whom credit should really be given.

7. With regard to the contemporary state of Ireland in the *Topographia;* on this, see Rollo, *Historical fabrication,* 253–55.

8. See in particular the *De invectionibus* (ed. J. S. Brewer in *Giraldi Cambrensis Opera. Vol III* [London: Her Majesty's Stationery Office, Rolls Series, 1863]), in which Gerald claims that Hubert Walter, archbishop of Canterbury and his most hated personal antagonist, had

incautiously attempted to correct King Richard's Latin in public, only to provoke the bishop of Coventry to observe that it was the king and not the archbishop who was correct in his usage ("Accidit aliquando quod Anglorum rege Ricardo Latinis verbis hunc modum proponente 'Volumus quod istud fiat corum nobis,' praedictus archiepiscopus, qui cum aliis multis et magnis viris tunc praesens extiterat, regem corrigere volens ait 'Domine, coram nos, coram nos.' Quo audito, cum rex Hugonem Conventrensem episcopum virum literatum et facundum respiceret, ait ille 'Ad vestram, domine, grammaticam, quia plus valet, vos teneatis,' risu cunctorum qui aderant subsecuto" [1.5]). To these can be added other cursory references to Hubert's lack of literate skill: in attacking Gerald in writing, the archbishop made the foolish mistake of attempting to use letters against a representative of the truly literate and erudite ("[est] ineptum [et] dispendiosum et talioni obnoxium literatos viros literis offendere et in scripturis eruditos scriptis injuriosis ad scribendum provocare" [1.2]); the archbishop labored for an entire night to compose a single line of nugatory Latin verse in an effort to display his expansive learning ("archiepiscopus hunc quoque versum nocturna lucubratione fabricatum ad philosophiae suae grandis ostentationem... contribuit" [1.2]); and, rather than being nurtured in letters from an early age, the archbishop was trained in tyrannical oppression and financial extortion at the Exchequer, which Gerald considered a vulgar manifestation of the new bureaucracy ("vocatus [fui] a studio et archiepiscopus unde? A scaccario et quid scaccarium? Locus in Anglia publici aerarii, Londoniis scilicet tabula quasi quadrata, ubi fiscales census colliguntur et computantur" [1.4]; "a puerilibus annis quando in Donato vel Catone initialia literaturae fundamenta stravisse debuisset, publicis regni officialibus adjunctus pauperum oppressionibus et tyrannicis extactionibus invigilare non cessabat" [1.10]).

9. As Dimock observes, this self-endorsement was often pushed to the point of narcissistic presumption: "A man of strong impetuous feelings and violent prejudices, with a marvellously elastic self-confidence that nothing could put down, Giraldus looked down with sublime contempt upon everyone and everything that did not agree with his own notions; he had not an idea that anything he thought or said could by any chance be wrong; he could not imagine any one who differed from him to be other than a fool or a rogue; ready as he was to find fault with any one except himself, yet sometimes an unflinching partizan, but often a virulent antagonist, he was the man of all others whose nature rendered it simply impossible for him to write a fair history of any sort.... There is no argument sometimes in favour of what he is advancing too absurd for him, or too inconsistent with what he may have said a few pages before, or so many pages after; there is no assertion sometimes too bold, no invective against an opponent too virulently unjust, no imputation of the basest motives too manifestly unreasonable, and no assumption of the vilest and most horrible calumnies as certain truths too atrocious for him" (*Giraldi Cambrensis Opera. Vol. V,* lxiv–lxv); "I think no equal case of multitudinous repeating from himself, as the most excellent of all writers, and the most worthy to be followed,—such, it is plain, Giraldus considered himself,—is to be found in the whole compass of authordom. Vain and proud of their productions, as many authors may have been, no other ever attained to the exquisite vanity of Giraldus, to his unassailable faith in his own supreme excellencies as a writer" (*Giraldi Cambrensis Itinerarium Kambriae et Descriptio Kambriae,* lxviii). Later in his career, Gerald ceded to an almost comical paranoia, as the virulent critic of established governance gave way to the equally self-absorbed voice of an ill-appreciated grandeur that saw itself hounded by the base machinations of inferiors. In *Gerald of Wales, 1146–1223* (Oxford: Clarendon, 1982), 63–66, Robert Bartlett summarizes Gerald's steadfast belief in his own victimization, mentioning in particular his suspicions against Archbishop Hubert and William Longchamp, effective viceroy of England during the protracted absence of Richard the Lionheart. Perhaps more revealing than these two cases, however, is Bartlett's summary of biographical information culled from the *Speculum duorum*, in which Gerald reports how his own nephew and a friend attempted to bribe him by threatening to disseminate a selection of his written criticisms of the Angevins and his more inflammatory perorations against those in power (64).

10. For the dating of the successive redactions of the *Topographia* and the amplitude of the additions to the third, see Dimock, *Giraldi Cambrensis Opera. Vol. V*, xi–xxiv, and *Giraldi Cambrensis Itinerarium Kambriae et Descriptio Kambriae*, x–xi.

11. See, again, Dimock, *Giraldi Cambrensis Opera. Vol. V*, lix–lx.

12. "Verumtamen, quoniam res gesta per interpretem non adeo sapit aut animo sedet, sicut proprio et idiomate noto prolata, alicui, si placet, lingua simul et literis erudito, ad transferendum in Gallicum ocius non otiosus liber hic noster committatur: qui forte fructum laboris sui, quoniam intelligi poterit, assequetur, quem nos quidem, minus intellecti, quia principes minus literati, hactenus obtinere non valuimus."

13. "Multa, magister Giralde, scripsistis, et multum adhuc scribitis: et nos multa diximus. Vos scripta dedistis, et nos verba. Et quanquam scripta vestra longe laudabiliora sint, et longaeviora, quam dicta nostra, quia tamen haec aperta, communi quippe idiomate prolata, illa vero, quia Latina, paucioribus evidentia, nos de dictis nostris fructum aliquem reportavimus, vos autem de scriptis egregiis, principibus literatis nimirum et largis obsoletis olim et ab orbe sublatis, dignam minime retributionem consequi potuistis."

14. "Unde et vir ille, eloquio clarus, W. Mapus, Oxoniensis archidiaconus, cujus animae propitietur Deus, solita verborum facetia et urbanitate praecipua dicere pluries, et nos in hunc modum convenire solebat" (proem to the second redaction).

15. It is the general consensus today that John could read, if only with difficulty. On this issue, see Galbraith, "The Literacy of the Medieval English Kings," 201–38, who somewhat ingenuously presents John's attested purchase of books for a personal library as proof of high literate accomplishments (214). Thompson, *The Literacy of the Laity*, 179, approaches this issue with greater circumspection, although he uses Gerald's testimony as a counterargument. It should be noted that the purchase of books does not necessarily imply a desire, or even an ability, to read them, and that, even if this first point is viewed to be untenable, the ability to read does not necessarily presuppose the ability to understand the complexities of what is being read.

16. Cataloged by Broich in "Heinrich II. als Patron der Literatur seiner Zeit," 27–203.

17. "Vir... litteratus ad omnem decentiam et utiliatem, linguarum omnium quae sunt a mari Gallico usque ad Jordanem habens scientiam, Latina tantum utens et Gallica" (*De nugis curialium*, ed. Thomas Wright [London: Camden, 1850], 5.6).

18. "Princeps eloquentissimus, et, quod his temporibus conspicuum est, literis eruditus" (1.46).

19. For what it is worth, Gerald implies as much in *Itinerarium* 1.6, although in a characteristically extravagant context. Apparently, a momentous encounter took place in Cardiff between Henry and a mysterious (perhaps ghostly) figure who greeted the king in English ("qui et regem in haec verba quasi Teutonice convenit, 'God holde þe, cuning'") and proceeded to expound at length in the same language. Although Henry had to have his French reply ("dixit lingua Gallica") translated by one of his retainers, he had clearly understood what had been said.

20. "Tibi, vir inclite, Hugo Lincolniensis episcope, quem religio pariter et literatura commendant, laborem nostrum per horridos Kambriae fines non illaudabilem in duabus particulis scholastico stilo tam digerere quam destinare curavi" (first preface).

21. "[P]rincipibus parum literatis et multum occupatis . . . vacuo . . . et infructuoso labore peregi."

22. "Hibernicam Anglorum regi Henrico secundo Topographiam ejusdemque filio et utinam vitiorum non succedaneo Pictavensium comiti Ricardo Vaticinalem Historiam . . . peregi."

23. "Ad curiam igitur a studio, peccatis exigentibus, a rege vocatus [sum], cui nihil minus menti quam non mentiri, nil desiderio magis quam decipere, quam differre, quam sequentium animos et obsequentium dilationibus cruciare."

24. "De principis instructione tractatum edere me compulit id praecipue, quod in principum moribus et praelatorum, qui alios tam exemplo quam potestate regere tenentur et informare, quod digne reprehendi possit plus invenio. Quis enim hodie princeps, qui non indultam desuper potestatem ad omnes animi motus, ad omnem carnis libitum ac luxum, ad omnem pravae tyrannidis atrocitatem, indifferenter extendat, et, tanquam quicquid libet liceat, velut aequis ambulantia passibus posse pariter et velle non metiatur? Quis hodie princeps, qui regum inunctionis sacramentum, qui coronam et sceptrum et insignia singula, quid sibi velint, attendat? Proinde et in veterum scriptis principes illiterati tanquam asini censentur coronati." Obviously, the general tenor of this passage (and of the work it introduces) anticipates the resentment that led to the writing of the Magna Carta. For illuminating comments on the relationship between Gerald's political thought and the baronial stipulations imposed on John, see Bartlett, *Gerald of Wales,* chapter 3.

25. See the notes to chapter 2.

26. "Cumque ibidem de variis hominum in lupos mutationibus sermonem produxerit, demum subnectit: 'Nam et nos, cum essemus in Italia, audiebamus talia de quadam regione illarum partium; ubi stabularias mulieres, imbutas his malis artibus, in caseo dare solere dicebant viatoribus, unde in jumenta illico verterentur, et necessaria quaeque portarent, postque perfuncta opera iterum ad se redirent: nec tamen in eis mentem fieri bestialem, sed rationalem humanamque servari. Sicut Apuleius, in libris quos Asini Aurei titulo inscripsit, sibi ipsi refert accidisse, ut accepto veneno, humano animo permanente, asinus fieret.'"

27. Again, with added emphasis: "De aniculis quae juvenem asinum *videri fecerunt*"; "Hae hospitem, si quando solus superveniebat, vel equum, vel suem, vel quodlibet aliud *videri faciebant*"; "ephebum asinum *videri fecerunt*" (2:171).

28. "Daemones igitur seu malos homines sicut nec creare, ita nec naturas veraciter mutare posse, simul cum Augustino sentimus. Sed specietenus, quae a vero Deo creata sunt, ipso permittente, commutant; ut scilicet videantur esse quod non sunt; sensibus hominum mira illusione captis et sopitis, quatinus res non videant sicut se habent, sed ad falsas quasdam et fictitias videndum formas, vi phantasmatis seu magicae incantationis, mirabiliter abstrahantur."

29. "Sciat autem in primis quod laicis haec et parum literatis edita principibus plano facilique stilo solam desiderant ad intelligentiam explanari."

30. "[Q]uae major inscitia quam illa, quae ad evidentiam indicanda proponimus, ignotis sermonum ambagibus et intricatis quibusdam verborum involucris abdere potius et velare; et ut singulari scientia scioli videamur et soli, aliis tanquam videndo non videntibus, et intelligendo non intelligentibus, eo ipso quo intelligi debemus ut non intelligamur elaborare?"

31. "Et cum esset singularis, interrogaverunt eum hi qui cum eo erant duodecim, parabolam. Et dicebat eis: 'Vobis datum est nosse mysterium regni Dei; illis autem qui foris sunt, in parabolis omnia fiunt: ut videntes videant et non videant, et audientes audiant et non intelligant'" (*Biblia Sacra iuxta Vulgatae exemplaria,* ed. A. C. Fillon [Paris: Letouzey et Ané, 1887], Mark 4.10–12; the translation is the Revised Standard Version [Nashville, Tenn.: Thomas Nelson, 1972]).

32. See Rollo, *Historical Fabrication,* 255–65.

33. See ibid., 265–72.

34. "[Livor] objicit enim in hunc modum: lupum introducit cum sacerdote loquentem, bovina humano corpori depingit extrema, mulierem barbatam" (*Expugnatio,* "Introitus in recitationem").

35. "Scio tamen et certus sum me nonnulla scripturum quae lectori vel impossibilia prosus, vel etiam ridiculosa videbuntur. Sed ita me Dii amabilem praestent, ut nihil in libello apposuerim cujus veritatem vel occulata fide vel probatissimorum et authenticorum comprovincialium virorum testimonio cum summa diligentia non elicuerim." The "utterly impossible or even ridiculous things" to which Gerald refers obviously include the talking wolf, the ox-man, the bearded lady, and the women with unnatural desires, which are documented in 2.19–24. But they are also quite possibly some, if not all, of the following (references to chapters of book 2): an island on which any creature of the female gender at once drops dead (4); an island on which no one dies (4); a sanctuary that cannot be entered by women and chickens (4); an island on which women cannot give birth (4); an island on which corpses do not rot and that is uncongenial to mice (6); a well with waters that dye the hair gray (7); a well with waters that turn wood into stone (7); subaquatic churches with round towers (9); a fish with golden teeth (10); a willow tree that bears apples (28); Saint Kevin's pet blackbird (28); Saint Colman's unboilable ducks (29); a church with wine flowing from one of its walls (30); a colony of fleas condemned by Saint Nannan to inhabit only one field in Connacht (31); a bell that invariably returns to its favored location when moved (33); an enclosure that cannot be entered by men (36); a book written by an angel (38–39); a speaking and unmovable crucifix (44–46); a demented clairvoyant living in Ferns called Fantasticus (47); and a fire that cuts off people's legs (48). To these can be added diverse phenomena that Gerald considers beyond the confines of Ireland, such as the waters of a Sicilian well that attack anyone wearing red clothes (8), an English hind with golden teeth (10), and Welsh and Scottish crones who make milk-raiding expeditions in the guise of hares (19).

36. "Habeat hic igitur et praesens tempus quod laceret, et posteritas quod laudet; habeat hoc quod laedat, illa quod legat; habeat hoc quod damnet, illa quod amet; habeat hoc quod reprobet, illa quod probet."

37. "Verum qui talia tam vehementer abhorret, legat in libro Numeri asinam Balee locutam, et prophetam increpantem."

38. "Advertat autem sanius et attendat, juxta Ieronimi sententiam, multa in scripturis incredibilia reperiri, nec verisimilia, quae nihilominus tamen vera sunt."

39. "Quamdiu ergo gens ea mandata Domini custodierit, et in viis ejus ambulaverit, tuta manebit et inconvulsa. Sin autem, quia proclivis est cursus ad voluptates, et imitatrix natura vitiorum, ad nostros ex convictu mores forte descenderint, divinam in se quoque proculdubio vindictam provocabunt."

40. See Rollo, *Historical Fabrication,* 265–71.

41. To cite the entire passage once again, this time with the appropriate emphasis on cause and effect: "[Livor] objicit enim in hunc modum: lupum introducit cum sacerdote loquentem, bovina humano corpori depingit extrema, mulierem barbatam, hircum amatorem et leonem. *Verum* qui talia tam vehementer abhorret, *legat* in libro Numeri asinam Balee locutam, et prophetam increpantem" (*Expugnatio,* "Introitus in recitationem").

42. Baldwin was "vir quidem valde litteratus," and Walter and Robert, "vires litteratissimi"; both references are from the "Ad capitulum Herefordense de libris a se scriptis," respectively 410 and 412.

43. On Baldwin, see the *De rebus a se gestis* 2.20 ("[archiepiscopus] librum leg[ebat] et perleg[ebat]"); on Walter and Robert, see the "Ad capitulum Herefordense," 412–13 and 413 ("[Walterus] libenter audiebat et inspiciebat"; "[Robertus] leg[ebat] et releg[ebat], satiarique legendo seu fatigari vix val[ebat]").

44. "Aquam si vel crudam potes, vel corruptam jejunis naribus olfacias, mors imminet"; "Terram nudo vestigio teras, mors imminet"; "Auram nudato capite liberius carpas, si frigida penetrat, si calida perturbat, mors imminet"; "Marmori minus caute insideas, mors imminet."

45. "Cibum majori in quantitate sumas, mors in januis"; "Vinum non aquatum bibas, mors in januis"; "Nec tantum cibaria et pocula, verum etiam vestes, sellae et subsellia, veneno suspecta sunt."

46. "Infestant aspides et viperae; infestant dracones; et solo invisus visu, soloque timendus aspectu basiliscus. Infestat seps, serpens exiguus, modicitatem tamen malitia supplens. Non solum enim carnem, sed et ossa veneno consumit."

47. "Habeat igitur oriens venenosas, habeat toxicatas opulentias suas. Nos, cum aurea rerum mediocritate, quae et usui decenter suppetat et naturae sufficiat, omnes orientales pompas sola aeris nostri clementia compensamus. O Dei donum in terris incomparabile! O inaestimabilem, et nondum intellectam mortalibus gratiam divinitus collatam!"

48. "Homines igitur isti cum nascuntur, non accurate, ut assolet, nutriuntur. Nam praeter alimenta, quibus ne penitus deficiant, duris a parentibus sustentantur, per cetera fere cuncta naturae relinquuntur. Non in cunabulis aptantur: non fasciis alligantur: non frequentibus in balneis tenera membra vel foventur, vel artis juvamine componuntur. Non enim obstetrices aquae calentis beneficio vel nares erigunt, vel faciem deprimunt, vel tibias extendunt. Sola natura quos edidit artus, praeter artis cujuslibet adminicula, pro sui arbitrio et componit et disponit. Tanquam itaque probans quid per se valeat, fingere non cessat et figurare, quousque in robur perfectum, pulcherrimis et proceris corporibus, congruis et coloratissimis vultibus, homines istos provehat et producat."

49. "Medicorum opera parum indiget insula. Morbidos enim homines, praeter moribundos, paucos invenies. Inter sanitatem continuam, mortemque supremam, nihil fere medium."

50. "Sicut enim Gallia Britanniam, sic et Britannia Hiberniam, aeris tam serenitate quam subtilitate longe praecellit. Quanto namque ad euri partes magis acceditur, tanto coeli faciem quo purior et subtilior, tanto penetrabilior et inclementior aer illustrat."

51. "Cumque ipsam multum Anglici, multoque plus Hibernici cum admiratione conspexissent, demum Duvenaldus rex Ossiriensis, vir prudens in gente sua et fidelis, tunc forte praesens existens, cum grandi capitis concussione, gravique cordis dolore, verbum hoc eructavit: 'Pessimos in Hiberniam rumores vermis iste portavit.' Utensque tanquam prognostico vero, certissimum hoc signum esse dicebat adventus Anglorum, imminentisque conquisitionis et expugnationis gentis suae."

52. See *Expugnatio* 2.20: "Circa id ipsum temporis, apud Waterfordiam, rana reperta fuit, cum multa gentis illius admiratione; sicut *Topographia* testatur." This comment is inserted into a narrative of the principal events of 1177–79; see Dimock's marginal notes to pages 348–49.

53. "Inter omnia vermium genera, solis non nocivis Hibernia gaudet. Venenosis enim omnibus caret. Caret serpentibus et colubris; caret bufonibus et ranis; caret tortuis et scorpionibus; caret et draconibus. . . . Nec mihi mirandum videtur quod vermium istorum, sicut et piscium, avium, et ferarum quarundam naturalem defectum terra patitur. Sed hoc stupore dignum occurrit quod nihil venenosum aliunde advectum unquam continere vel potuit vel potest."

54. ". . . statim verso ventre, videntibus et admirantibus multis, medii crepuerunt et interierunt."

55. "Legitur namque in antiquis terrae istius sanctorum scriptis, quod aliquoties, experiendi gratia, serpentes in ollis aeneis delati sunt. Sed quam cito medium maris Hibernici cursum transmeaverant, exanimes et mortui reperti sunt"; "In tantum siquidem terra haec inimica veneno est ut, si aliarum regionum seu viridaria seu quaelibet alia loca pulvere ipsius aspergantur, venenosos abinde vermes procul exterminat"; "Corrigiae quoque terrae istius, non adulterinae sed verae, et de coriis animalium quae hic nata sunt factae, contra serpentum bufonumque morsus, in aqua rasae et potae, efficax remedium ferre solent."

56. "Vidi oculis meis corrigiam hujusmodi, strictam et arctam, bufoni circulariter periculi causa circumpositam. Ad quam perveniens et transire volens, statim tanquam capite percussus retro cecidit."

57. "Quinimmo omnia pene quae de eadem insula sunt, juxta Bedae assertionem, contra venena valent. Asserit enim se vidisse 'quibusdam a serpentibus percussis, folia codicum, qui de Hibernia fuerant, et ipsam rasuram aquae immissam, protinus totam vim veneni grassantis, totum inflati corporis absumpsisse ac sedasse tumorem.'"

58. "Quanto ad circii zephyrique partes magis vergitur, gleba sterilior, sed aura salubrior." Similar sentiments are expressed in almost identical terms in 1.3.

59. "Terra triticea; piscibus marinis, vinoque venali copiose referta; et, quod omnibus praestat, ex Hiberniae confinio aeris salubritate temperata.... Non itaque mirandum, non venia indignum, si natale solum, genialeque territorium, profusioribus laudum titulis auctor extulerit."

60. On the advent of the ancestors of the Gaelic population, see *Topographia* 3.6–7.

61. Gerald expatiates on the degeneracy of the Irish in *Topographia* 3.19–22.

62. "Juxta antiquissimas igitur Hibernensium historias, Caesara neptis Noe, audiens diluvium in proximo futurum, ad remotissimas occidentis insulas, quas necdum quisquam hominum habitaverat, cum suis complicibus fugam navigio destinaverat; sperans, ubi nunquam peccatum perpetratum fuerat, diluvii vindictam locum non habere. Amissis itaque quas in comitatu habebat naufragio navibus, una, qua cum viris tribus et quinquaginta mulieribus vehebatur, nave superstite, primo ante diluvium anno ad Hibernica litora forte devenit. Sed licet acute satis, et laudabili in femina ingenio, fatalitatem declinare statuerit, communem tamen interitum et fere generalem nullatenus potuit evitare. Litus igitur, in quo navis illa primum applicuit, navicularum litus vocatur; et in quo praefata tumulata est Caesara, usque hodie Caesarae tumulus nominatur."

63. "Verumtamen cunctis fere per diluvium jam deletis, qualiter rerum istarum, et tam eventus quam adventus memoria post diluvium retenta fuerit, non indignum videtur dubitatione. Sed qui historias istas primo scripserunt, ipsi viderint. Historiarum enimvero enucleator venio, non impugnator. Sed forte in aliqua materia inscripta, lapidea scilicet vel lateritia, sicut de arte musica legitur ante diluvium inventa, istorum memoria fuerat reservata."

64. The canonical history of written language is found in Isidore of Seville's *Etymologiae,* a text that, we shall shortly see, Gerald certainly knew: "Nosse poss[umus] linguam Hebraicam omnium linguarum et litterarum esse matrem.... Hebraeorum litteras a Lege coepisse per Moysen; Syrorum autem et Chaldaeorum per Abraham." The text is from the edition of W. M. Lindsay, *Etymologiarum sive originum libri XX,* 2 vols. (Oxford: Clarendon, 1911); here, 1.3.

65. "A nomine vero praedicti Heberi, secundum quosdam, Hibernienses nomen traxerunt; vel potius, secundum alios, ab Hibero Hispaniae fluvio, unde provenerant. Dicti sunt etiam Gaideli; dicti sunt et Scoti. Sicut enim antiquae referunt historiae, Gaidelus quidam, Phenii nepos, post linguarum confusionem apud Nembroticam turrim, in variis linguis peritissimus fuerat. Ob quam peritiam rex Pharao filiam suam Scotiam ei sociavit uxorem. Quoniam igitur Hibernienses ab istis, ut aiunt, originalem lineam ducunt, a Gaidelo et Scotia Gaideli et Scoti, sicut et nati sunt, sic et nominati. Gaidelus iste, ut aiunt, Hibernicam linguam composuit. Quae et Gaidelach dicitur, quasi ex omnibus linguis collecta."

66. "Inventor fuit musicae consonantiae, sicut in Genesi legitur, Jubal, de stirpe Caim, ante diluvium. Qui et dictus est 'Pater canentium in cithara et organo.' Et quia Adam audierat prophetasse de duobus judiciis, ne periret ars inventa scripsit eam in duabus columnis, in qualibet totam, una marmorea, altera lateritia: quarum altera non dilueretur diluvio, altera non solveretur incendio." The first period is lifted from the history of music that Isidore gives in *Etymologiae* 3.16.

67. "In musicis solum instrumentis commendabilem invenio gentis istius diligentiam. In quibus, prae omni natione quam vidimus, incomparabiliter instructa est. Non enim in his, sicut in Britannicis quibus assueti sumus instrumentis, tarda et morosa est modulatio, verum velox et praeceps, suavis tamen et jocunda sonoritas. Mirum quod, in tanta tam praecipiti digitorum rapacitate, musica servatur proportio" (3.11; "De gentis istius in musicis instrumentis peritia incomparabili").

68. "Hibernia quidem tantum duobus utitur et delectatur instrumentis: cithara scilicet, et tympano."

69. "[Cithara] manibus clamat, sine ore loquitur."

70. "Hinc accidit ut ea, quae subtilius intuentibus et artis arcana acute discernentibus internas et ineffabiles comparant animi delicias, ea non attendentibus, sed quasi videndo non videntibus et audiendo non intelligentibus, aures potius onerent quam delectent."

71. "Nam et ipse mundus harmonice dicitur esse compositus"; "Et coelum ipsum sub harmoniae fertur modulatione revolvi"; "Ipsas quoque bestias, necnon et serpentes ac volucres, et phocas etiam marinas, ad auditum suae modulationis musica provocat harmonia"; "Sine musica nulla disciplina potest esse perfecta. Nihil enim sine illa" (all transposed from Isidore, *Etymologiae* 3.17).

72. See *Topographia* 3.10, in which Gerald documents the allegedly primitive Irish practice in horseback riding, warfare, agriculture, metallurgy, industry, and trade. It is to be noted that this chapter immediately precedes and prepares the revelation of musical supremacy in 3.11, "De gentis istius in musicis instrumentis peritia incomparabili."

73. "Notandum vero quod Scotia et Wallia, haec propagationis, illa commeationis et affinitatis gratia, Hiberniam in modulis aemula imitari nituntur disciplina."

74. See Rollo, *Historical Fabrication,* 284–89.

75. "Mirum quod, in tanta tamque praecipiti digitorum rapacitate, musica servatur proportio"; see also *Topographia* 3.11, quoted above.

76. "Hinc accidit ut ea, quae subtilius intuentibus et artis arcana acute discernentibus internas et ineffabiles comparant animi delicias, ea non attendentibus, sed tanquam videndo non videntibus et audiendo non intelligentibus, aures potius onerent quam delectent."

77. On Gerald's complex relationship with the Brythonic Welsh and his tendency to ascribe to the Cambro-Normans (including first and foremost himself) their admirable qualities, see Rollo, *Historical Fabrication,* 277–302.

CONCLUSION

1. That Geoffrey wrote the *Historia regum* to warn against the political and economic chaos that threatened to engulf England after the death of Henry I has been well argued by Schirmer, *Die frühen Darstellungen des Arthurstoffes,* passim, and Jean Blacker, "Transformations of a Theme: The Depoliticization of the Arthurian World in the *Roman de Brut,*" in *The Arthurian Tradition: Essays in Convergence,* ed. Mary Flowers Braswell and John Bugge (Tuscaloosa: University of Alabama Press, 1988), 54–74. Even though we may assume that Geoffrey expected some remuneration for the *Historia regum,* he never directly countenances financial reward in his various dedications. See, for example, his dedicatory prologue to King Stephen and Robert of Gloucester (ed. Wright, 3–4).

2. Warren, *Henry II,* 89, maps the following as the Continental territories that Henry controlled in c. 1160: Normandy, Brittany, Maine, Anjou, Poitou, Touraine, Châteauroux, La Marche, Auvergne, Limousin, Aunis, Saintonge, Angoulême, Périgord, Agenois, Gascony, Cahorsin, and Armagnac. As Warren also points out, however, Henry's dominion over some of these lands was contested and scarcely enforced, particularly in Armagnac and the counties forming the Auvergne.

3. See again, Warren, *Henry II,* 74, 143–44.

4. The primary twelfth-century accounts of this conflict are provided by Jordan Fantôme in his vernacular verse chronicle, ed. Richard Howlett as the *Chronique de la guerre entre les Anglois et les Ecossois,* in *Chronicles of the Reigns of Stephen, Henry II, and Richard I,* 4 vols. (London: Her Majesty's Stationery Office, Rolls Series, 1884–89; reprint, New York: Kraus, 1964), 3:202–377; and William of Newburgh, *Historia rerum Anglicarum,* 2.27–38.

5. I myself consider this tendency, particularly with regard to William of Malmesbury, Gaimar, and Wace, in *Historical Fabrication,* chapters 1–4.

6. For the linguistic complexion of twelfth-century England consult V. H. Galbraith, "Nationality and Language in Medieval England," *Transactions of the Royal Historial Society,* 4th series, 23 (1941): 113–28; Rolf Berndt, "The Linguistic Situation in England from the Norman Conquest to the Loss of Normandy (1066–1204)," in *Approaches to English Historical Linguistics: An Anthology,* ed. Roger Lass (New York: Holt, Rinehart, and Winston, 1969), 369–91; William Rothwell, "A quelle époque a-t-on cessé de parler français en Angleterre?" in *Mélanges de philologie romane offerts à Charles Camproux* (Montpellier: C. E. O. Montpellier, 1978), 2:1075–89; Douglas A. Kibbee, *For to Speke Frenche Trewely: The French Language in England, 1000–1600: Its Status, Description, and Instruction,* Amsterdam Studies in the Theory and History of Linguistic Science, Series 3: Studies in the History of the Language Sciences 60 (Amsterdam: Benjamins, 1991), 8–26; and Ian Short, "On Bilingualism in Anglo-Norman England," *Romance Philology* 33 (1980): 467–79.

7. For a perspective of Anglo-Angevin society, see Richard Mortimer, *Angevin England: 1154–1258* (Oxford: Blackwell, 1994), 194–234. The Norman contribution to Insular culture has been analyzed by D. J. A. Matthew, *The Norman Conquest* (New York: Schocken, 1966), 219–97; Jack Lindsay, *The Normans and Their World* (London: Hart-Davis and MacGibbon, 1974), 279–367; Ann Williams, *The English and The Norman Conquest* (Woodbridge, England: Boydell, 1995), passim; and Judith A. Green, *The Aristocracy of Norman England* (Cambridge: Cambridge University Press, 1997), especially 254–383.

8. "En l'isle de Gersui fui nez, / a Chaem fui petitz portez, / illoques fui a letres mis, / pois fui longues en France apris" (*Le Roman de Rou,* "Troisième partie," 5305–8).

9. See *De rebus a se gestis* 1.2 and 2.1.

10. Two factors make it difficult to define Benoît's place of birth. First, there were several towns bearing the name Sainte-Maure or Sainte-More during the period. Second, Benoît's vernacular displays no dialectical traits that can be definitively associated with one region: while recognizably of western/central France, it could conceivably represent a normalized, literary version of any of the dialects spoken between the Ile-de-France and

Poitou. Constans, *Le Roman de Troie,* 5:190–91, states that Benoît was from Sainte-Maure near Poitiers (meaning that he would have been a native of a territory that came under Angevin control during his adult life), but his argument is suggestive rather than definitive. Ultimately, moreover, such speculation is irrelevant to the Insular and Norman themes of Benoît's works.

11. Rollo, *Historical Fabrication,* chapter 9.

12. For John's biography, see again the forematter of Nederman's translation of excerpts from the *Policraticus.*

13. In addition to Alain, several other Latin authors working in the French domains during the period consider magic and literacy in the general terms I mention. Guibert of Nogent revised the *Gesta Dei per Francos* in the 1110–20s to accommodate a biography of Mohammed, in which the Islamic prophet is depicted as a manipulative forger who propagates his seductive words with the aid of demonic familiars; see *Gesta Dei per Francos,* ed. J. P. Migne, in *Patrologiae cursus completus: Series latina,* vol. 156 (Paris: Éditions Migne, 1853), cols. 689–93. Hugh of Saint Victor—probably German by birth but active in France—inserted a chapter on magic into book 6 of his final redaction of the *Didascalicon,* a treatise on categories of knowledge that frequently addresses the responsibilities of the literate; see *Hugonis de Sancto Victore Didascalicon de studio legendi,* ed. Charles Henry Buttimer, Studies in Medieval and Renaissance Latin 10 (Washington, D.C.: Catholic University of America Press, 1939), 6.15. The works of both authors could be productively engaged in the terms I have proposed.

14. Rollo, *Historical Fabrication,* chapters 6–8.

15. Ibid., chapter 3, especially 81–92.

16. For the dating of Chrétien's five romances, see Anthime Fourrier, "Encore la chronologie des oeuvres de Chrétien de Troyes," *Bulletin Bibliographique de la Société Internationale Arthurienne* 2 (1950): 69–88.

17. The edition of *Brut* used will be that of Ivor Arnold, Société des Anciens Textes Français, 2 vols. (Paris: Société des Anciens Textes Français, 1938–40). Reference will be to line number only.

18. On Wace's use of the First Variant rather than the Vulgate for the greater part of his translation, see Leckie, *The Passage of Dominion,* 25–27, 104–9.

19. "Maistre Wace l'ad translaté / Ki en conte la verité / Si cum li livres le devise" (7–9).

20. It is unclear whether Wace is here referring to the Brythonic tales that William of Malmesbury categorized some thirty years earlier as *nugae* and *fabulae* (see *Gesta regum* 1.8) or to the new genre of Gallo-Romance narrative represented, for example, by the roughly contemporary *Tristan* of Thomas. In this latter context, it can be noted in passing that Thomas himself attests a process of diversification similar to that intimated by Wace and recognizes that he too has embellished the paradigm:

Ici diverse la matyre.
Entre ceus qui solent cunter
E del cunte Tristran parler,
Il en cuntent diversement.

[At this point, the material diverges in the renditions given by the various storytellers who recount the tale of Tristan.]

E diz e vers i ai retrait:
Pur essample issi ai fait
Pur l'estorie embelir,
Que as amanz deive plaisir.

[I have rendered the story in words and verse, and I have given it greater beauty to create a version that should be pleasing to those in love.] (Thomas, *Tristan*, ed. Bartina H. Wind, in *Les Fragments du "Roman de Tristan": Poème du XIIe siècle*, Textes Littéraires Français, 92 [Geneva: Droz, 1960], respectively "Douce," lines 840–43, and "Sneyd 2," lines 830–33.)

21. Rollo, *Historical Fabrication*, 109–35.

22. Ibid., 161–63.

23. For Chrétien's relationship with Wace, see Donald Maddox, *The Arthurian Romances of Chrétien de Troyes: Once and Future Fictions* (Cambridge: Cambridge University Press, 1991), 8–34.

24. Here and in all subsequent references to Chrétien's *Cligés*, I cite the edition of Wendelin Foerster in *Christian von Troyes: Sämtliche Werke*, vol. 1 (Halle: Niemeyer, 1884). Reference is to line number.

25. Wace also addresses the toponymic history of England in *Brut*, 1175–200, and in *Rou*, "Troisième partie," 7–14.

26. Despite the impression I give in translating, line 35 is ambiguous. As the "vint" of line 33 demonstrates, it was possible in Old French to use a singular verb to refer to two balanced subjects; accordingly, lines 33–35 could just as validly be rendered "It was then Rome that inherited chivalry and the sum of learning, which *have* now come to France."

27. See *Brut*, 9587–13009. The equivalent victories are described in *Historia regum*, 148–76.

28. "Talia michi et de talibus multociens cogitanti optulit Walterus Oxinefordensis archidiaconus, uir in oratoria arte atque in exoticis historiis eruditus, quendam Britannici sermonis *librum uetustissimum* qui a Bruto primo rege Britonum usque ad Cadualadrum filium Caduallonis actus omnium continue et ex ordine perpulcris orationibus proponebat. Rogatu itaque illius ductus, tametsi infra alienos ortulos falerata uerba non collegerim, agresti tamen stilo propriisque calamis contentus codicem illum in Latinum sermonem transferre curaui" (prologue; emphasis added).

29. See again Freeman, *The Poetics of "Translatio Studii" and "Conjointure,"* 91–139.

30. For the Latin, see the notes to chapter 2, note 30.

31. This is Chrétien's own word for the magical draught; see lines 3251, 3259, 3310, 3316, 3340, 3364. In the twelfth century "poisons" conveyed the sense of its later doublet "potion," rather than the modern resonances of the term.

Index

Medieval Cultures

Volume 22
Michelle R. Warren
History on the Edge: Excalibur and the Borders of Britain, 1100–1300

Volume 21
Olivia Holmes
Assembling the Lyric Self: Authorship from Troubadour Song to Italian Poetry Book

Volume 20
Karen Sullivan
The Interrogation of Joan of Arc

Volume 19
Clare A. Lees
Tradition and Belief: Religious Writing in Late Anglo-Saxon England

Volume 18
David Matthews
The Making of Middle English, 1765–1910

Volume 17
Jeffrey Jerome Cohen
Of Giants: Sex, Monsters, and the Middle Ages

Volume 16
Edited by Barbara A. Hanawalt and David Wallace
Medieval Crime and Social Control

Volume 15
Kathryn Kerby-Fulton and Denise L. Despres
Iconography and the Professional Reader: The Politics of Book Production in the Douce "Piers Plowman"

Volume 14
Edited by Marilynn Desmond
Christine de Pizan and the Categories of Difference

Volume 13
Alfred Thomas
Anne's Bohemia: Czech Literature and Society, 1310–1420

Volume 12
Edited by F. R. P. Akehurst and Stephanie Cain Van D'Elden
The Stranger in Medieval Society

Volume 11
Edited by Karma Lochrie, Peggy McCracken, and James A. Schulz
Constructing Medieval Sexuality

Volume 10
Claire Sponsler
Drama and Resistance: Bodies, Goods, and Theatricality in Late Medieval England

Volume 9
Edited by Barbara A. Hanawalt and David Wallace
Bodies and Disciplines: Intersections of Literature and History in Fifteenth-Century England

Volume 8
Marilynn Desmond
Reading Dido: Gender, Textuality, and the Medieval "Aeneid"

Volume 7
Edited by Clare A. Lees
Medieval Masculinities: Regarding Men in the Middle Ages

Volume 6
Edited by Barbara A. Hanawalt and Kathryn L. Reyerson
City and Spectacle in Medieval Europe

Volume 5
Edited by Calvin B. Kendall and Peter S. Wells
Voyage to the Other World: The Legacy of Sutton Hoo

Volume 4
Edited by Barbara A. Hanawalt
Chaucer's England: Literature in Historical Context

Volume 3
Edited by Marilyn J. Chiat and Kathryn L. Reyerson
The Medieval Mediterranean: Cross-Cultural Contacts

Volume 2
Edited by Andrew MacLeish
The Medieval Monastery

Volume 1
Edited by Kathryn L. Reyerson and Faye Powe
The Medieval Castle

David Rollo is associate professor of English at the University of Southern California. He has previously taught at l'Université Française de l'Océan Indien (La Réunion), at Dartmouth, and at Agnes Scott College, where he was Adeline Arnold Lordians Professor and Chair of Modern Languages. He is also the author of *Historical Fabrication, Ethnic Fable, and French Romance in Twelfth-Century England.*